Through the MOONgate

Through the MOONgate

Muse Norcross Kotenev

toExcel

San Jose   New York   Lincoln   Shanghai

Through the MOONgate

Published by toExcel

For information address:
toExcel
165 West 95th Street, Suite B-N
New York, NY 10025
www.toExcel.com

Photos property of Muse Norcross Kotenev.
Graphics: Joanna N. Coke

ISBN: 1-58348-389-6
LCCN: 99-65403

Printed in the United States of America

Acknowledgement

I would like to thank several of my friends without whose advice, critique and assistance this book would not have been possible:

Walter R. Howell, my editor

Valery Grey, my untiring efficient typist

Jean Gollay, my invaluable adviser

Joanna N. Coke, my daughter, for the graphics used in this book

Preface

In China, the "Moongate" is a circular entrance through which you walk on the way to a temple, monastery, or palace. It also may lead into a secluded garden. Here, a radiant splash of red, yellow and white roses in full bloom or a splendid array of soft pink peony petals may delight you. But some of these gardens are devoid of flowers. Instead, various small and large rocks of bizarre shapes and colors meet your gaze. It is the valuable collection of a connoisseur owner, who seeks in quaint rock formations the diversity of creation.

Thus, I, too, perceive events in life. Each episode is tantamount to stepping through a "Moongate" into a garden. Some visits leave pleasant memories; others leave pain. Yet each experience is a valuable part of the total tapestry of one's being.

Prologue

I looked up at the steel-gray sky as gusts of the northern wind shook our ship, making it strain at its lines. Wrapping my blue fox jacket more tightly around my shoulders, I turned to check on my two little girls. We were standing on deck waiting for our ship to pull out of Tsingtao, China.

It was January 15, 1949.

Our ship, the *U.S. Empire State*, a small sea-going freighter, had arrived two days earlier. It had been hurriedly unloaded of its cargo of wheat, and now was about to depart. All other steamers had already left Tsingtao because Tsingtao and its surrounding area were cordoned off by the Fifth Communist Army of Mao Tse-tung, creating a panic in the city. The repatriation of United States citizens was in full swing. The sailors were frantically packing, crating and conveying their possessions to the ships. Only the presence of the United States Seventh Fleet deterred the Communists from taking Tsingtao.

Like a flock of white geese at rest the fleet was riding at anchor in the harbor. Lately, however, these ships were prepared for imminent departure. The crew had been restricted from going ashore and the engineers were standing by, awaiting only the admiral's commands to start the diesel engines.

As I watched the stevedores rush up and down the gangway, scurrying with the boxes and baggage of our ship's sixteen passengers, my heart filled with anxiety and sorrow. I knew that my two daughters and I might not see China, our home, again. Tears welled up in me at the realization that I was also parting, perhaps forever, from my parents. My uncertain future in the United States, and that of my little girls, loomed like a dark cloud over me.

As I clung with one hand to the rail of the vibrating ship, trying to shield my daughters from the biting wind, I recalled an afternoon with my Father. He had spoken to me gently but incisively.

"Daughter," he had said in his velvet-toned voice, "you are a widow of twenty-nine. Your husband, may his soul rest in peace, left you with no financial security. America is the place for you. It is your duty to save your children from the doubtful times ahead under the Communists here."

Father's voice was deep with emotion. For a few seconds he remained silent before he concluded: "Yes, in the United States you will be safe. Make every effort to get there. There is no other way!" he insisted. "Be courageous! Live honorably as your Mother and I have always done. Life will lead you as it has us. Trust it."

Life, or destiny, led me as I dutifully yielded to my Father's wishes. Miraculously, I had obtained my passport and received my visa to the United States only the morning before the *U.S. Empire State* was to depart, and that same afternoon I had been able to purchase the last available tickets for our voyage to America.

An hour before I kissed my Father for the last time. He was sitting in his favorite green armchair, unable to rise because of his paralyzed legs. As I bent over him, he covered his face with his hands to hide his anguish. My Mother, in the corner on her knees, was sobbing before the icon of Serafim, our patron saint.

I tore myself away with difficulty and ran with my children to the waiting cab. As the chauffeur started the engine, I looked back at the white-shingled, two-storied house where we had lived for the past two years. I was gripped with sadness. Tears streamed down my face.

"Mama, Mama, why are you crying?" Regina, my five year old, asked, looking frightened.

"Don't be afraid, dear. Everything will be all right," I said as calmly as I could, drawing both girls closer to me.

Now, on the deck of the ship, I became keenly aware of how similar my fate was to my parents'. They had hastily departed from St. Petersburg in 1917, fearful of the Revolution and the new Soviet Government of Russia, and fled to Siberia. They, too, had been fortunate to obtain passage on what was the last transport leaving the city…

I made the sign of the cross and braced myself. Whatever the future might bring, my life could not hold more stirring and dramatic experiences than it had so far.

1

The Beginnings

A "white polar bear" played an important part in my entrance into this world. That is, to be precise, a "white polar bear rug." Years later, in Tsingtao, before my departure from China in 1949, my Father testified to this.

At that time, my good friends, the Kushnareffs, were selling what they could in their own preparations for leaving China. Among these possessions, I saw a white polar-bear-skin rug. For some inexplicable reason, pictures, movies, and figurines of this majestic animal had always caught my imagination, and now, seeing this large skin for sale, I wanted to have it.

"How much is it?" I asked Tatiana Mihailovna Kushnareff.

"Only one hundred and fifty United States dollars," she answered. I caught my breath. The price was steep. At this time United States currency had high value and one could live very comfortably in Shanghai for an entire month for U.S. $25—small apartment, maid servant, food and utilities included. One hundred and fifty dollars was also quite a chunk out of my meager savings. Notwithstanding, I reached for my purse and unhesitatingly counted out the bills.

Tatiana Mihailovna counted the money carefully, then folded the twelve-foot-long skin with the head and mouth opened, teeth showing in defiance, and fastidiously wrapped it in a large blue cotton cloth.

"Be sure always to keep it in blue—this way the fur keeps its whiteness," she instructed. She helped me to carry the bundle to the pedicab awaiting at the gate of her garden.

When I arrived at my parents' house I unraveled the parcel. Father, sitting in his usual place, the green armchair, looked startled. He placed his monocle to his left eye and with his right hand, brushed his short-clipped moustache.

"Hmmm," he uttered as he gently patted the fur. I noticed that he had a strange, whimsical expression on his face.

"The Kushnareffs sold it to me. You know I always wanted it," I explained.

"You were conceived on a similar rug," Father murmured with a faraway look in his eyes.

"What did you say?" I was sure that I had not heard him correctly.

"Yes, it was in Siberia while we were fleeing to the Far East during the Revolution. You were conceived on it."

"Oh, Father!"

"Yes, that's so. You see, the bed at the inn where we were staying squeaked loudly, and there on the floor of the room was this perfectly beautiful skin. Your birth nine months later coincided perfectly."

Father again patted the bear lovingly and thoughtfully.

"A bear!" I whispered to myself as I left the room. "A denizen of harsh Nordic lands. What a symbol of survival and endurance!"

And so, nine months later, at midnight on January 16, in the year 1920, in Vladivostok, Russia, I was born.

My parents had just arrived in this fine city on the east coast overlooking the shores of the Sea of Japan and the end of the Trans-Siberian Railway. They had traveled 5,720 miles from St. Petersburg in quest of refuge from the turbulent revolution in western Russia. To the tired, travel-worn bodies and souls of Anatol and Lubov Kotenev, Vladivostok, at this time luxuriating in abundance and prosperity, seemed to be a veritable Shangri-La to them.

Father remembered the house. It was surrounded by a thicket of wild grapes and stood against a backdrop of hills. Before them, stretching for miles into the distance, was a splendid beach.

Two months later, according to Russian tradition, I was taken to the cathedral to be baptized. Mother vividly remembered the ceremony and the unusual circumstances in which I received my name.

She, my Father, my Godfather, Colonel Nazadze, and Mother's maid Liza, with me in her arms, entered the vast Russian Orthodox Church with heads bowed in reverence. Mother could recall the lights from the hundreds of candles illuminating the solemn visages of the saints and the Blessed Virgin with little Jesus in their richly embossed silver overlays. The royal doors of the iconostasis were ablaze with gold and silver decorations.

Father Ignaty, the priest, was to perform the ceremony. He was sumptuously attired in a vestment woven with gold thread. A heavy gold chain and a bejeweled cross hung on his chest. He stood to the left of the royal doors, near the marble baptismal font. At his side was his assistant, Deacon Afanasy, in a more modest liturgical garment, white trimmed with yellow and blue thread. He was swinging the censer.

Father Ignaty greeted us, bowing ceremoniously. Our group returned his bow in unison. Deacon Afanasy also bowed as he kept swinging the censer backward and forward, filling the air with the pungent aroma of frankincense.

"What will be the name of this humble slave of God?" Father Ignaty inquired, his deep voice smooth as velvet.

"Magdaleine," replied my Father.

"No, no," my Mother protested.

Father Ignaty raised his eyes. He arched his bushy eyebrows. "Then what will be the name of this humble slave of God?" he asked again.

"Magdaleine," my Father repeated, but his voice was less confident.

"NO! NO!" cried my Mother with determination. "Magdaleine was his sister who died when she was fifteen. It would be most inauspicious to have the baby named after her."

Father Ignaty looked perplexed. He turned to my Father, who shrugged his shoulders.

What a dilemma! Father Ignaty lifted his eyes heavenward. Thus he stood for a few seconds as if expecting an answer from above. He must have received it, for suddenly his face brightened.

"The Book! The Book of Names!" the good Father cried. He turned to the Deacon. Deacon Afanasy nodded his head approvingly and quickly stepped through the royal doors into the sacristy. Everyone could hear the sounds of the opening and closing of drawers and cabinet doors, and then the good Deacon emerged looking triumphant.

In his left hand he was holding a thick, well-worn, brown leather tome with a curiously wrought metal clasp.

Father Ignaty made a sign of the cross over the holy book before receiving it into his hands. Carefully, he unclasped the old lock, and slowly started to turn the vellum pages.

"M-M-M," he kept mumbling, as he sought the page with names beginning with the letter "M." At last he found it. Down the page with his index finger he searched. M…M…M…His finger stopped. He grasped me from Liza's arms as he made his announcement.

"This child, God's humble slave, will be named Muse!" he declared. And to preclude further discussion, he removed my blanket, and dipped his right thumb into a cup of oil which Deacon Afanasy extended to him. He anointed my feet, the palms of my hands, and my forehead. Then, with rapidity and deftness, while holding my nose and mouth closed with one hand and my body with the other hand, he immersed me, naked, three times into the Holy baptismal water in the font, chanting, "In the name of the Father, the Son, and the Holy Ghost, I name this humble slave of God…MUSE!"

Mother told me that I screamed with all the strength that my newborn lungs could muster. Unperturbed, Father Ignaty passed me dripping wet into the towel held out by my Godfather.

"Here she is! Muse!" Father Ignaty's voice resounded throughout the cathedral.

My Mother liked the name.

2

My Parents' Journey to China

It all began in 1917 when my parents boarded the train in St. Petersburg and started an arduous journey. Delays along the way at stations, the ever-present fear of railway service possibly being suspended, and watching the steady dwindling of their financial resources added to their fears and anxiety that they might not reach their destination, which was China. There, my Father was hoping to find refuge for himself and his small family. Those were fearful days. The Revolution, with Lenin at the head, was tearing Russia apart. Members of the nobility like my Father were being eliminated. Everyone who could was fleeing in fear for his life. Father's nostalgic memories of his youth as an Imperial Cavalry officer in command of a small detachment of Cossacks, attached to the Russian Embassy in Peking, in the years from 1902 to 1904, and the memory of the Russian-Japanese War when he was wounded in his spine, were drawing him back to the Far East and China.

In time, after many difficulties, my parents did reach China to start a new life in Shanghai. This busy European port on the Wang Pu River became our home. Yet Russia and that long, arduous journey across Siberia remained ever fresh in my Father's mind.

Years later, after dinner with friends, fellow Russian emigrants, these memories would be relived. Each emigré had his tale to relate.

Father, like his friends, loved to recall those momentous events in Russia. It was painful to remember. Each episode was, for him, like a pearl on a string, and the memory of the hardships that had been surmounted gave him a sense of pride in his ability to overcome difficulties. No doubt it also gave him courage to continue to adjust to adverse conditions, and to pursue new goals.

One day in Shanghai, as he was sitting comfortably in his overstuffed armchair, holding a cigarette between his long, well-manicured fingers, I remember approaching him.

"Father," I asked, "was it imperative for you and Mother to leave Russia and risk the uncertainties of distant lands?"

With an effort, he lifted his right leg to cross it over his left knee. After finding the right position, he turned to me. Even now I can see his fine face with its short-clipped graying moustache, his aquiline nose and deep-set eyes—a faraway look in them.

"There was no other way for your Mother and myself, if we were to stay alive." Father nodded his head pensively and for a few moments was silent. Then, as the details of those days started to crowd in on him, he began to relate to me what had prompted his decision to leave St. Petersburg and undertake the long journey across Siberia to the Far East.

3

Father's Memories

"Those were frightful days!" Father told me. "Tsar Nicholas II had just abdicated and the Provisional Government of Alexander Kerensky had been established. Times in Russia had become ominous—demonstrations by the masses, laborers' strikes, the plundering of shops and residences in the cities by unruly hoodlums, and the vandalism and the brutal slaughter of cattle by the peasants in the countryside. All order was breaking down. The police and the military, despite their efforts, were losing control." Father knit his brow and an expression of repugnance appeared on his face as he visualized those times.

"One event in particular influenced my decision to leave Russia," he continued. "I was attending an assembly in the Tauride Palace, the Headquarters of the Government, as a delegate to the Kerensky Provisional Government from the St. Petersburg Ohta District.

"The grand ballroom was ablaze with light from several magnificent crystal chandeliers. On the white walls edged with gold, hung portraits of royalty in elaborately carved frames. The vastness and luxury of the surroundings dwarfed the delegates as they crowded around the podium in the far left corner of the room. In their black suits and long frock coats they resembled dark beetles on the polished checked parquet floor.

"Alexander Kerensky—tall, blond, dapper in his immaculately fitted tailcoat and high-collared white shirt with black satin cravat—presided from the podium. His opening speech emphasized the importance of solidarity and speedy decisions. He pointed to the urgency of taking steps to restore order in the country. All of the delegates applauded. Everyone seemed to be in accord.

"As each delegate had the right to be heard, one speech followed another. Some delegates aroused enthusiasm while others received a few polite claps. As speech after speech continued, everyone listened attentively. The clock struck nine, and then ten, and still the speeches persisted monotonously, with nothing conclusive being reached.

"I began to notice boredom and frustration among the delegates. They started to gather into groups—the Mensheviks, the Bolsheviks, the Social Revolutionaries, the Cadets. Snide remarks and ugly innuendoes were being exchanged. Here and there high-pitched voices could be heard. I realized that tempers were flaring up. No one was paying attention to the speakers!

"'Gentlemen! Gentlemen! I beg you to restrain yourselves!' Alexander Kerensky called out, hitting the top of the podium again and again with his gavel. It was useless. By now the delegates, forgetting all decorum, were confronting each other with hatred in their eyes. They were shaking their fists and swearing. The Bolsheviks, the adherents of the Marx and Engles doctrine of Communism, were especially conspicuous in their aggressive behavior toward the Cadets, the nobility and the intelligentsia.

"In utter consternation, I watched the chaos in the hall. Suddenly, I realized that what I was witnessing within these palatial walls, could happen on a much greater scale should the Kerensky Government collapse. And at this point it was showing distinct signs of disintegration. It was obvious to me that Russia was on the brink of disastrous happenings. Members of the nobility, like myself, who stood for the old social order, would become targets for extermination by the 'New Masters,' and I was certain that the 'New Masters' would be the Bolsheviks...

"Our ancestors, the Kotenevs, date back to the early times of the Boyars, owners of large tracts of land, 'the pillars of the realm,' as Russians referred to them. The Kotenevs' homestead was in the ancient city of Kostroma. As the eldest son of a noble family, I was educated in a cavalry school. It prepared me to be an officer in the Imperial Military Corps. I commanded a detachment of Cossacks during the Russo-Japanese War in 1904. In Manchuria, during an attack against a Japanese redoubt, I was seriously wounded in the spine. Though I was left with paralyzed legs, it did not prevent me from entering the University of Moscow and graduating with a degree in Law.

"Despite being a wounded veteran, and having been elected to represent Ohta District by majority vote, I was sure that I would not be protected from persecution by the Bolsheviks. There was no doubt in my mind that I would become one of the victims of a Revolution, which was fast rearing its head.

"What then would become of your Mother? There was only one way to survive and save her. We had to leave Russia immediately. But where could we go? I remembered Siberia, a vast region, rich in natural resources, a boundless area full of possibilities for an enterprising individual.

"There had been rumors of a railroad strike. The trains, however, had continued to run on schedule and the Trans-Siberian train was leaving St. Petersburg the next morning. That was the train we had to take. It might have been the last. This was in October, 1917. Anything could have happened.

"Not waiting for the end of the assembly, and as quickly as I could, I made my way to the entrance of the palace where a sentry summoned a carriage for me. It delivered me to the bronze gate of our red brick apartment building. The night watchman unlocked the massive oaken door. The clock in the foyer struck twice as I stepped into the vestibule of our apartment.

"It grieved me to awaken and disturb your Mother. But if we were to leave on the morning train, we had to hurry. I knew that all this would throw her into confusion. She was so very young, only twenty years old, and had lived a sheltered life. Your Mother and I had been married only one year earlier.

"Her father, Annany Terentieff, was a successful merchant, owner of the Terentieff Vodka Distillery, an imposing group of buildings in Ohta. He ruled over his family with an iron hand, yet showered them with all the luxurious comforts and blessings that his millions permitted. Your Mother was a pampered child. At first, Annany Terentieff wavered about giving his blessings to our marriage."

I was curious about how my grandfather looked. "Father, do you remember Annany?" I interrupted.

"He was a rugged individual with a shaggy dark beard, bushy eyebrows, and a pair of cold, calculating eyes. He had his hair cut short in the peasant style and he always dressed as a peasant, clad in an embroidered white shirt buttoned on the left shoulder and wide blue or black trousers tucked into high leather boots. When he went out, he wore a cap with a shiny black visor. It was easy to take him for a serf recently arrived from the country, and this is what he was, except that he had come to St. Petersburg many years before."

Father looked straight at me and after a moment of silence continued. "Your grandfather, on your Mother's side, belonged to the few amazing Russian peasants who, in their teens, dared to leave their villages. Annany, with a sack on his back containing a small icon, a piece of bread, and a bottle of water, had stepped onto the dusty road and walked for hundreds of miles from his village searching for a better life, a life without perpetual hunger and the fears of an indentured serf, a slave on an estate.

"Some masters of large estates in Russia, who could spare a man or two, actually encouraged their strong, young, energetic peasants to try their luck in the cities. If the man was successful, the master was sure to receive a yearly payment for his partial liberty. Eventually, if his man did well, the master could expect a goodly sum for the man's complete freedom.

"Annany had not disappointed his lord. With relentless energy and purpose, ingenuity and cunning, starting as a mere factory laborer, he rose to become the respectable owner of many properties and a prosperous distillery...quite an achievement that very few men have been known to have accomplished, men with wills of steel and uncompromising direction. This is how I will always remember him.

"Your Mother was his sixteenth and the youngest of his children. She was his favorite. She alone could sway him a little, as she had done to marry me.

"How could you, a young nobleman, have married the daughter of a former indentured serf? Wasn't it unusual?" I asked, knowing how structured society had been in Russia.

"No. It was not unusual for Russian nobility to marry rich merchants' daughters, even though society considered such marriages not particularly desirable, a sort of misalliance. Annany Terentieff had promised a sizable dowry and, of course, he had extensive connections amongst the merchants of Ohta. Besides, your Mother's beauty attracted me. So, who can blame me, a beginning lawyer in the district, a man of talents but modest means, when one of Terentieff's sons-in-law, with whom I had business dealings, suggested such a union? Understandably, I was more than agreeable.

"At first, Annany looked somewhat askance at his favorite daughter marrying me, a cripple, especially as there were several other wealthy merchant suitors. But, for a former indentured peasant to be related to nobility by the marriage of his daughter was quite an honor. Nevertheless, he wavered.

"'Luba, keep in mind that you will be a nurse to a cripple for the rest of your life,' Annany told your Mother.

"But your Mother insisted. She had met this handsome, tall, elegant lawyer and was smitten." My Father stopped and looked at me with a twinkle in his eyes. "Your Mother answered: 'So what if he cannot walk with ease? He is kind and intelligent. Besides, it is an honor, Father!'"

"After a few anxious thoughts, Annany gave his consent. To be related to nobility was too good to pass up. But he stipulated a condition. He told your Mother: 'I will give my blessings, but without a dowry.'

"You see, he could not forego a little bargaining." Father laughed. "His shrewd nature felt that in this particular case, giving a dowry might not be such an advantageous transaction.

"'I don't need the dowry,' I told the matchmaker who brought me Annany's conditions. Besides, by then I was too enamored with the young, beautiful girl, my junior by sixteen years." Father smiled.

"Russian nobility was not very practical," I remarked.

"No, they were notorious for their impracticality. Their honor was always above any other consideration," Father laughed. "Well, the wedding took place with all appropriate ceremony in the great cathedral. Golden crowns were held over our heads as we pronounced our vows and, according to ancient Slavic tradition, the choir glorified ecstatically the Lord on High while the priest swayed his incense burner, saturating the air with fragrant frankincense."

"What happened when you arrived home from the meeting in the Tauride Palace?" I interrupted.

"I am coming to that point," Father answered. "In the apartment, I went straight to the bedroom. I remember hearing the ticking of the grandfather clock in our living room. It made me realize how little time we had to pack and prepare for our long journey. I switched on the small electric lamp on the dressing table and, as carefully as I could, approached the bed. Your Mother was fast asleep." Father stopped. A pleasurable memory made him smile again. "Your Mother was so lovely," he murmured. "Thick, curly auburn air framed her face, a face that a friend had once described as a classical Russian beauty with bow-shaped eyebrows, large periwinkle-blue eyes outlined by thick long lashes, a fine small nose and sensuous full lips.

"I placed my hand gently on her shoulder half uncovered by the blanket. 'Luba, Luba,' I called to her. She opened her eyes.

"'What is it, Anatol?' I could see she was startled.

"'Wake up!' I told her, with as calm a voice as I could muster. 'There are things to attend to! We must pack! We are leaving on the morning train.'

"Your Mother stared at me with fear and disbelief. 'Have you lost your senses?!' she asked softly.

"'No, I am all right. But things are not well in Russia,' I told her, trying with difficulty not to frighten her completely. 'We must catch the early training leaving for the East. It may be the last one. Go awaken Liza! She will help you collect your furs, jewels, gold, silver objects, and clothing for winter and summer. We may be travelling a long while. And don't forget to tell Liza to bring food along, like bread, sausage, cheese.'"

Liza would later be my nurse. She was a sturdy, blond, blue-eyed country girl with a ready smile. She had come, as custom prescribed, with my Mother into her new home as a personal attendant, and was expected to remain with her for the rest of her life attending to household duties.

"Your Mother understood that something serious must have prompted my decision," Father continued. "Without further questions, she pulled on her lace dressing gown, slipped her feet into her silk slippers, and hurried to Liza's room.

"In no time suitcases were brought in, cleaned and dusted; valuables and clothing collected; and victuals with a couple of bottles of wine were placed into a basket. Sheets, pillows, and blankets found their places in duffle bags. Barely dawn, everything was ready.

"The sun was just rising above the horizon when our cabby stopped at the arched entrance of the Trans-Siberia Railway Station. As a delegate of the Government with credentials, I had no difficulty purchasing tickets on the Siberian Express.

"The porters, with our luggage under their arms, formed a phalanx and spearheaded us through a dense crowd of soldiers and passengers on the platform, and into our compartment. As a third whistle shrilly announced the train's departure, I put my arms around your Mother. Bravely, she tried to compose herself, but tears streamed down her cheeks. It was overwhelming to realize that we might not see St. Petersburg again.

"The train's wheels turned faster and faster as it picked up speed.

"'Oh, God!' your Mother exclaimed.

"But there was little I could do to comfort her. I, too, felt that we were moving into a great unknown and the future seemed like a gigantic chasm ready to engulf us!

"Only Liza, with her staunch peasant fortitude, acquired with generations of suffering, did not lose her composure. She said firmly, 'Let us trust God and pray!'

"We made the sign of the cross and lowered our heads.

"'Lord help us mortal sinners!' Liza's prayer was in the old traditional Russian manner.

"'Yes, guide us and protect us, Lord, I implore you!' I added silently.

"I remember that, little by little, a confidence that all would be well crept into my being. 'Amen,' I said aloud and turned to look out of the window to hide my emotions. Trees, houses, church cupolas, and fields with distant hamlets flickered by as the train sped on its track along the River Neva towards the East."

For several minutes Father was silent. I could see that he was trying to recall the details of that journey.

"What a relief it must have been to know that you were on your way to safety," I remarked, to prod him along.

Father shifted to a more comfortable position in his armchair. "At first it was," he continued. "But then, suddenly, two armed soldiers and an impressive-looking Cossack with a rifle in his hand and a revolver in his belt, unceremoniously entered our compartment. There was not much I could do. Staring at us in silence, they squatted on the floor close to the window. Hearing a commotion in the corridor, I looked out of the door. The corridor was thronged with soldiers. It was impassable.

Father sighed. "Besides the Russian Revolution, there was the First World War. The Germans were pressing on Pskov and the whole Russian Northern Army was pushed back. Thousands of soldiers, with and without weapons, some with machine guns, were deserting their units and flooding the trains in an attempt to make their way back to their villages. Not only the staterooms, but even the toilets, were filled with men. They hung in baggage nets, clung to wagon roofs, and clutched to the skimpy railings of the small platforms between the wagons. The farther the train got from St. Petersburg, however, the less crowded things became. Somehow, everyone found a spot for himself. With difficulty, it became possible to reach the lavatory.

"A few stops later, before Stanka Station, the Cossack managed to leave the train and return. He returned looking extremely worried.

"'Your Honor,' he whispered to me, 'in the next compartment there are several commissars. They are heading for the Murmansk Line. One of them has given orders to have our wagon disconnected at Stanka. That station, like all others, is packed with people who have been waiting for weeks for space on a passing train. We will be stranded.'

"'Pass the word around,' I told the Cossack.

"'I did already. Do you hear the noise?' There was a loud buzzing of voices in the corridor.

"'I fear the dolts will get scared when it comes to business. You are an officer. If you take command they will listen to you,' the Cossack whispered.

"What to do? I knew that only drastic action could save the situation, so I opened the door of our compartment and called out, 'Comrades!' The buzz stopped. 'You have heard that there are plans to cut us off at Stanka. Place guards on platforms and connectors! Prepare machine guns and load your rifles! Send men to control the engine wagon! UNDERSTAND?'

"The door of the next compartment opened. A man in a black leather jacket looked out. 'What is this, Comrades, a riot?' he started to say. But the Cossack in my compartment shouted over my shoulder, 'Give him a punch in his mug! Lock the door and guard it!'

"The soldiers in the corridor became excited. The man in the leather jacket quickly slammed his door and turned the key.

"'Let him sit there until the train leaves the Stanka Station!' shouted the Cossack, and for emphasis, he let loose several colorful curses.

"The train started to slow down. The wheels screeched as it came to a stop. Everyone dashed to the entrance. Some soldiers dragged their machine guns, others cocked rifles.

"After several minutes, our Cossack, who had left our compartment and had participated in the confusion, returned. 'All is in order, Your Honor,' he informed me. 'We've taken the station. There is a guard at the telephone. The Station Chief is shaking with fear. The engineers are taking on water and coal for the train. Our people are helping.'

"Only when the train started again did I breathe easier.

"'What are we going to do with these?' our Cossack asked, inclining his head in the direction of the locked stateroom.

"'Take them off the train at the next half station!' I directed.

"At the next stop the frightened commissars were taken off the train and, so that they could not communicate with other stations, our farsighted Cossack destroyed the telegraph.

"Nevertheless, I was in a constant state of anxiety and expected the worst to happen, perhaps at the next stations, Vologda or Viatka, where I suspected that there might be a garrison of soldiers. Fortunately, all went well. We were machine gunned as the train passed Viatka. The soldiers responded with their rifles. Unhappily, some of their machine guns, with which they had been armed, turned out to be faulty.

"I was glad to see that the Cossack in our compartment retained his morale. 'Sort of late to stop us now. Turn, Gabriel, turn,' he kept repeating. He had named the train's engine Gabriel. Gabriel did reach Omsk, where, after wishing our fellow passengers all the best, your Mother, Liza and I left the train."

Very little is known of the events that took place in Siberia, that vast region of Russia, during the years 1917 to 1920. They are replete with political consequences and human interest.

I am imparting the details of these years as described by my Father in his memoirs, **Big Trifles and Little People**, written in Russian.

Anatol Kotenev - 1918

Luba, Muse's mother, at age 20

Omsk-Siberia

In Omsk, my parents found the streets windswept and freezing. Heavy icicles hung from the edges of roofs, threatening to fall on the pedestrians who, bundled in shawls and heavy scarves, hurried over the wooden walks constructed along the streets to circumvent the high snow piles in winter and the slush and filth in the spring.

With difficulty, Liza found a carriage and they started out to look for a place to stay. From one inn to another, from one guest house to another, they searched in vain. The town was overcrowded with people who, like themselves, were escaping from the ominous changes in Russia. Everyone they met on the streets and asked for information, looked at them suspiciously before hurrying off without so much as a word. The Siberians were highly distrustful of Russians from European Russia. They blamed the political troubles on them.

Father remembered that they were half-frozen and disheartened when he had an idea. He had caught sight of a sign. "DOCTOR—OBSTETRICIAN, receives 8 to 11." He looked at his watch. It showed ten. "STOP!" he shouted to the cabby.

The waiting room was cozy and warm. They huddled for a while near the large iron stove in the middle of the room. Finally, the door opened and a pleasant-looking gray-haired man in a white linen doctor's smock invited them into his office.

"We need advice, Doctor. It is in the field of hygienics. I will pay you well," Father addressed him.

Peering over his spectacles, the doctor looked at them curiously. "What do you mean? I do not understand."

"What should a young couple require if death from cold and hunger threatens?" Father explained, trying to be humorous. "We have been driving through the streets in the sub-zero temperature in quest of a room. And have found nothing, not even a suggestion. Everyone runs from us as if we had the plague."

"Ah! Now I understand. Wait here. I will be back." The doctor left the office for a few minutes. "Good news!" he exclaimed when he returned. "There is a room at the European Hotel. The owner is one of my patients. I just called her on the telephone."

Father reached into his side pocket for his wallet.

"No, no, that is not necessary. I give advice without charge. If in the future you will need someone to assist in childbirth. Well, that will be another matter." He looked meaningfully at my Mother. Everyone laughed as they shook the good doctor's hand.

The room at the European Hotel was not a room. It was more like a slit in the wall, and a dark one at that. However, my parents were not in a position to grumble. After a cup of hot coffee with fresh cream and a bagel, followed at noon by a very decent lunch of grouse in sour cream with raspberry jam, they made peace with their accommodations, except for one thing.

They were puzzled by a strange detail: wide metal stripping on all doors. One morning, meeting a janitor in the corridor, Father inquired as to the reason for the stripping.

"Rats," the servant answered calmly.

"RATS?!" Father exclaimed, alarmed.

"Yes," the janitor answered in a nonchalant manner, as if it were of no importance. "They chew through the doors and enter rooms at night. You see, as soon as wheat is shipped off to Russia, rats come into town."

Yes, indeed, there were rats. My parents could hear them chewing on the wood at night. They were especially numerous in the toilets, trying to get to the water. Everyone staying in the hotel had to bang and clatter to frighten them off before entering the toilets.

Fortunately, the stay in Omsk ended as soon as my parents, through an old connection, obtained tickets on a train to Biysk, a lovely rural town. Here they intended to stay awhile. But lawlessness was reaching even this distant, peaceful Siberian region. Pillaging sailors, who had mutinied from the Vladivostok Navy made nightly excursions to Biysk. They even visited the inn where my parents had found a room, but after a talk with Liza they left them unharmed.

Siberia in 1918 was not included in the Soviet of Russia. This condition led to the formation of a White Siberian Army under General Kolchak. It was called the White Army, as opposed to the Red, with its red banner with hammer and sickle, under which the Revolutionary Army served.

As usual, the merchants had been approached by General Kolchak to fund the Army's needs. Only one merchant, Nikolai Asanov, realized the importance of maintaining it. He alone contributed. Sadly enough, later, when Siberia was taken by the Reds and Kolchak was defeated, Nikolai Asanov paid for his help with his life.

The next city my parents reached was Biysk. Here they stayed for several months. Boredom was deadly. Biysk, with its unpaved roads, was drowning in mud. At last, at the end of April, a play was announced. Father and Mother decided to see it. It was fortunate that they did.

During intermission, as they stood by the refreshment counter, a young man in the uniform of a telegraph official approached them.

"Are you by chance Kotenev from St. Petersburg?" he inquired politely. "There is a telegram for you at the office. It arrived two days ago but we could not locate you."

The next day Father picked up the telegram. It was brief and had no signature. All it said was "YOU ARE BEING SEARCHED."

That was enough. Prudence dictated the taking of the very next train to the farthest city to which they could obtain tickets. It was Irkutsk, one of the largest cities in Siberia, near Lake Baikal.

Irkutsk is a large industrial center and at that time was in a state of depression. The recent revolt of the Yunkers, a low military caste of the army, had left bad memories amongst the population. Everywhere one looked were the remains of burnt houses. Other buildings that had been spared had broken windows and bullet holes in the walls. At sunset all stores closed, leaving the streets dismal and deserted.

"Shouldn't we try to go farther east?" my Mother pleaded as they drove from the station to the hotel. The surroundings and the sight of pedestrians hurrying along, fearfully peering to the left and to the right, made her uncomfortable.

"Yes, Harbin would be better," Father agreed, aware also that their finances were rapidly diminishing. He knew that he would have to seek work soon, but in Irkutsk it certainly did not look promising.

To leave, however, they had to obtain permission from the Commandant's Secretariat. This was not easy. Because the city was under military control, security was tight. All exits were carefully scrutinized.

"We know you wounded officers. Once you are beyond the Lake you will immediately recuperate from your wounds," the clerk in charge rudely replied when Father requested permission to leave, giving health as his reason. Neither did appealing to his common decency move him. The clerk remained adamant in refusing to provide the necessary papers.

What a predicament! Father returned to the hotel most discouraged. No one slept that night. Even Liza, who usually remained optimistic, was turning on her squeaky cot behind the screen in the far corner of the room.

Fortunately, Father suddenly remembered that he was still counted as a Cossack of the Suvorov Area since the Russo-Japanese War, and therefore had the right to return there. With this in mind, he drove straight to the Irkutsk Cossack Headquarters where he expected to be treated better.

The man at the desk greeted Father politely and listened attentively. "It would be better if we gave you authorization as a Cossack Delegate traveling to Chita on our regiment's business. They have more respect for delegates," he said, and issued the necessary papers. With these in hand, Father went back to the previous clerk.

"Ha! So you have gotten yourself an authorization!" The clerk bristled with annoyance as he signed the permission for travel.

Early the next morning, my parents were sitting in the third-class wagon, the only passage available. Mother remembered the bare wooden bunks that stank of urine and dirt. Nevertheless, Liza arranged the bedding as well as she could and it was comfortable enough. The other passengers were doing the same. As the train sped through the endless Siberian forests, brooks, and distant hills, they felt relieved watching the picturesque region through the window.

All went well until the evening when Mother noticed the other passengers whispering in an animated fashion. At first, she did not pay much attention to it. But Liza did, and at the next station when she went to fetch hot water for tea, Liza returned looking frightened.

"Sir," she whispered to Father, "I heard that at the next stop, Slyudyanka, all documents are checked and officers are taken off the train. Someone by the name of

Savich, a Red commissar, is merciless. He sends the officers to the Cheremhorsky Mines."

With Mother's help, Father made his way along the corridor to find the train conductor to ask him if this was true. The train conductor would not give an answer at once. Only after a bank note was pressed into his half-opened hand did he whisper, "Your Honor, everything does happen. It is not our business, you know." He rolled his eyes meaningfully.

Depressed by this information, my parents could not drink their tea. That night, Father dreaded every stop. He could not sleep. Eventually, exhausted, he dozed off. How long he slept he did not know. The sun's rays were illuminating the countryside when he awoke. He looked around. The other passengers were calmly munching their bagels and sipping their tea.

"How far is Slyudyanka?" Father anxiously asked his neighbor to the left, a fat country woman with a kerchief tied around her head.

"Now you are asking!" the country woman raised her eyes. "We passed it long ago."

"What do you mean we passed it? What about Savich and the inspection of papers?"

"No one checked anything," another passenger explained. "I heard that the Commandant got drunk as a pig—so the train was not ordered to stop."

Father made the sign of the cross thanking the Lord for his protection. The world suddenly seemed to be a better place for the three of them.

The next stop was Chita, and then Harbin, where they arrived at night. The streets looked dismal, and only at occasional crossroads did they see a policeman. They began searching for lodgings and their Omsk experience was repeated, with only one difference—the weather was warmer and pleasanter. It was a balmy May night and the sky was studded with millions of twinkling stars.

The Revolution's influence had not yet reached this Far Eastern place and life was flowing in the old way. Gendarmes guarded the safety of the city, while on the main street elegant men and women were strolling about. One felt the peace and security. It was enjoyed by everyone, especially the Chinese residents, who had received the right to have their armed units in the area and were controlling the railway line.

General Horvat, the Chief in command of this area, lived with his family in a splendid manor house. In this luxurious residence, his wife, Camilla Albertovna, reigned supreme. She entertained lavishly and surrounded herself with all the pomp of royalty.

My parents stayed in Harbin for several months, during which time Father sought employment. One day he found himself in the Tsisicar Railway Station, where he had just arrived looking for opportunities. Here, by chance, he met an officer he had known during the Russo-Japanese War. Tambaur Malinovsky was his name.

Tambaur Malinovsky had been a senior officer of the Baikal Cossack Battery and had, at that time, been court-martialed for misusing government funds. He was eventually absolved. Now he was on the staff of Baron Ungern-Sternberg, the commander of the army in Siberia loyal to the old imperial regime. In obvious high spirits, he invited my parents to stay with him. Of course, they were happy to accept his invitation.

Tambaur's house, situated on a side street near the railway station, was unbearably cold. However, under the able supervision of his housekeeper, Maria Lvovna, who was an excellent cook as well, his meals were excellent and compensated for many inconveniences.

Tambaur loved to eat well and Father used to recall how his host could consume, at one sitting, unlimited quantities of pancakes, varenikys (dumplings), and many other fatty victuals, so typical of the kitchens of the Ukraine, the part of Russia where Tambaur had been born.

Strangely enough, his extreme corpulence, the consequence of his eating habits, did not diminish either his energy or his agility. When my parents would creep back to their room with difficulty after one of these gargantuan meals, Tambaur would be singing with gusto in his high-pitched tenor voice his Ukrainian songs.

One day he announced to Father, "I am short of money. The creditors are hounding me. The Baron promised to pay, but today is the seventh of the month and not a kopek have I seen."

"What about the Japanese?" Father asked, knowing that Japan was one of the countries that was interested in these parts of Siberia.

"As soon as they freed the Baikal Lake Region from the Soviets, they stopped supplying us with money," replied Tambaur. "They are saying, 'You can support yourselves. This region is the richest in the world.'"

"Maybe they are correct," Father answered. "Remember how the Cossack Ottomon Semenov used to obtain his providence. You know there may be legal ways," he added. Tambaur's tiny sharp eyes had a strange gleam in them.

"Why not?" Father continued. "The Military units could take it upon themselves to supply the inhabitants with various merchandise. Harbin and Manchuria are crammed with it. Beyond Baikal, to the west, there is no sugar, tea, or flour because the railway is transporting provisions only for the military."

"But where would we get the capital for these commodities?" Tambaur asked, scratching his beard.

"One can start with small sums and gradually increase them," Father answered, confident that it could be done.

"How much do you think we would need to start?"

"One, two hundred thousand rubles."

Tambaur became glum. "We don't have such financiers in this region." he mumbled.

"They can be found." Father's instinct told him he was right. "Why, your Baron Ungern-Sternberg, the Commander of the Rifle Brigade, the Cossack Unit and the Artillery, must have funds."

Here the conversation ended. But ten days later Tambaur came home all excited. "Your idea impressed the Baron," he announced to Father all smiles. "The Baron would like you to come to his headquarters at Dauria immediately."

The next morning they were both sitting in a railway car on the way to the Baron. Father had mixed feelings about this visit to the man about whom many rumors were circulating. Baron Ungern-Sternberg's eccentric and unpredictable nature was well known. Still, Father was hoping that the meeting might lead to something constructive.

"What can I expect for my efforts?" Father asked Tambaur while they were having dinner in the dining car.

"I suppose a percentage of the net profits. But all these arrangements you must settle only with the Baron himself," Tambaur replied, as he shoved a huge piece of steak into his mouth.

5

The Baron

General Baron Ungern-Sternberg occupied one of the largest barracks. A more dismal place would be hard to find. Not a tree, not a bush, nothing but a bare expanse of land as far as the eyes could see. Water had to be carried from a well a mile away. In the summer water had to be brought by train. How the Command could have chosen such a location for the Rifle Brigade, the Cossack Unit, and the Artillery, was hard to comprehend.

"What a damned place!" Even the Baron—who was usually indifferent to nature's beauties and weather, hot or cold, and who always wore the same light cape over the same shabby uniform—complained.

In Dauria, besides the Baron's units, there was also a small detachment of Japanese. Officially, they were serving as a guard unit, but unofficially they were observers of what went on in the Baron's unusual forces, which included wild Mongol horsemen and their just as strange-looking officers.

Once, in a moment of confidence, Tambaur elucidated the situation. "You think these are Mongolian officers? Not at all. These are Japanese. Out of the wild robber Mongol tribes they form military units loyal to Japan, preparing them to hit in the rear of China or Russia, depending on whom Japan might be in conflict with. It is being arranged with methodical care and cunning."

Father and Tambaur were met coldly at the Baron's headquarters. Father felt an air of distrust everywhere, and the vast, cold, unfriendly buildings with their bare dirty walls and few furnishings added to the depressing atmosphere. Here no one laughed. Everyone spoke in low voices and those who entered on business, tried to accomplish it as quickly as they could. The Baron's name was whispered. Should he himself enter the room, everyone tried to make a quick exit.

Father noticed that Tambaur Malinovsky had also changed. He sucked in his protruding belly and seemed to move like a rolling ball while holding up his saber at his side.

"Please enter!" the Baron beckoned.

They walked into a large room, with only a desk and several chairs in the middle of it. This was the Baron's study and dining room. At their entrance, they watched the Baron rise and come around his desk with an outstretched hand.

He was a tall, young, blond officer with an unruly lock of curly hair on his forehead, a perfect representative of the Teutonic race in the prime of manhood. His short moustache was carefully clipped and his gray sports shirt had the officer's medal of Saint George pinned to it on his chest. He looked piercingly at Father with his steely grayish-blue eyes.

"Tambaur spoke to me about you," he addressed my Father. "I like your plan. I am convinced that the present speculation on goods will soon be stopped. All will be in military hands. The time is coming for Military Socialism."

"You are quite right, General," Tambaur interjected respectfully and inclined his head as if in anticipation of hearing more. But the Baron stopped him short.

Turning to Father, the Baron said, "We will speak in detail later. You, Staff Captain Kotenev, I shall expect you for supper this evening!"

Tambaur Malinovsky clicked his heels, bowed and backed out of the room.

"I will send you Neimann. He will arrange a room for you and whatever you will need." With these words the Baron terminated the meeting.

Neimann, the Baron's orderly, came in. He was a stolid-appearing German and was loyal to the Baron like a dog, and the Baron trusted him. They always conversed in German.

In no time Neimann arranged for a room and had brought into it a bed, bedding, pillows, and even a small rug. In the evening he came again to inform Father that the Baron was waiting. The Baron and Father had supper alone. Their business arrangements were agreed upon in minutes.

"I trust you. Tomorrow you will receive money to proceed as planned," the Baron told Father at parting.

The next morning, the Baron called his Cossack treasurer. "Give the Staff Captain Kotenev one hundred and fifty thousand rubles."

The treasurer, a man of about fifty, with graying hair and a care-worn face, opened his eyes wide in amazement. "But, Baron, I do not have such a sum in my safe box!" he stammered.

Baron Ungern knit his brow. For a minute he looked pensive. "Take from the other…"

"Yes, sir!" And the treasurer retreated backward toward the door.

"Where is the receipt?" Father asked when the Cossack treasurer brought him a leather sack containing 150,000 rubles' worth of opium-smelling Russian Bank Notes, which his Mongol guard had counted out.

"If you like, sir."

"What do you mean?" Father was surprised by his attitude.

"This money is under the personal jurisdiction of the Baron. He doesn't require receipts. It's given on trust."

Baron Ungern-Sternberg was a most remarkable man, a man out of his times. Motivated by dreams alien to everyone around him, he was disliked and misunderstood.

In a time when the old order in Russia was crumbling and the new order established by the Revolutionaries under Lenin was beginning to penetrate even the remotest corners of Siberia, Baron Ungern was trying to forestall this change in the Far East and Siberia. Commanding the military forces in the region, which were still loyal to the old regime, he, like Baron Vrangel, another general of German descent, who commanded loyal forces in the south of Russia, fought to the last what was to be a losing battle. Remaining true to himself, Baron Ungern thereby eventually met a tragic end. He was strange, unpredictable, and often mad—as he seemed to everyone who came in contact with him—but still, he remained a knight without reproach, true to his own principles.

In his staid family of Ungern-Sternbergs, this sullen man—a cruel, if not sadistic soldier, yet devoid of avarice—was considered an "enfant terrible." His family did not like to think about him. He had been educated in the Marine Corps School, from which he entered the Baikal Cossack Division located near the Pacific Ocean.

The appearance of this young descendent of Teutonic knights, infused with ideals and a sense of honor that few understood in our prosaic century, in the midst of coarse Cossack officers, was, in truth, a tragedy.

The Baron's parents, wealthy Baltic landowners, sent him a sizeable monthly stipend. He gave everything away, helping everyone who asked, often remaining penniless himself. He dressed badly, forgot to shave, and at times, even to comb his hair. Frequently deep in his own thoughts, he was a stranger to everything that surrounded him. Once he disappeared. Ordering his horse to be saddled, he rode off. After months of searching he was traced to Mongolia.

Apparently, some Mongols picked him up in the desert near Hingan. He was sick and dying from starvation. They took him to the nearest Buddhist monastery, where the monks nursed him back to health. How and why he was in Hingan remained a mystery. He himself disliked talking about it...

An Unpredictable Situation

Several weeks later, Father stopped in Verhneudinsk, where he had ordered the tea, sugar, and flour in accordance with the agreement with the Baron. He was having breakfast at the Station Manchuria when he saw Peter Isaev, someone he had known both before and during his Russian-Japanese War days. Isaev had been the Commandant of that Station even in the days of the Tsar. He looked worried when he approached Father's table.

"What is it with you?" Father asked him, inviting him to sit down.

"Finish your meal and come with me to my study," he replied, looking around apprehensively.

In his study, after first carefully closing the door, Isaev turned to Father. "What has happened between you and the Baron?" he asked.

"Nothing. We made a business arrangement. I have not seen him in several weeks. Why do you ask me these questions?" Father was beginning to feel uncomfortable.

Isaev opened the middle drawer of his desk and took out a paper which he handed to Father. Father stared at it in disbelief. It was an order for his arrest.

"This is ridiculous! I have not done anything! What about our business agreement? I have to pay my Chinese merchants for their products!"

"There is nothing that I can do. The Baron is most unpredictable." Isaev gestured with his hands, indicating his helplessness. Then he left the room.

Father remained alone, totally bewildered, worried about what would happen to my Mother should he be arrested. After several minutes there was a knock on the door and a young officer, a colonel, entered. He asked for Colonel Isaev.

"He will be back soon. Would you like to wait for him?" Father waved him toward an empty chair. He was surprised that such a young man would be a colonel. He seemed a mere boy. One might have mistaken him for a girl with his curly light blond hair and long eyelashes. Father could not control his curiosity.

"How old are you, Colonel?" he asked.

"Twenty-five. But please do not call me Colonel. Just Stepanov. The times for ranks have passed. We are mere executioners," Stepanov finished with a smirk on his face.

So this was the famous Stepanov, the Commander of the Armored Cars of General Ottoman Semenov. The man who carried out dangerous assignments for the General. Father remembered stories about Stepanov's cruelties, more severe even than Baron Ungern's.

"Maybe you are not looking for Colonel Isaev, but for me," Father said. "I am Staff Captain Kotenev."

"You are Staff Captain Kotenev?" Stepanov looked surprised. "I am supposed to bring you back to the Baron."

Meanwhile, Isaev had returned. He stopped abruptly at the door upon seeing Stepanov in the room.

Stepanov turned to Isaev. "Maybe, Colonel, you can explain something to me."

"Why don't we go into the corridor?" Isaev took Stepanov by the elbow as he led him out. After several minutes, Isaev returned alone. "You will go back with Stepanov," Isaev. "Don't be afraid. You can trust this creature. He has his own grudge against the Baron to settle."

Colonel Isaev was correct. One could trust Stepanov. Late that evening, he and my Father finally arrived at the Baron's barracks. The lights were still on. Stepanov went in first. Father stayed in the half-lit entrance hall not knowing what to expect. Soon Stepanov returned.

"All is well," Stepanov told him. "Baron Ungern asks you to enter."

Father opened the door and stepped in irresolutely.

The Baron greeted him in a friendly manner. "Very glad to see you," he greeted Father. "Please come in and take a seat."

The room was the study, now made into a dining room. The Baron's desk was covered with a white tablecloth and set for dinner. About ten officers sat around it. Father sat down and Neimann brought him a glass of wine.

"Splendid, tomorrow we will talk," the Baron explained. "Right now I must leave." The Baron got up and departed with the rest of the officers. Father was left alone. Despite Neimann's entreaties he could not eat anything.

The next morning Father was still in bed when Baron Ungern came into his room.

"Don't get up. We can talk just as you are!" The Baron leaned his back against the side of the tall Russian stove, with his hands in his sleeves.

"You must help me to execute two persons according to the law," he began. "Lawfully, you understand. There are these silly details that control the actions of men which have brought us to this sad state in Russia. You are a jurist and will be able to manage. I am tired of hearing 'The Baron is crazy,' 'He is a beast,' 'He shoots people without a court hearing.' All right, let them have a court session!"

"But, Baron, I am not a good jurist and am not versed in the laws of military court," Father protested.

"Nonsense! You are intelligent. That's enough. My Chief of Staff will give you all necessary information!"

"But, sir, you must have better-informed people on your staff," Father tried again. Baron Ungern knit his brows.

"I knew it! They told me you would never agree and that you would never come back to Dauria. That is the reason I ordered your arrest. When you finish the case you can go to Verhneudinsk or wherever you desire."

There was nothing Father could do but hope for the best and trust the Good Lord to carry him through. The Chief of Staff, Colonel Aksimov, a former Gendarme, informed him that the man and wife that the Baron wanted to be convicted were the Savelieffs. They were accused of sabotage and espionage on behalf of the Bolsheviks.

"I know very little about Court Martial regulations. Besides, I wonder if this case really belongs under military procedure," Father explained to Colonel Aksimov.

The Chief of Staff shrugged his shoulders and told Father, "I was ordered to wait for your arrival. The couple is in the guardhouse. Do you order me to bring them?"

"All right. Bring them!"

Two Mongols in bright blue wadded cotton trousers and jackets, with rifles slung over their shoulders, dragged in an officer in a torn and dirty overcoat and a young, disheveled blond woman. They looked pale and emaciated. Father ordered the Mongols to leave, as he did not want them present during the interrogation. These precautions were not out of place in Dauria.

"Your name, rank, and age?" he asked the officer, after both sat down.

The man answered all questions in a straightforward manner. Then suddenly his voice cracked. "Why all this comedy? I know that Baron Ungern will shoot me. But I plead for my wife!"

"It will all be done according to law. I must ask you the details and the reason you were found so close to the restricted area, which was posted with signs," Father replied.

"We were careless and wandered into the area not knowing the danger," the officer explained without hesitation. "We are new here and on the way to my battalion in Chita. We have been kept for two weeks under intolerable conditions. I request that my Commander be notified," the young officer answered without hesitation.

He gave his own battalion commander's name. Everything pointed to the likelihood of it having been a mistake and that, indeed, they had wandered unknowingly into the area.

Father's decision was that the couple was not guilty and that they should be released.

The next morning, Father went to see Baron Ungern-Sternberg.

"Baron," Father said, after greeting him, "of course, you can shoot these people, but not according to the law."

"Why?!" The baron puckered his lips.

"Because what they did does not merit capital punishment."

"I don't care! They will be punished and you have to prove their guilt!" the Baron blazed. He turned abruptly to leave, but before he reached the door, he suddenly turned to Father. "Are you positively sure that they are innocent?"

"Yes, sir."

For a brief moment the Baron stood irresolute. Then, suddenly, he looked at Father with a piercing glance. "You are sure they are innocent?" he repeated without taking his eyes off Father's.

"Yes, sir," Father replied, looking back with the same unswerving gaze.

"All right, I trust you! Release the prisoners!" The Baron walked swiftly to the door and was gone.

The Savelieffs were released that same day.

This incident made Father decide to split with the Baron, sell the merchandise he had bought, pay off the Chinese creditors in Harbin, return to the Baron the sum he had given him, and pay Tambaur Malinovsky his promised percentage. He considered that it was best for him to leave with my Mother for Vladivostok. Father feared that the next disagreement with the Baron might not end as well.

The market in Verhneudinsk, which opened on the 21st of January, was known for its huge crowds and the multimillion-ruble exchange of money. But in 1919, when Father arrived, because there were not as many people in the area and the market for the tea, wheat and sugar that Father had purchased, was limited, he sold very little. What hurt him was the distrust he met as an agent of Baron Ungern. Large Siberian firms would not do business with him. Fortunately, however, Father did sell enough to pay the Chinese creditors.

Having sent a report regarding the situation, Father received, in return, instructions from the Baron to donate all the money to the cultural institutions educating the Buryats, the indigenous Siberian population. Baron Ungern was imbued with the idea of providing schools for the Buryat children, printing newspapers, and even founding a university. More than 400,000 rubles, a sizeable sum even at that time of ruble depreciation, were sent to the Chairman of the Buryat Cultural Association.

Baron Ungern-Sternberg's end was sad. He did oust the Chinese troops from Mongolia and took Urga, but he unexpectedly moved to the north toward Verhneudinsk where his forces were badly beaten by the well-organized and well-equipped Bolsheviks. A group of his soldiers rioted. The rioters attacked him at night. They bound him with ropes and handed him over to the Bolsheviks. In Novo-Nikolaevsk, the Baron was tried and executed.

If the Baron had moved to the West into the steppes and not to the North, he might have survived. At that time, neither China nor the Bolsheviks were of sufficient strength to capture him there.

But Baron Ungern-Sternberg was incapable of practical considerations, and as a result, his life came to an end in the same unpredictable and insane manner as he had lived.

7

Siberia: 1918–1920

Everyone confidently awaited the help and intervention in Siberia from Russia's allies, the English and the Czechs. Everyone believed that the European partners for whom Russia had spilled so much blood during World War I, would come to help save Russia from the claws of Communism. Or, at least, that they would come to save their millions of tons of supplies still unpaid for by the Russian government. There was still another reason for assisting Russia. It would provide an opportunity to snap up the regions of Sakhalin or Komchatka. Of course, these thoughts no one uttered.

Still, Russia's allies delayed. So did Japan, which, more than the others, should have been interested in the Far Eastern regions.

The Bolshevik Army, gradually moved eastward into Siberia. Soon their red banner with hammer and sickle was flying over many Siberian cities and towns. During this period the Bolshevik Army pressed forward. Discord among the commanding officers of the loyal "White" troops, constant desertion of White soldiers to the Bolshevik side, plus the weak, irresolute leadership of Admiral Kolchak, the White Commander in Chief, were the causes of its final defeat.

Everyone who could was fleeing. My Father and Mother would have been stranded if it had not been for several friends, staff officers, who had at their disposal a couple of train wagons. They took my parents along. My parents took with them the remaining crates that had contained tea and sugar. Out of these crates they constructed a small cabin on Tiumen station where they lived for two weeks until they were able to take a train to Vladivostok. Before leaving, Father sold the last of the tea at very cheap prices to the local peasants.

8

My Parents Flee to China

Then came the memorable day in late January when the sound of cannon shots was heard. The Revolutionary Red Army had finally reached even this distant city, and captured it. General Rozanov, the White Army Commander of the Vladivostok forces, fled on one of the Japanese ships. At the roll call at the Fortress by the new masters, only Colonel Nazadze, my godfather; Father; and two younger men remained.

Colonel Krakovetsky, the new Bolshevik commander, offered to permit them to stay, but Father declined. He realized that sooner or later his former connections to Baron Ungern-Sternberg would become known. This fact alone would be enough to warrant his execution. Many White officers were shot for less. Therefore, it was best to leave for Manchuria.

China, too, beckoned. Father remembered when, as a young officer in 1902, he was attached to the Russian Embassy in Peking. Without difficulty, Father purchased tickets on the train to Harbin. With a few other passengers, they found comfortable seats in the second-class wagon. All seemed to be going well when suddenly the doors of the compartment swung open and two armed Red commissars entered.

"We are here to inspect the luggage!" they announced and started to open every suitcase, sack, and package, confiscating anything that they deemed illegal.

By this time my parents had little money. Mother's jewelry had long ago been sold to provide for necessities; however, Father had a revolver, a Browning. Mother had placed it in the small brown valise. The gun was their only security, and Father had heard that the Chinese paid good prices for weapons and ammunition in Harbin.

With dread Father was watching the commissars approach them to begin their search. First, they picked up several bundles, opened one suitcase, then another, finally turning to the small brown valise. Father caught his breath. The commissars turned it upside down. There was nothing in it but some clothing. Father looked at Mother. She was sitting calmly, staring out of the window.

Strange, he thought. What happened to the revolver?! Father looked at Liza. She, too, was looking out of the window, holding me on her knees.

Now one of the commissars noticed that the pad on the bunk near Mother had a bulge near the wall. The commissar was about to pick the pad up...THE REVOLVER! flashed in Father's mind! Mother had hidden it between the pad and wall while everyone's attention was distracted.

"Oh, let it be, Comrade!" Father drew the commissar away from the seat. "The conductor will arrange it. Besides, the third bell is about to ring." Mercifully, at that very moment the bell did ring, announcing the departure of the train. The commissars hastened to the door.

The train started with a jolt. There was the rumble of the wheels. Father wiped cold sweat off his forehead. They were on their way to Harbin and, eventually, Shanghai, China.

9

Shanghai, China

My earliest memory of Shanghai is of our flat of two small rooms, a tiny, five-by-six-foot kitchenette, and a shower stall with a portable toilet. The apartment was intended, originally, for the servants of a large brownstone town house, located on one of the main thoroughfares of Shanghai. Narrow, steep—almost perpendicular—stairs led up to our apartment. How my Father negotiated them daily with his crippled legs, without complaint, is a wonderment to me.

Our landlord was a Portuguese named Da Silva. Despite his affluent-sounding name, he could not have been much better off than ourselves, judging by the quantity and quality of the strange-looking people he lodged. They would peep out of their nooks and crannies as Liza and I passed through the corridor to the main entrance door.

Father and Mother occupied the larger of our two rooms, which also served as sitting and dining area. Although smaller, Liza's and my room above did have some advantages over theirs. It had a window into which the sun penetrated, and there was a view of the lane beyond the high wall encircling the backyard. This lane was a source of constant entertainment for me. I was only four years old, and Liza would let me stand on a chair so that I could watch the activity outside.

In contrast to the wide noisy road in front of our town house—where the tooting of horns, the screeching of car brakes, and the angry exclamations of the pedestrians mingled with the shrill whistles of a British policeman on the corner, which were the usual raucous noises of a busy Chinese street—life in our back lane passed serenely.

At break of day the "honey-dew cart" would announce its arrival by an indescribable potency of odor—the contents of chamber pots and portable latrines collected from house to house. There was the sound of swishing whisk brooms and splashing water as the cartman conscientiously cleaned each container after emptying the contents into his two large vats. Not one drop was wasted, for this was precious stuff, eventually finding its way into the fields to be spread as fertilizer. What luscious lettuce, carrots, cabbage and spinach grew as a result of it! Never have I eaten more flavorful vegetables than in China.

The day was still in its infancy when the iceman arrived. Under the cover of a thick burlap, he hauled huge blocks of ice on his two-wheel horse-drawn cart. For the price of several coppers, the driver would chop off the size necessary to fit into the icebox.

Later, about midday, the wheelbarrow-restaurant man arrived. Unfurling his white canopy, he placed folding tables and benches under it, and then proceeded to prepare his specialties over a charcoal brazier. Delicious smells of mysterious ingredients would drift into my window as he stirred the contents of a cauldron with his chopsticks, all the while singing out the day's menu and prices.

The food must have been enticing and the price just right, for, in no time, customers would occupy his benches, ready to be served the bowls of noodles and tofu, and the promised delicacy of the day.

My favorite participant in the life of our lane was the fritter vendor. He arrived about four in the afternoon, a veritable artist. The Chinese children loved him. They came swarming from all directions when the jingle of his bells announced his approach.

Into a deep pig-iron cooker bubbling with hot oil, the fritter vendor would throw ribbon-like shreds of dough. In a few seconds the shreds turned gold and puffed out. He would wait for just the right moment, and then out of the spattering oil he would snatch a piece of cooked dough with his tongs. Lifting each strip, he gave a sudden twist of his wrist and—voilà!—beautifully convoluted six-inch golden fritter was formed. They were crisp and sweet and melted in one's mouth. The Chinese children stretched out their little arms with coppers in their hands. Occasionally, Liza, too, would buy one for me.

The most spectacular of our visitors, however, was the bird peddler. He came later in the day carrying cages tied cleverly in tiers on each end of a long bamboo pole, which he balanced on his shoulder. The cages contained canaries, finches, parakeets, chickadees, and the most prized, the black birds. They could sing in many ways, and sometimes even talk like humans. The old men on the block would gather to examine and listen to the feathered tribe.

In China, collecting birds and training them is a venerable hobby. In the parks I have seen respectable-looking Chinese gentlemen, clad in black silk gowns and small round silk caps with jade or amber buttons on the peaks, holding up exquisitely made wooden cages with birds. These gentlemen were proudly exhibiting their pets. Even competitions were held and prizes were given to the owners of the birds that performed the best trick or surpassed in singing.

We, too, had a cage with golden finches. Father took care of them and enjoyed watching them frolic. I suspect that it was a way of taking his mind off his worries. This was a trying time for him. After months of searching, Father had finally found a position as an interpreter translating Russian into English at the Shanghai Court. It had to have been taxing work because he had started to learn English only since we had arrived in China. Father memorized one hundred words a day. Mother, not understanding a single word, would test him. I could hear them practicing for hours in the evenings.

"Necessity is a great mover to achievements," Father would tell me. "You can do anything if you put your mind to it!" he would add. At that time I did not quite understand the full significance of these words, but as I grew older they would come into my mind in times of need.

And so, he did achieve. Not knowing English well, but relying on his previous knowledge of court procedure, Father would translate the testimonies of the wretched Russian emigrants, who had been arrested for petty thievery, forgery, or prostitution. He tried to help them by presenting their declarations in such a way that frequently their cases were dismissed.

The judges were not unaware of this, but, like Father, they, too, understood that in most cases dire need had forced the men and women to turn to these unsavory practices. Times were difficult for the thousands of Russians who had been forced to escape from the Bolsheviks during the Russian Revolution. Perseverance and fortitude were needed to create a life for oneself. Jobs were scarce. There was no help for the needy and not everyone was adequate to the task.

Soon Father became acquainted with a sizeable number of these less respectable members of the Russian emigrant community. I remember several occasions when, sitting next to him in a rickshaw, as we were driven along one of the main streets, some bedraggled-looking individual on the sidewalk would lift up his tattered hat to salute. Father always acknowledged these greetings by lifting his own hat and bowing. "That is one of my special connections," he would joke.

"But, Father, he looks so horrid!" I would protest.

"My dear, despise not a beggar's plight. One knows not what may lie ahead of thee," he would quote an old Russian proverb.

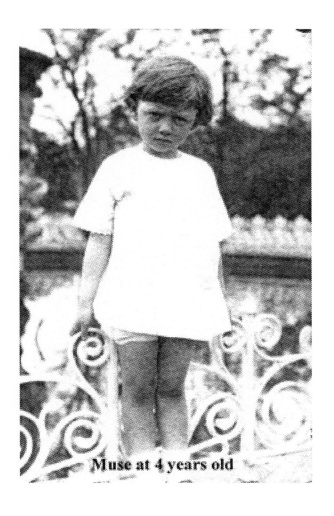

Muse at 4 years old

10

Our Life Style
Takes A Step Upward

Father's English steadily improved and eventually he authored several books in English. When I was about five, his abilities were recognized. Father was appointed Head of the Shanghai Municipal Council's Archives, under the British Colonial Service governing the British Concession of Shanghai. Shanghai territory had the British International Concession, the French Concession, and the Chinese City.

With this advancement, our life style also took a step upward. We moved to a two-storied house at the end of a cobblestone street called Range Road. It had a balcony and a garden. Instead of a tiny shower stall and a portable latrine, we now had two full bathrooms with tremendous bathtubs on lion's paw feet, and water toilets.

Each time someone pulled the wooden handle hanging on the long chain of the water tank near the ceiling, a thunderous burst of water rushed down the copper pipe into the toilet bowl. It swirled loudly for a minute or two and then, with a gluck, gluck, gluck, drained out, giving notice throughout the house that someone had just attended to nature. (It is curious how trivia such as this remains in one's memory when much more important moments sink into oblivion.)

The new house seemed very grand to me. Across from the imposingly arched entrance door rose a wide staircase. Its polished banisters and railing of dark mahogany lent a note of luxury. I loved to slide my hand along the shiny, satin-like surface as I climbed up to the second floor where the front room with a balcony was assigned to Liza and myself. My parent's bedroom and our dining room were on the first floor, to the right of the entrance.

The rooms were spacious and the ceilings high. A fireplace or cook stove in every room kept us warm in winter. The house was pleasing in every way, and yet a strange, unexplainable atmosphere prevailed in it, especially on the second floor.

Our tenant, in the small room off the first flight of stairs, noticed that his coal stove was red with heat one summer day. Upon inspection, he discovered that the stove was cold and empty. Pale as a ghost, he rushed to tell our cook-boy in the kitchen. Together they scrutinized the little pig-iron stove. There it stood, cold and gray. Soon after, our tenant left us.

There were also mysterious voices calling people by name. Several persons had heard this phenomenon downstairs when there was no one present on the second floor. The most unnerving occurrence, though, was experienced by my Uncle Vsevolod, who had recently arrived from France. He was a battle-scarred veteran Legionnaire, six feet two inches tall, a hero who had earned the Medal of Honor for bravery while fighting the Moors in Africa.

He had remained to guard the house while our family temporarily moved into the center of Shanghai for safety during a political disturbance caused by one of the Chinese War Lords. On the second day, early in the morning, he appeared at our rooms with his valise in hand, swearing in perfect Parisian French, vowing that he would never set foot in the house again. He explained that he had gone peacefully to bed at a normal hour of the evening, but that no sooner had he turned off the light in his room when the door creaked open.

Thinking that perhaps he had not closed it properly, Uncle Vsevolod turned on the light, and before his unbelieving eyes, the door to his room slowly closed. Upon inspection, he found no one in the corridor. He checked the doorknob and it was in order. He returned to bed and turned off the lights. Again there was that unmistakable creak and the sound of the door opening. Once more he turned on the light while the door slowly swung itself back. This was too much for my Uncle. He got out of bed, dressed, and packed his valise. He waited for the break of day sitting up with the light on.

My Father was politely skeptical, but I believed my Uncle, for I, too, always felt uncomfortable when left alone in that room. On the other hand, my insecurity might have stemmed from causes engendered by human, not supernatural, beings.

Three events closely following one on the other had, at this time, greatly affected my world. The first was the arrival of my German Grandmother, my Father's mother, from Russia; the second, my beloved Liza's sudden departure; and third, Uncle Vsevolod's coming from Paris, adding considerable tension to our household.

11

My German Grandmother

My Grandmother, Emma Ivanovna, as everyone respectfully called her, was a very proper lady. She arrived from the south of Russia via the Black Sea, having traveled through the Suez Canal, around India, through the Strait of Malacca, around Singapore, and up the east coast of Asia. The route was long and tedious, but she survived unscathed, and grateful to the man who had helped her, a Soviet commissar, in whose house she had been employed as a governess to his armless boy.

It was a good and kind family where Grandmother had found refuge and work as a governess after my parents had departed. Her charge was a ten-year-old boy who was born without arms. Despite his birth defect, he was exceptionally intelligent, gentle, and handsome, with an endearing manner. My Grandmother always remembered him with great tenderness.

"He would use his feet as hands and could write and draw beautifully," Grandmother recalled with a tender smile on her stern, handsome face.

Grandmother arrived just before Liza left us. I remained under her guidance for the next several years and she, more than anyone, was responsible for shaping my character. She instilled in me a love of order, cleanliness, perseverance and discipline. She imbued me with an uncompromising sense of what was right and what was wrong. Later in life, this discipline gave me strength and endurance. But at seven years of age, becoming my German Grandmother's charge was a traumatic experience, particularly because I was to lose my Liza.

The plain-looking, kindhearted peasant girl was not just a nurse to me. After my birth, and I was the only child, when my Mother started to show signs of emotional instability, Liza was entrusted with my well being. I had a wet nurse, but Liza gave me the warmth, love, and protection a child requires. As I grew, she was my constant companion. We took walks together, played together, went to church together, and she shielded me from my Mother's unpredictable outbursts of temper. At the end of the day, after making a sign of the cross over my head, in keeping with the Russian Orthodox tradition, she tucked the blanket around me. Then, turning the lights out, she carefully crept into our large double bed. Feeling her next to me, I drifted into a peaceful sleep.

I loved Liza dearly and she returned my affection by gently indulging my every whim. And so it continued until I noticed that Liza, on her days off, was paying a great deal of attention to her appearance. She had embellished her simple gray Sunday dress with a lace collar and cuffs, and she had started to curl her short blond hair with curling irons. She also began to come home much later than she had before.

Then one evening I heard my Mother downstairs shouting, "YOU CAN LEAVE! THE DOOR IS OPEN!"

Tears were streaming down Liza's cheeks as she ran into our room. The next morning, Liza packed her little brown suitcase and, after giving me a quick hug, she left. That same afternoon my Grandmother took her place in my room.

I was stunned. "Where is Liza?" I asked.

"Liza is to be married to an English gentleman," Grandmother answered curtly.

"Are we going to her wedding?"

"I don't think so."

"Doesn't she want me at her wedding?!" I asked, bewildered. "Doesn't she?!"

Grandmother did not answer. She shrugged her shoulders and continued with her sewing.

Much later I did find out that, of course, we were all invited to Liza's wedding ceremony, but that my Mother had prevented any of us from attending.

Soon after, Liza's husband, a Customs official, was transferred to Hong Kong. Liza did come to say goodbye. She looked elegant in her fashionable beige suit and her black wide-brimmed hat. She did not stay long. She hugged and kissed me in silence, and in the next minute she was gone. I was inconsolable. It was the last time I ever saw her...

My strong-willed, highly disciplined Grandmother and my emotionally unbalanced mother could not see eye to eye. Consequently, with frequent confrontations, my Mother became progressively more nervous and emotionally unstable. Father was too busy earning a living, and later was too engrossed in his writing and social work, organizing and directing a center for needy Russians, to have time for me. Only in my teens did he talk with or counsel me.

Grandmother, stepping into this gap of parental negligence, performed her task splendidly, with all the dedication to duty intrinsic to her Teutonic blood. She was a true daughter of her father, Johannes Robert von Horst, a German mining engineer and prospector, who came to Russia in the latter part of the reign of Catherine the Great. He pioneered and discovered the Lena Gold Field Basin and became its managing director.

At nineteen, my Grandmother married a widower, my Grandfather Michael Ivanovitch, a notary public in Krasnoyarsk. She brought up his son from his first marriage, and gave birth to my Father, my uncle Vsevolod, and my Aunt Magdaleine, who died when she was fifteen.

Grandmother must have been fifty-seven when she arrived in Shanghai, an age considered respectably elderly at that time. Grandmother personified this image to perfection. There was not a hint of frivolity in her behavior or in her appearance. Her dresses, worn down to her ankles, showed no waistline. They were dark blue, gray, brown or black, and only one had a tiny pattern of blue flowers. Long sleeves were the order of the day, changed during summer for comfort to a wide cape collar.

Grandmother used no makeup. She did not need it—her skin was clear and fine, and her lips were naturally red. She arranged her graying hair in a bun with several strange-looking waves in front. The waves were her only touch of vanity and she cultivated them conscientiously. Every night I would watch her dampen her hair, then divide it into equal strands, which she rolled around a carefully folded piece of paper, before tying it with a string. I used to wonder how she could sleep with her head covered with row on row of stiff paper knots, but she did.

Despite her unique manner of dressing, or perhaps because of it, Grandmother always looked very distinguished and I was proud to walk with my hand in hers down the street to catch a trolley which would take us on our weekly trip to the Russian library, situated across town on the Avenue Joffre, in the French Concession.

It was a modest-looking building with shelving to the ceiling, crowded helter-skelter with books. Here, translated into Russian, reposed the literature of the world. Our weekly norm was two or three books. Grandmother, an avid reader, selected them with care. It was a mixed diet. She read to me history, biography, the classics, and once in a while, a romance. Romantic stories were Grandmother's favorites, though she saw to it that we did not overindulge in them.

Grandmother especially savored Werner's Victorian novels, and I enjoyed listening to her reading with feeling about the difficulties of life in manor houses, standing amidst magnificent gardens, where the young, beautiful governess of the many children of the widowed lord fell in love with the estate's handsome gardener, while the widowed lord of the manor was in love with her. I never worried how these complications would end, as the books always finished in a most gratifying manner. At the right moment, by chance, it would be discovered that the lord of the manor was not the lord at all. He was the son of the former gardener switched at birth by mistake with the real lord's son. So the present handsome gardener becomes the lord and there is no mistaking whom the beautiful governess marries. Ah!! What a denouement! The tender, sentimental heart of my seemingly austere Grandmother was gratified. And so was mine.

Order reigned supreme in my Grandmother's world. Liza's gentle permissiveness was gone forever. When I was seven, my Grandmother decided that it was time for me to become literate. Once a week, on Monday, my Russian teacher would arrive. He was a former colonel in the Russian Imperial Infantry. He was destitute. Father wanted to help him, so he hired him to teach me reading and writing in Russian. Judging by the amount of food the Colonel consumed at our dinners after our lessons, I suspected that the repast was part of his tuition fee.

Well, teach me he did. And now I am grateful for it. But at the time, I dreaded my lessons. The Colonel approached his assignment as a teacher in the same spirit that he must have had when training his peasant boys to become soldiers. He would steady his pale blue eyes on me, wrinkle his forehead, bend his bald head down and command, "LET'S START!" I had to read what he pointed out with the tip of his pencil. Woe was me if I had not previously acquainted myself with the words.

"REPEAT AFTER ME!" he would announce. Repeat I would, over and over again, until I thought I would scream. However, strange as it might seem, this method achieved wonders. In no time I was reading the children's books tolerably well and writing quite satisfactorily. My Russian lessons lasted several months, then suddenly stopped—not because I became totally literate, but because my Colonel found a more lucrative position and, probably, a more elaborate fare. I sincerely hoped so.

Muse and Grandmother Emma Ivanova

12

My Uncle Vsevolod

In the meantime, Uncle Vsevolod arrived in China when I was eight years old. Grandmother was forty-two when Uncle Vsevolod was born. He was her pride and joy, and there were good reasons for it. Uncle Vsevolod was, without exaggeration, one of the most handsome of men. He was six feet two inches tall, with an athletic body, blond, blue eyed, graceful in movement—a veritable Greek god. Always elegant, an excellent dancer and an amusing conversationalist. Women could not resist him, and he could not resist women. How Uncle Vsevolod remained a bachelor for such a long time was a puzzlement to everyone who knew him; unless it was his one flaw, not apparent at first glance, but a hindrance to stable relationships.

He had the quickest temper, which could burst out at the slightest provocation. Our dog seemed to sense his unbridled temper and would slink out of the room when he entered. Grandmother excused this character defect as the result of an unfortunate and tragic accident in his youth.

At sixteen, Vsevolod and his best friend had gone hunting. Mistaking a crouching shadow behind a tree for a deer, Vsevolod aimed his gun and shot several times in that direction. To his horror, he found that he had killed his friend, not an animal.

No doubt this incident did leave a lasting scar on him. Over time, however, Vsevolod managed to overcome his initial trauma. He finished his academic education tolerably well. Excelling in sports, he even trained as a diver for the Olympics. Unfortunately, the Revolution in Russia broke out, and Uncle Vsevolod had to escape like many other Russians.

He made his way to France, where he joined the French Foreign Legion. In Morocco, as a lieutenant leading an attack with his company, he was wounded in the temple by the Moors. The bullet bypassed his brain, but left him partially blind. The French government awarded him the coveted "Legion d'Honneur," a medal given for special bravery in action. No doubt his impaired sight increased his lack of self-control.

My Father, twenty years his senior, did not see eye to eye with his younger brother. Grandmother always took the side of her youngest son, which added fuel to their disagreements. My Mother, being as she was, added to the tension, turning our home into a veritable battlefield, especially at dinnertime. Fortunately, after several months, Uncle Vsevolod found a position with the Shanghai Health Department, which enabled him to rent an apartment for himself.

13

A Lesson Well Learned

That year in September, as I was six years of age, Grandmother considered me ready to enter the kindergarten at the Shanghai Public School for Girls. This was where I learned one of my most valuable lessons.

It had to do with colored pencils, a coloring book, and six strands of colored yarn. We had used these objects during class, but when the other girls returned them to the teacher, I did not. An irresistible urge to keep them made me hide everything in my desk. When the class was over, I smuggled my treasures out of the room.

As usual, Grandmother picked me up from school. Her sharp eyes noticed at once that I was carrying a package. She inquired as to what it was. I told her. She asked me if the other girls were also permitted to take their supplies home. I told her no. Grandmother knitted her brows and was silent all the way home.

That evening after dinner, I heard Grandmother consulting with Father. Father looked grim. He turned to me and said, "Grandmother tells me you brought some things home from school today."

"Yes," I said.

"Did they belong to you?" he asked.

"No," I said.

"Then come into the other room!"

I did. Father closed the door behind us and took off his leather belt. "Take off your pants!" he ordered. I did.

"Come here!" he said. I did.

Father placed me over his knees with my bare buttocks upward and smacked me with his belt several times, not too slowly or lightly.

"This is so that you will remember that we do not take what is not ours," he instructed me. "We respect others and their property. Now, put on your pants!" I did.

What an invaluable lesson several sharp strokes of a belt can be! How well and how lastingly a belt can impress a set of values on that exposed area. It certainly did for me.

"We may not have money," my Father told me, "but we preserve high standards. What would a man or woman be without culture and dignity?"

Lady of Culture

So a lady of culture I was to be, and, of course, the Shanghai School for Girls that I had been attending until now, was, at this point, considered inadequate. As a result, I was enrolled in the Convent of the Sacred Heart, an elite Catholic institution run by nuns for girls of good families. Father had to obtain several letters of introduction testifying to the fact that I was indeed a girl from a "good" family and endowed with all the virtues appropriate to my birth. Finally, I was admitted.

"We groom our young ladies for society," said the Headmistress, Mother Foy, stately in her black nun's habit, with a white wimple on her head over which was draped a black veil dropping to the ground.

And groomed we girls were. At lunch, in the cavernous dining hall, we had to sit with backs straight, no elbows on the table. No talking, no loud chewing, no slurping from the soup spoon or from the cup was permitted. The fork and knife had to be held just so, and the food had to be eaten without soiling the outer rim of the plate. Any breach of this etiquette was immediately observed by the "Mother-in-Charge," who sat on an elevated platform, alert for any transgression.

CLAP! CLAP! CLAP! would go her wood clapper, an instrument made out of two thin squares of wood, similar to Spanish castanets, whenever she espied a culprit.

Ah! What an efficient instrument was the clapper! Just as the Spanish dancer is attuned to the sound of the castanets, our ears were attuned to the sound of the clapper when the Mothers-in-Charge wished to make their wishes known.

CLAP! CLAP! CLAP! and the girls sprang up from their chairs. CLAP! CLAP! CLAP! with the emphasis on the third clap, meant "Silence!" and the girls froze. CLAP! CLAP! CLAP! CLAP! (left right, left right) and the girls marched in tempo. One definite, loud CLAP! meant "Class dismissed!" and the girls closed their books and filed out of the classroom.

Our discipline extended to our uniforms. Summer and winter, long-sleeved white-cotton blouses, over pleated navy-blue serge skirts eight inches from the floor, with a triple-folded hem to allow for growth, was the prescribed apparel. Black cotton stockings and black laced shoes completed the ensemble.

Each Friday we received ribbons for our appearance and good behavior. Pale blue was the coveted color. It was almost always present on my chest.

Scholastic subjects such as mathematics, geography, history and French were given some attention, but the emphasis was on religion, Catechism and Gospel. Mother Foy was the instructress.

One of these classes witnessed my downfall. It was not that I did not know my subject. I was excellent in it. Mother Foy delighted in my answers and I loved her for it. But one day, during the Catechism class, Mother Foy was expounding on Catholicism and suddenly mentioned that only Catholics would go to heaven when they died.

My sense of fairness, so laboriously instilled by my Grandmother, was aroused. I raised my hand.

"What is it, Muse?" Mother Foy asked.

"Even if the non-Catholic was a good and honest man, he still will not go to heaven?" I asked.

"Even!" was Mother Foy's curt reply.

"But why?" I persisted, indignant at the obvious discrimination.

Mother Foy looked annoyed. For a moment she seemed to waver. "Come and see me during the recess!" she said, and CLAP! went her clapper, loud and clear, which meant "Class dismissed!"

I went to her study during the recess. Mother Foy was not too friendly. She spoke briefly about many things but eluded the subject I had come to discuss. I dared not press her. Besides, the importance of who goes where after death was not a pressing matter for me at that time. I was only twelve years old.

I told my Father about this episode, however. "Hmmm," he uttered and pensively looked through the window at the sky.

That Friday, when the ribbons for achievements were given out, I did not receive one...

For a while, it continued to go well for me at the Convent of the Sacred Heart. I stepped in tempo with the clappers. My skirt was precisely eight inches from the floor and I wore the long-sleeved white-cotton blouse over the heavy navy-blue serge skirt. I asked no questions during the Gospel and Catechism class. In other words, I was an exemplary pupil, fitting perfectly into the ranks. But fate, destiny, kismet—whatever you want to call it—had planned it otherwise.

After school was dispersed for the summer, there was a yearly celebration. The girls were required to be present to participate in a procession, which was followed by a High Mass in the convent chapel.

Shanghai was frightfully hot during these months. Therefore, my Grandmother had decided that I should dispense with the uniform and wear a light summer dress.

It was a pretty dress of pale gray cotton fabric with a forget-me-not print, just below my knees in length, with a cape collar covering my arms down to the elbows. On my feet I had white socks and white pumps with tiny heels. A very demure sort of garment for a proper girl of twelve, I thought.

After the procession, we gathered in our study hall. I noticed that some girls wore their uniforms; others had nondescript dresses with sleeves. It did not strike me as odd that I was the only one with a cape. But there was someone who did notice this. It was the Mother-in-Charge of our study hall, Mother Morgan.

"MUSE!" I heard my name called. I lifted my eyes.

There stood Mother Morgan, stretched to her full five feet. Her sharp beady eyes were riveted on me. "MUSE, COME HERE!" Her high-pitched voice suddenly pierced the silence in the room.

I stepped forward, wondering what I could possibly have done.

"LOOK AT HER! WHAT A DISGRACE!" Mother Morgan was pointing at my dress and feet.

Blood rushed to my head! I was crimson from embarrassment.

"Look at her bare arms and stockingless legs! Muse! Get your hat and stand outside the chapel during Mass!" she commanded.

I heard girls giggling behind my back. Some even laughed outright. I felt humiliated. My pride was hurt. Without a word I left the hall. I took my hat from the cloakroom, but I refused to stand outside the chapel. I went home. How I reached our house I do not remember. Our house was quite a distance from the convent.

"You are early," I heard my Grandmother remark questioningly, as I tried to slink past her up the stairs.

"What happened?" my Father inquired at dinner, looking at me suspiciously.

"Father, I am not going back to that school." I told him what had happened.

"Hmmm" was all he uttered, and, with a quick gesture, sliced the roast on his plate.

I did not return to the elite Convent of the Sacred Heart. Instead I went back to the school for the "hoi polloi," the Shanghai Public School for Girls. Whether or not I would be a lady when I grew up was left to my Grandmother and to life's future grooming.

15

The Shanghai Public School for Girls

The Shanghai Public School for Girls was an imposing two-story, sand-colored building that stretched for a sizeable block on Jessfield Road on the edge of the British Concession. The school had no particular advantages in education and it certainly did not claim them. Under the supervision of a formidable, buxom English lady, Miss Alexander, the school imparted to its pupils just enough knowledge to step into life's vortex. Should the pupil have ambitions for higher education, she had to pass additional British college entrance examinations.

Our school also had special uniforms, a navy-blue pleated jumper over a white blouse; however, neither the length of the jumper nor the fabric of the blouse was compulsory. The length of sleeves was also left to the discretion of the wearer.

We had no study halls. Our classrooms were spacious and the windows were wide. These rooms were our homes for the entire year. The teachers of various subjects came and went.

Our teachers were well-meaning ladies from different parts of the globe, assiduously trying to impart their subjects to the motley crowd of girls from every strata of life and from different nationalities and cultures. But it was not only for their efforts in instruction that I remember my teachers. It was their unique personalities that are most strongly imprinted on my memory.

Take, for instance, Miss Monday, our French teacher. How could I ever forget her? During one of her French classes, as she was elaborating on the finesse with which one pronounces certain French words, I was deeply engrossed in a novel held below my desk on my knees. Suddenly, something hit me on my head. I looked up. A roll of papers kept together with an elastic band lay at my feet.

There, near her blackboard, stood Miss Monday, looking smug, obviously pleased at her marksmanship. Her jet-black eyes were riveted on me. The girls roared with laughter. Miss Monday said not a word; she just stared. I got her message. Sheepishly, I placed my novel inside my desk. For the rest of the class I paid closed attention to the lesson.

Miss Monday was "sans pareil." She was five feet four inches tall, with a back straight as a rod. Her hair was jet black, cut page-boy style. Her nose was a beak, and her deep-set eyes were dark and very shining. She came from the United States and must have had American Indian blood within her veins, so completely did she resemble an Indian warrior. All that was lacking was a feather in her hair.

Miss Monday dressed modestly. Her only noticeable indulgence was silk stockings, steel-gray in color. They were particularly effective as she marched with firm long strides down our halls to her next class. To see her bottle-shaped legs in the steel-gray stockings, glistening with every step, was quite a memorable sight.

Miss Monday also had a gentle side to her nature. It was not too apparent, but her voice would soften when she spoke of children, home, and weddings. She was a spinster; however, it was not difficult to surmise that under her Indian-warrior appearance beat the tender heart of a woman who longed to marry, have a home and children.

"Who would want her? Look at her!" the girls would whisper, aware of her longings.

Well, someone did. One morning the school was assembled in the gymnasium. As we stood in neat lines, Miss Alexander entered and took her place on the stage.

"Girls!" she announced, "I am here to tell you important news. Miss Monday is not Miss Monday anymore. She is Mrs. Anderson."

A ripple of amazement trickled down our lines. "The man must be blind!" someone whispered loudly enough for everyone to hear. Everyone snickered.

"Class dismissed!" Miss Alexander called out. One could see that she, too, was suppressing a smile.

Strangely enough, it soon became known that Miss Monday had, indeed, married a man who was nearly blind. He attended one of our school festivities.

Several months passed. Miss Monday, that is, Mrs. Anderson, was visibly blossoming. Her clothes became more stylish and her stockings matched the color of her skirts. Then, unexpectedly, there was a substitute teacher of French. The substitute was boring in comparison to Mrs. Anderson. Happily—at least for us—this situation did not last. One morning we were again assembled in the gymnasium.

"Girls! " Miss Alexander was visibly ill at ease. "Girls!" she repeated. "I have to announce that Mrs. Anderson will be back to resume her French classes. She will be known as Miss Monday."

"Good heavens! The man must have regained his sight," the girls whispered.

And, sure enough, we did hear that Miss Monday's husband had had surgery and had regained most of his vision. Whether it was because of seeing the light of day, and with it, his wife, or for some other reason that we will never know, the marriage ended shortly after in divorce. Miss Monday returned to teach us.

Now, as she made her way down the long corridors to her classes, her steps seemed less assured. Her eyes also had lost some of their fire, or so it seemed to me. But she never relinquished her zest to impart to us the lyrical quality of the French language. And she also understood her students well.

On my last report card, her notation was: "Muse can do wonderfully when she wants to, but she seldom wants to." At that time, the criticism was to the point, and Miss Monday showed her perception.

Perhaps Miss Monday eventually did find someone perceptive enough to see below her Indian-warrior appearance and discover her many good, gentle qualities. I sincerely hope so.

There were two other teachers, Miss Cumberland and Miss Cordelle, who I remember well. Both were typical "blue stockings." They always wore their hair pulled back in knots, wore tweed suits, and used no powder or lipstick. It was their pasts that were unusual. These ladies had been nuns in the same convent.

Why these soft-spoken, straight-laced women had renounced their vows and left the comfort and protection of the Catholic Church can only be guessed. It had to have been a momentous decision that took great courage. The Shanghai Public School for

Girls benefited by it, myself especially. Miss Cumberland and Miss Cordelle were superior teachers.

Miss Cordelle taught us art. She gave me special assignments for encouragement. A pen-and-ink rendering of a "Chinese Street Scene" which I did received a prize. That award speeded me on in my artistic endeavors.

Miss Cumberland was our English instructress. She never tired of correcting my essays and emboldened me to write.

I will always be grateful to have had these two ladies cross my path.

16

Friends

"A life without a friend is a life not worth living," wrote Elbert Green Hubbard.

I am fortunate to have had my life enriched with lasting friendships.

Marianna Schvaikowsky and Ludmilla Merkuloff were my playmates since we were four.

Marianna, a pretty girl with curly auburn hair and expressive hazel eyes with long eyelashes, was an avid reader. Her prodigious memory retained what she read and enabled her to recite at our social gatherings whole passages from the Russian classics.

I still remember the poem, "The Monkey," by our Russian poet Lermontov. It was about a small monkey behind bars in a zoo, pining for her far-off tropical land and the trees and branches upon which she had swung. Marianna's presentation had such sensitivity that it made me cry.

Marianna's mother, Anna Vasilievna, as she was properly addressed, was my Mother's closest friend. Marianna's father, Sergei Illyich, was a talented musician; a handsome, charming man when sober, but a terror when not. Sadly enough, this change occurred whenever he could lay his hands on money, which would happen on the last day of each month when he received his salary from the Shanghai Philharmonic Orchestra, where he was the English horn player.

Maestro Pacci, the Italian conductor, overlooked Sergei Illyich's alcoholism and his absences from rehearsals, because Sergei Illyich was a valuable member of the symphony orchestra. He could adjust scores, could substitute for the conductor, and he also played several other instruments.

Anna Vasilievna forgave her husband's transgressions and waited patiently for him to return to his normal charming self. Eventually, to save the family from starvation, Sergei Illyich's salary was given directly to his wife. This condition lasted for a while, until one day Sergei Illyich left Shanghai for Harbin, deserting his family and the orchestra. We never heard from him again.

Adversities destroy some people, but make others stronger. Anna Vasilievna belonged to the latter. A fine seamstress, she started a small business in her room and in time became quite skillful in creating women's apparel.

When the Chinese Communists took over China, Marianna and her mother had to leave. Marianna, with a daughter of her own by then, and her mother made their way, first to South America, and finally to the United States, where they settled in California.

That these two courageous women accomplished this feat with limited means is a testimony to their resolute spirit.

Those who possess this attribute are fortunate, indeed. They come through their adversities with flying colors, as did my very dear friend, Marianna Schvaikowsky.

Ludmilla Merkulov's life was a different story.

Ludmilla was a true Slav in appearance: light blond hair, blue eyes, and a spotless pale complexion. She was vivacious, light hearted, good in sports, and very popular with boys.

Ludmilla and her widowed mother lived with Ludmilla's elder married sister, Lydia, and her German husband, Richard Boerstling, a prosperous dealer in Chinese artifacts. Their residence was a large townhouse on Rue Bourgeoit in the French Concession.

Lydochka, as we lovingly referred to Lydia, was beautiful, but very neurotic. For days she would keep to herself on the second floor in her "boudoir," propped up by a multitude of lace pillows on her "chaise lounge." At these times, everyone in the household would tiptoe so as not to disturb her.

Richard Ivanovich, as everyone called Richard Boerstling, bore this Russian melodrama stoically. He was a dutiful husband and a good son-in-law. He was a good provider and the family lived in considerable comfort, lacking nothing. Richard Ivanovich's only weakness was horse racing, and every Sunday he would disappear to the race course to bet on the horses. Sometimes he won; sometimes he lost. Whatever, Richard always returned home punctually in time for dinner.

Years passed. We were growing up. China fell into difficult times. There was the war with Japan in 1937. Richard Boerstling's import-export business faltered. He stopped going to the races on Sunday. Lydia had to give up some of her servants. The family tightened its belts.

One day the doorbell rang. Lydia's only servant, the cook, was busy so Lydia went to see who was at the front door. She opened it. Before her stood a young Chinese woman who said in fairly good English, "I would like to see my husband."

"I think you have made a mistake. This is the Boerstling residence," said Lydia.

"Yes, I know. Mr. Boerstling is my husband. These are his children." The Chinese woman pointed to four children of various ages standing behind her.

"His children? I don't understand!"

"Yes, his children. He came to see me every Sunday, but now he has stopped. I have no money to support them."

"OOOOOYY! *Boje moy*!! [My God!]" Lydia cried. "I am fainting! I am fainting!" She clung to the opened front door in true dramatic Russian style.

The cook came running from the kitchen. Lydia's mother rushed down from the third floor. They managed to get rid of the Chinese woman.

Lydia retired to her "boudoir" and remained incommunicado on her lace pillows for some days, but she did not file for divorce.

When my Father heard of Richard's indiscretions, he looked pleased. "Hmmm," he mumbled, and added, "I am so glad to know that Richard Boerstling is neither a fool nor a saint."

My friend, Ludmilla, married a handsome Spaniard, a Jai Alai player, Osa Gonzales. When everyone was leaving China in 1949 because of the threatening Communists, Ludmilla and her husband went to Mexico, where Osa had relatives.

Richard and Lydia Boerstling adopted a little boy. The last I heard of them was that they were in Germany.

We were unable to find out how it ended with the Chinese Sunday wife and her many little Boerstlings. Richard was a gentleman and must have made some provisions for his transgressions.

There was still another member of our little group who meant a lot to me in my youthful days. His name was Igor. He was five years older than I was. I met him when Marianna and her parents rented a room in Igor's father and mother's house.

Igor was not an attractive child, nor did his appearance change much when he was an adult. He was about five feet nine inches tall, lean, with definite Asiatic features— high cheekbones and somewhat slanting eyes. Both his parents, Nikolai Nikolaievich and Lubov Madestovna, were native Siberians of Mongolian strain. But despite Igor's not-too-prepossessing appearance, he had a certain attractiveness of his own.

He was energetic and mentally alert, a loyal friend who communicated his ideas well in his pleasant, deep-toned voice. He was also very entertaining with his tricks. In his remarkably long, nimble fingers, coins, handkerchiefs and cards appeared out of nowhere and disappeared just as magically.

In his early teens Igor became a "radio ham" and with time developed dexterity in fixing and building mechanical objects. He especially loved the radio. When other youths, graduating from school, were just starting to search for their direction in life, Igor, long before graduating, knew what he wanted to do. It was electronics. He was already employed as an announcer-mechanic by one of the local English radio stations, and was earning enough to help his, by then, widowed mother, and to take me frequently to the movies, each time picking me up and delivering me home in style, in a cab.

Igor's family, the Poliakoffs, were originally wealthy owners of the first electric power plant in the city of Irkutsk in Siberia. When their holdings were commandeered by the Bolshevik Russian Government, they fled and eventually arrived in Shanghai. Igor's father, a gentle, frail man, had difficulty adjusting to the privations of the first years in exile. He died of pneumonia. Lubov Madestovna was left to provide for Igor, his older bother Nikolas, and herself.

Made of tougher fiber than her husband, she was more than equal to the task. Before long, Lubov Madestovna found work as a helper in a bakery and coffee shop. With her indomitable energy, a friendly personality, and an innate ability to learn, she soon became the manager. Under her guidance, the shop expanded and became one of the favorite meeting places for Shanghai residents.

Muse and Marianna - 1927

17

Father Writes Books

Meanwhile, my Father's earnings were increasing. His first book, **Shanghai: Its Mixed Court and Council**, dealing with the extraterritorial rights of foreigners in the Chinese courts, published in 1925, and his second book, **Shanghai: Its Municipality and the Chinese**, published in 1927, met with considerable success all over the world, as foreign powers had enormous interests in China at this time.

The royalties, together with Father's higher salary, permitted us to move into more comfortable quarters, a large two-story apartment in an imposing granite building on Wei Hai Wei Road, a desirable residential area in the British Concession.

Our living room had a cathedral ceiling with a staircase leading to a small balcony on the second floor. This balcony became my observation post. Through the banisters I could eavesdrop unnoticed while there were gatherings taking place downstairs.

From here I watched Father's dinner party celebrating the successful sale of his books. The guests were Father's publisher and English and Chinese officials with whom Father had worked while writing these books. It was a grand affair. The ladies received a corsage of yellow roses and the gentlemen were given a carnation for their buttonholes. The dinner menu was lavish and was served in crystal bowls and on silver platters. There were Russian hors d'oeuvres of black caviar, a roasted pheasant as an entrée, and cream plombir for dessert. Wine flowed without stopping. I was unable to hear the speeches, but I did see guests rise with glasses in their hands to toast Father and heard everyone clapping enthusiastically.

In this apartment, our lives changed drastically. Seldom did an evening pass without several people attending our dinners. In a truly generous Russian manner, Father opened his doors to the less fortunate. Our house also became a meeting place for musicians, writers and artists, whose paintings were displayed on our living-room walls.

At this time, I also started taking piano lessons from the aristocratic-looking Professor Aksakov, a student of the famous Russian composer, Scriabin. I will never forget how bored he seemed as he puckered his lips and blew out clouds of smoke from his cigarette while I was trying to interpret "Für Elise." Poor man, he was forced to endure my lack of talent as well as listen to his other talentless pupils. Sadly, giving piano lessons was his only means of subsistence in Shanghai.

Living Room on Wei Hai Wei Rd.

18

Mr. Wu's Family

On one of the main Shanghai thoroughfares, the Bubbling Well Road, was a high masonry wall stretching for two long city blocks with an awesome-looking iron gate under a gable-roofed gatehouse. When anyone rang the large brass bell hanging on the gatepost, a small peep-window in the gate would open and the head of a guard appeared to scrutinize the visitor. After carefully ascertaining the nature of the visitor's business, the guard would slowly open the gate, to the grinding and screeching of its hinges.

Passing through the gate, the visitor found himself on a wide lane which led to a grand four-story edifice with tall gothic windows, marble terraces, and an imposing porte-cochere on the south end. The appearance of the building and the several tennis courts off a wide terrace on the west side reminding one of a luxurious European hotel; and that is exactly what it had been in the past. At the time when I was permitted entrance through the noisy gate, it was the private residence of Mr. Wu, a rich indigo-dye merchant, and his extensive family.

I must have been seven years old when I made my acquaintance with this interesting household by chance. I was caught by one of the guards who patrolled the grounds, while I was peering over the back wall which ran along adjacent to our Wei Hai Wei apartment complex. Our garages and the garbage bins with the ever-present piles of wooden crates, were perfect for climbing onto this wall. Here, perched upon it, I could observe what was below me: the fascinating corner of a rich Chinese residence—the loves, hobbies and menagerie of its family members.

Large yellow earthen tanks filled with exotic fish attracted my attention. Some fish had huge butterfly tails and monstrously large protruding eyes. Others shone like silver and gold as the sun's rays penetrated the water's surface. A little beyond, displayed in rows, I could see a collection of dwarfed trees. They were trained to grow no taller than a foot and a half, yet were perfect, curiously shaped pines, maples and birches. This group of trees was a valuable assemblage and the hobby of a cultivated Chinese gentleman.

But what I loved to watch especially was the kennel of the "Lion dogs." We know them as Llasa Apsos from Tibet. In the olden days Tibet used to send several dogs to the Chinese Emperor, as tribute, every three years. They were kept in the Forbidden City in Peking, protecting the Emperor's wives from intruders at night. I loved to watch the fluffy pups frolic in their pens and longed to have one of them as my pet.

One morning while I was so busily occupied, I was not aware that I, too, was being watched, until two guards approached me with a ladder. Very politely, in broken English, they invited me to come down. They told me that Mr. Wu's Number-One-Wife would like to see me. I could have run away, but my curiosity prevailed.

Obediently, I climbed down the ladder and followed the guards to the house. They led me through the main door of the porte-cochere into a cathedral-ceilinged hall where the morning sun was streaming through the tall gothic windows to the right. In front of me rose a winding staircase, and a little beyond, I saw two women standing by the open door of an elevator. The guards pointed to them, indicating that I should proceed.

The two nurses, or amahs, as they were called in China, beckoned me, giggling. Taking me by the hand, they pulled me into the elevator, which quickly raised us to the fourth floor.

"*Wu Tai-tai! Wu Tai-tai* [Mr. Wu's lady]," they repeated, pushing me gently through a door at the far end of a long corridor.

A strange, pungent odor enveloped me as I entered the room. The curtains on the windows were drawn and it took me a few seconds to discern a large couch standing at an angle to the opposite wall. On it a small woman was lying on her side. She was holding a long pipe with a bulbous end over a small burning oil lamp. A tiny piece of brown substance was attached to the end of the pipe; she kept touching it with a small sharp utensil. The brown paste sputtered as it burned over the flame, producing a thick yellow smoke which the lady inhaled. I guessed that she was smoking opium.

One of the amahs whispered something to the lady, who slowly sat up and passed her pipe to the servant. The amah immediately left the room.

With a very slow wave of her hand, as if in a daze, Mr. Wu's Number-One-Wife indicated to me to sit down on one of the armchairs covered with white slipcovers near the windows. I took a seat. By now, being accustomed to the semi-darkness of the room, I could see my hostess.

She was dressed in an old-fashioned, pleated, black silk Chinese skirt, over which she wore a white brocade jacket buttoned to the side. Numerous jade rings adorned her fingers and several heavy gold bracelets curled around her wrists. Everything about her reflected wealth and importance.

I noticed, too, her tiny feet, barely five inches long, in their tiny, pointed embroidered shoes. The custom of binding girls' feet so that they would grow no larger than a two-year-old child's had been forbidden by the late Manchu government; but many wealthy Chinese families still continued that practice and despite the horrible anguish it inflicted on the child, it had been a tradition for centuries. Tiny feet did become a great pride of a Chinese lady, and her swaying manner of walking, which she had to cultivate to keep balance, was considered especially alluring as well as a sign of a privileged upper class. Peasant and lower-class women in China did not bind their feet.

As I watched Mr. Wu's Number-One-Wife, the door opened and two young girls burst in. Both were dressed in black trousers and white jackets, a proper young Chinese girl's attire.

"How do you do? I am Grace," the tallest girl addressed me in faltering English. She extended her hand to shake mine. "This is my younger sister, Alice." She pointed to the other girl.

Alice, with two long braids falling down her chest, also shook my hand. Number-One-Wife looked pleased.

"*Hoa! Hoa!* [Good! Good!]," she kept repeating, then added something I could not understand. I saw that her teeth were yellow from smoking.

"My Mother say you come visit us often," Alice translated. "My Mother ask why you look over wall. Must come through gate."

"I love to watch the puppies," I explained. Grace translated what I had said to her mother, who nodded approvingly.

"Come often. Speak English with us. We want to know English."

"I will," I answered. "I will be very happy," I added, bowing to be proper.

On this positive note our conversation ended. The amahs brought me tea and sweetmeats on a large black lacquered tray. Grace offered me a cup, holding it in both her hands as etiquette prescribed.

Having finished drinking tea, I bowed with my hands clasped in the proper manner…That was the beginning of my many visits to the Mr. Wu's household.

I discovered that the building was divided by floors. Each floor had its own kitchen, cooks, a nursery, and a sizeable staff of servants. Appropriately, the fourth floor, the top, was the domain of the Number-One-Wife and her children. The third floor was for the Number-Two-Wife and her children. The second floor was, of course, for the Number-Three-Wife and her progeny. Mr. Wu also had several concubines. Their rooms were at the far end of the second floor.

Judging by the number of children by each wife, Mr. Wu divided his husbandly attention fairly and conscientiously. I noticed that peace and harmony prevailed. The children shared the large schoolroom on the first floor. They gathered daily to learn reading and writing. Their teacher would pull out, at random, large white cards with black ideograms on them and would call, in a singsong way, the sound and meaning of the Chinese character on each card. The children repeated after him. In China, the schoolroom is a bedlam with everyone calling out as loud as he or she can, after the teacher.

To read the newspaper requires the knowledge of at least four thousand characters, while to read the classics requires forty thousand. It takes years of memorizing to be as proficient as the literati. When a man does achieve this feat, however, and becomes a scholar, he is treated with the utmost respect by everybody.

Mr. Wu's wives, children and visitors gathered when actors or storytellers performed. These times were great events in the household and an opportunity for gossip and conviviality.

In a most friendly manner, the wives and concubines came together. They conversed amicably and, at the same time consumed pounds of sunflower seeds, candied fruits, and sesame cakes. Meanwhile their servants continuously filled their cups with hot tea. The children ran about shouting and playing. No one really paid any attention to the performers, who, in their elaborate costumes, with masks on their faces, strutted and pranced about on the elevated platform. With exaggerated hand movements, in high-pitched voices, they melodramatically recited episodes of intrigue, murder, and the heroic deeds of emperors and generals during the times of ancient history.

Everyone present was well acquainted with the stories, so these gatherings were only an excuse to break the monotonous routine of a large, old-fashioned Chinese household, where every member had to behave as it had been prescribed by Master Kung, Confucius, the philosopher who lived from 551 to 479 BC

But the diversions of the family that I most enjoyed, not without ulterior motive, were the shopping trips to the largest department store in Shanghai, the Wing On and Company, located on Nanking Road, in the company of Mr. Wu's Number-One-Wife, who would take me with her.

We rode out of the compound through the iron gate in a cavalcade. In the first car, an ancient Chrysler, high on the wheels, with room enough for a child of seven to stand upright, rode Number-One-Wife, with Grace and Alice comfortably seated on the red plush seats. I perched on a folding stool in front of them. An armed guard with a pistol at ready sat next to the chauffeur. In the car behind us rode several servants with tea kettles and hot-water bottles to warm hands in the winter, or fans or umbrellas in the summer. Wraps, handkerchiefs and other objects of toiletry were also available. The third car, bringing up the rear, was reserved exclusively for guards. All these precautionary measures were necessary for protection from kidnapping, a frequent occurrence and ever-present possibility in China when I lived there.

Thus we arrived at the main entrance of the Wing On and Company, where the Manager was awaiting us with several of his staff. The manager bowed constantly, showing great respect, as he conducted the numerous members of our party through the various departments. Mr. Wu's Number-One-Wife examined this and she touched that, and if something attracted her fancy, she would casually wave her hand. Immediately, the boxes of candies, condiments, stationery, yards of fabric, toys, bric-a-brac, perfume and cosmetics were wrapped as gifts and then given to the attending amahs to be carried.

In China, one's status dictates that he extend his generosity to friends and family. The richer and more important the person, the more generous he or she had to be. Mr. Wu's Number-One-Wife adhered to this custom. Her credit was limitless. The Manager of Wing On knew that the bills would be settled no later than the eve of the next Chinese New Year. Not to comply with this tradition meant a great loss of face for a Chinese gentleman. He would lose credit, but what was worse, he would lose the respect of society.

I loved these shopping trips because I always returned home with many gifts. Whenever I visited Mr. Wu's household I never left empty-handed. Mr. Wu's Number-One-Wife gave me lengths of silks, curious birds from the aviary, fish from the tanks, and finally, one day, in a basket, a Lhasa Apso puppy. We called her Mimi. She had long silky light beige fur. With time she became the mother of our own family of "Lion dogs." When Father retired into the Laoshan Mountains in Shantung Province, we had four of them.

My friendship with Grace and Alice continued for several years. I was present when Grace was married. I watched as she entered the phoenix-sedan-chair, elaborately draped with red and gold silk curtains, made especially for brides. In it she was carried away to her husband's home. A noisy procession followed. Musicians blew trumpets and cymbals crashed, striking every other step, while a long line of carriers conveyed the dowry, enormous red chests with household goods and an endless array of wide trays with fruit and victuals.

Alice, too, had her wedding and so did Samuel and Johnson, the sons of Mr. Wu's Number-Two-Wife. Their wives rode through the iron gate in the phoenix-chairs accompanied by their numerous dowry carriers.

With Grace and Alice gone, my visits to the residence became less frequent. Besides, my family had moved away from the apartment on Wei Hai Wei Road to the French Concession.

Then one day when I was about thirteen years old, I decided to pay Mr. Wu's Number-One-Wife a visit. To my surprise, I found the iron gate wide open. In the house, servants ran to and fro packing trunks and boxes. Everyone looked bewildered. I took the elevator to the fourth floor. Number-One-Wife sat in the middle of her empty room. Tears were streaming down her cheeks. I realized that something terrible must have happened. It had. Mr. Wu had lost his fortune gambling. Dice and mahjongg games were often the ruination of many prosperous families. Now Mr. Wu's family was being divided into smaller households. Sadness overwhelmed me.

Number-One-Wife noticed my presence. In silence she rose and bowed to me. I bowed to her. In a halting voice she said something to a servant. The amah escorted me to the elevator and through the cathedral-ceilinged hall. I walked slowly down the lane to the gatehouse and out to the street.

How often I wondered what happened to the tanks of exotic fish, the magnificent collection of dwarf trees and the menagerie of Lhasa Apso dogs. Soon after my last visit, Mr. Wu's residence was torn down. In its place, rows of ugly gray town houses were built.

The Europeans considered this to be progress and the civilizing of ancient China.

19

Problems at Home

As I mentioned previously, my Mother's emotional condition was highly unpredictable. As I was growing up and the years passed, Mother's periods of depression and delusion became more severe and more frequent.

When calm, my Mother was the kindest and the most generous of women. She was a gracious hostess and a superb cook. On the shortest notice she could prepare the best of meals for unexpected guests. I had a strong suspicion that Father's tolerance of her excesses was because he relished her culinary talents. Father enjoyed a tasty dish and Mother could prepare it, competing with any trained chef. The saying, "The way to a man's heart is through his stomach," must be true.

Mother's admirable qualities, however, did not make her easier to live with, and peace in our house hung precariously by the thinnest of threads. A harmless word could arouse Mother into uncontrollable fury. A friendly conversation with Grandmother could end in a fit of hysteria. Most exasperating, though, were the times when we watched Mother develop one of her delusions. It was especially frustrating because in Shanghai there were no means to help her. There were no psychiatrists and only limited accommodations for mentally disturbed patients in the local hospitals. The Chinese mentally ill were kept in institutions worse than prisons.

So, one day, seeing that Mother was winding up for one of her "crescendos," Father invited a recommended physician, who claimed some expertise in psychiatry, to our Wei Hai Wei Road apartment.

I was watching through the banisters of the balcony in the living room, my observation post, when the expert arrived.

He was a large, pot-bellied man with an untidy reddish-brown beard. Entering the living room and greeting my Father and Mother, he made himself comfortable by the window in my Father's favorite green armchair. Lee, our cook-boy, brought him a cup of tea. The physician drank it slowly; I could hear him slurp as he drank. Then, after having blown his nose into a large, not-too-fresh-looking handkerchief, he turned to Mother, attempting to draw her into conversation.

But Mother had grown suspicious of this strange man in her living room. Father had casually mentioned that a new friend would be stopping by, but she sensed that there was more to it. She would not answer any of his roundabout questions. After several futile attempts, the physician finally gave up. He got up from the chair, bowed to Father, and pompously sailed out through the entrance door, stopping only long enough on the way to drop over his shoulder to Father, "The bill for my services will be sent."

Father was furious. Mother looked pleased with herself. She might have been a little crazy, but she was no fool.

The next day, a messenger brought Father the bill, It was considerable. Attached to the bill Father found a note, which read: "Your wife, Lubov Koteneva, has a malady called CYCLASTIA." How the good physician discerned this malady was a mystery to all of us. His trained eye must have picked up information even though all he did was sit in Father's favorite green chair and drink tea. But, he might have been correct. Indeed, Mother's periods of emotional disturbance did come in cycles. I remember one such occasion.

We noticed that Mother began developing an intense love for the Bible. She walked with the revered book in her hand, and fervently studied the lives of the saints and ancient hermits. This sudden thirst for all things holy was due, we discovered, to her interest in Father Gregory, a tall, gaunt man with a scraggly beard and untidy blond hair falling down to his shoulders, and a cassock worn thin at the elbows. Once when he visited us on my Mother's saint's day, a day celebrated by Russians, I recall a distinct aroma hanging like a cloud around him. It might have been spirit, but definitely not holy. Nonetheless, Mother was totally captivated by him.

The Russian clergy were poorly paid. Their sustenance had always depended upon the generosity of the congregation. So, Mother showered the man with homemade bread, cakes, and cookies. During Lent she prepared fish stews for him, and on holidays, roasted chickens. The poor prelate's mostly empty stomach could hardly resist such temptations, so he accepted her gifts. By accepting her providence he inflamed Mother's ardor for the gospel even more. She started to hound the poor man with discourses on the inspired writings of the Apostolic Fathers. Finally, Archbishop Makary, fearing gossip and scandal, stepped in. He had Father Gregory transferred to a far, undisclosed corner of his archbishopric.

My Father closed his eyes to these happenings. He escaped into his writing and his social activities, helping the poor Russians. Eventually, Mother calmed down. Yet there were also periods when Mother's obsessions came closer to home. Mother would suspect Father of infidelities. She would follow him at a distance and spy on him around street corners. When he returned home she would confront him with accusations of all sorts. Then plates, cups, or anything within her easy reach, would be toppled to the floor.

These scenes affected me terribly. I remember once standing before them and begging them to have pity on me. Father looked at me and I saw understanding in his eyes. He quieted down, but Mother continued.

Despite my pleading, these encounters did not stop and I lived in constant dread of these scenes. I lost my appetite and developed a pain in my stomach and had nightmares. At school, my grades dropped, and the music and art classes had to be discontinued. My sickly appearance convinced Mother that I was suffering from an incurable disease.

So off she carted me to an Indian herb specialist. But the herbal concoction he gave me did not help, so we went to a psychic healer. His mantric incantations were of no avail either. Finally, at Father's insistence, I was taken to our good Dr. Kuznitsoff, an amiable, gray-haired gentleman and an experienced general practitioner. He was well acquainted with our family problems, as this was not the first time I had been taken to him with these symptoms.

To assuage Mother, the good doctor would go through all the customary procedures. With great deliberation, he would place his pince-nez on his bulbous nose, and with his stethoscope he would listen to my lungs and heart. He would thump on my chest with his knuckles and make me say "Ahhh."

Impressively wrinkling his forehead, Dr. Kuznitsoff would utter a long "Hmmm." Then, after a significant pause, he would say in a deep voice, "Yes, Muse must be placed in the hospital."

Mother would be elated. Now she had no doubts that I was ill.

Father did not protest. Part of his employment benefits was free hospitalization for the family. Besides, in those days there lurked, constantly, the fear of tuberculosis, which was widespread. Therefore, I would be taken and admitted into the Shanghai General Hospital. There I slept soundly and, with the help of a special diet and a variety of vitamins, I gained weight. In no time, I regained my normal appearance.

Meanwhile, at home, Mother's cycle tapered off. After a couple of weeks I would return home to a much calmer atmosphere. That is, calmer for a while, until the next episode.

One of these was spectacular. It occurred one Easter holiday, a celebration of great importance in a Russian household. Russians celebrate Easter more than Christmas. Days before Easter, our house was buzzing with preparations. Special *kulichis* (cylindrically shaped pound cakes) were baked. Cream cheese mixed with almonds and candied fruit was pressed into pyramid shapes—*pashas*, and colored eggs were dipped in dyes and decorated. Ducks and chickens were roasted. Various tossed salads, pickled herring, red caviar, and fish in aspic were garnished to be displayed on platters. All this abundance was placed on the best embroidered tablecloth on the dining-room table for consumption by guests.

In the pagan times of Russia's past, Easter was a Spring festival, celebrated by the ancient Slavic tribes as the harbinger of spring and the renewal of life and nature's procreation, after the long, arduous winter freeze. When Russia became Christian, this pagan jubilation took on new aspects, becoming the celebration of the resurrection of Christ.

According to tradition, there is a midnight service in the church on the eve of Easter Sunday. It is customary to be dressed in new clothing. Mother had ordered for me a lovely blue dress with a pink collar and cuffs. For herself she had purchased a long formal white gown of crêpe de Chine.

At eleven o'clock, our whole family proceeded to the Saint Nicholas Church on Rue Cornelle. It was a lovely building with five blue onion-shaped cupolas on its roof and a wide arched entrance inlaid with gold mosaic. We took our places on the right-hand side of the main door close to the raised platform prepared for the Archbishop to speak from.

There is nothing more impressive or so uplifting to the soul than this Russian Orthodox Easter Midnight Mass. The vast interior of the church was filled with celebrants all dressed in their holiday finery. The carved and gilded "Royal Doors" in the center of the iconostasis opposite the entrance and the whole church were ablaze in the light of hundreds of candles burning on tripods before the many icons of the benevolent-looking saints and the Holy Mother with the child Jesus.

On the balcony above, the choir was chanting an ancient Slavonic hymn a cappella as the Royal Doors opened and His Eminence, Archbishop Makary, stepped out in all his magnificence. His cape shone with gold and silver embroidery. On his head his miter sparkled with jewels and pearls. On his chest, below his snow-white beard, reposed a heavy gold Byzantine cross. Two tall deacons, impressive with their thick dark beards but in more modest attire, accompanied him.

The Greek Orthodox worshippers always stand in church. Only occasionally do they kneel when special prayers of supplication are recited. Now, as the Archbishop with the two deacons stepped toward the platform, everyone bowed in unison. The air was pungent with the incense from the deacons' censers.

I was on my knees, listening to the Archbishop's sonorous voice chanting an ancient prayer. Closer and closer he came to the platform and I saw that he was about to step up, when suddenly, he stopped short. His voice broke off. I also heard someone whisper, "Who is that?!" The whisperer sounded horrified.

I looked up and there, in the middle of the platform…who should be standing but my Mother. In the light of the crystal chandelier over her head, she looked dazzling in her white crêpe de Chine dress.

The Archbishop's face was expressing consternation. The deacons were swaying their censers faster than ever. I hid my own face behind Grandmother.

"For God's sake, get her down!" I heard Father telling Uncle Vsevolod.

But before my Uncle could do anything, the deacons came to their senses and resolved the problem. They grasped my Mother under her arms, lifted her, and carried her out of the church. Mother did not resist. She was in an ecstasy…

I could not help being glad that this time it had been a beautiful, holy experience for her, and that, perhaps, there would not be a scene at home. And, indeed, peace did rein for a while.

For many days, Mother imagined herself to be the reincarnation of Jesus. Her disposition became angelic, and she went about her household chores blessing everything and everybody.

That Easter day, when our guests arrived to partake of our holiday buffet, Mother was graciousness itself. Naturally, no one mentioned the incident in the church. Neither did Father. He was relishing the excellent food that Mother had prepared and the unusual peace…

20

Tsingtao

My life was not only one of stress and depression. There were also happy times. Some of these times were our summer excursions to the north of China.

Shanghai summers are unbearably hot. The temperature frequently rises to 100 degrees and higher, while, on the periphery of the city, the evaporation from the stagnant waters in the swamps and canals creates a stiflingly humid atmosphere. Not even a leaf stirs. Ignoring decorum, the inhabitants of my time in Shanghai sat in front of their open windows and doors clad only in the scantiest of clothing. They fanned themselves frantically with circular palm-frond fans as they drank cup after cup of hot tea, causing them to perspire in an attempt to lower the temperature of their bodies.

During these oppressive summer months of June, July, and August, everyone who could escaped to a sea resort. Tsingtao, in the northern province of Shantung, famous as the birthplace of Confucius, was one of these places. It was twenty-four hours by sea from Shanghai, and small Japanese vessels sailed regularly.

I was eight or nine when my parents and I traveled, for the first time, to that lovely sea resort. The *Dairen Maru* sailed at noon.

I remember watching from the promenade deck the red, blue, green, and yellow confetti strands stretch between the passengers on board and their friends on land; and as the ship pulled farther way, the strands tore into cascades of multicolored pieces falling into the water, as we steamed off down the Wang Pu River.

To the left and right, dismal gray factory buildings and endless rows of warehouses crowded our view. Farther along, towards the delta of the river, the banks became greener. Charming hamlets, with their yellow straw-thatched roofs, dotted the checkerboard of rice paddies, and soon after, the smell of the sea was heavy in the air.

At last the ship reached the delta and the shores faded out of sight. The waters suddenly changed from the yellow-brown of the river to the clean blue-green of the East China Sea. Here white-crested waves appeared and the ***Dairen Maru*** began rolling gently from side to side.

The ***Dairen Maru*** was a good and sturdy ship, exuding the strong smells of its cargo, salted cabbage and dried fish.

The passengers were divided into two classes. First class provided a comfortable cabin on the promenade deck, and all of the amenities of ocean travel. Second class, for a much lower price, provided space for passengers either in the bowels of the ship, should weather be rough, or allowed them to arrange folding cots or deck chairs on the poop deck. Weather permitting, it was an ideal journey, a veritable picnic. This was how my family liked to travel.

We arranged ourselves, like the other passengers, comfortably wrapped in blankets, in our folding chairs. A Japanese sailor passed around a kettle of water to brew tea. Everyone opened their baskets. Out came herring, Russian potato salad, cabbage rolls, and *pirozhky* (turnovers) with various fillings of beef, fish, or chicken with rice. Conviviality prevailing, bottles of vodka and wine appeared. There was the sound of clinking glasses and someone would invariably start to sing. Before you knew it, a chorus was formed. "Volga Boatman," "Stenka Razin," and many other lovely old ballads, full of nostalgia for the far away homeland of Russia, would fill the air.

I loved to listen to these songs as the ship plowed its way onward, heaving and bobbing. At night the sky was a dome of brilliant stars. Looking up into the vastness above and listening to the strains of the music, my eyes became heavy with sleep...

Next morning, the sun barely above the horizon, I awakened with a start. The sea was glowing with gold, orange, and purple hues as the undulating waves reflected the sun's rays. Most passengers were preparing their breakfasts. Again the pitchers of hot water were brought by the Japanese sailor and my Mother served us bagels with cream cheese. Having finished our morning breakfast snack, we prepared ourselves for the arrival in Tsingtao.

By nine o'clock, specks appeared on the horizon and, as the ship steadily proceeded at ten knots, the specks soon grew larger. By ten o'clock the specks became the silhouettes of mountains, the Laoshan Range on the Shantung peninsula, projecting eastward into the Yellow Sea.

By ten thirty, our ship was entering a wide harbor. On the starboard side were the shores of the city, bespeckled with multicolored houses. On the portside loomed a large green island that shielded the port from strong winds, creating a well-protected bay. At this point, a pilot boat approached. It steered our ship around a long promontory of land, and then pushed us into position along the dock of Tsingtao.

In no time, stevedores heaved the gangplank to the ship. It settled in place with a loud thud. The first-class passengers were the first to disembark. We, from the poop deck, followed. Father, who had to be half-carried, was the last to step ashore.

Finally, after much ado collecting our boxes, baskets, suitcases, and bundles of bedding, we took a taxi and were on our way to The Sea Villa, the inn owned and operated by Misha and Natasha Petrovsky, a former Russian Cossack officer and his energetic, buxom, blond wife.

Tsingtao is a curious city. It is in China, yet there is nothing Chinese about it. On either side of the broad, well-paved central street are buildings and shops of typically Germanic style, with high gabled roofs and walls of granite or brick. Several blocks away from the central area there is a park where, amid a grove of spreading linden trees, stands a rustic pavilion of the kind that you would expect to see in German villages or towns, where on Sundays a brass band plays the "Um-pah-pah."

Still farther, overlooking the esplanade along the seashore, are several imposing Baroque-style foreign buildings. The Japanese Consulate is the immense white neoclassical edifice on the corner of the street. Up the hill from it is a long, two-story red brick structure that was formerly a German military hospital, now serving as a school. Most impressive are the old German fortifications dating back to World War I. Constructed on a promontory south of the city, they are awesome. Their ominous-looking cannons peep from the high ramparts.

The reason for the Teutonic influence was that Tsingtao had been built by Germans for Germans in the early years of this century, when the European powers were acquiring large tracts of land and concessions in strategically important locations, all obtained at gunpoint as reparations for the misdemeanor of the Chinese populace. Germany took the Tsingtao area as compensation for the death of a German missionary priest slain in the interior of China.

All this was ancient history by the time we spent summers in Tsingtao. The Catholic priests and Protestant missionaries could proselytize their religions unmolested. Tsingtao and its surrounding vicinity had long ago been returned to their rightful owners, the Chinese. Only the architecture of the buildings reminded one of the days when Germany had had a footing here. The fort had become just another oddity to visit on weekend outings, while the rustic pavilion in the park had become a home for pigeons who built their untidy nests under its eaves.

When we visited Tsingtao, most summer residents spent their time on the splendid beaches, or they gathered for sandwiches, tea and hot chocolate on the wide terrace of the Strand Hotel. Here at five o'clock the orchestra played popular music and people danced. At seven everyone went to dress for cocktails and dinner. Evening gowns for ladies and tuxedos for the gentlemen were the "mot d'ordre" of the day.

In our inn, a pink-colored stucco Sea Villa overlooking a modest-sized beach at the north of town, life was simpler. The guests were Russian emigrants of modest means and unassuming habits. We sat on the narrow terrace, and drank only hot tea served from a copper samovar by Natasha Petrovsky. We watched the sunset and at times there was music from a gramophone. No one dressed for dinner. The meals were served on checkered red-and-white oilcloth tablecloths. I doubted, however, that the chef at the Strand Hotel prepared as tasty a spread as did Misha Petrovsky. The Strand Hotel garnished their delicacies with a flair, whereas our *zrazu po Polski*, *pohlebka iz robu*, or *cotlety iz kuritzutoene* were unceremoniously piled on platters, and the Russian *borscht* soup had to be scooped out of a communal tureen. But the taste of these dishes would not fail to satisfy the palate of the most finicky of gourmets.

The Sea Villa's accommodations were comfortable. The rooms were spacious and clean. The iron beds with horsehair mattresses were sturdy. My bed, in a far corner of the room, under the window, behind the massive wardrobe, reminded me of a hammock. Nonetheless, I slept soundly enough once I discovered the right position for my body.

On the whole, it was a good place to stay if one overlooked one slight inconvenience not unusual in old-fashioned, reasonably priced hotels, which had on each floor only one bathroom and one privy, located at the far end of a long corridor. In the event of an emergency, should you not desire to use the "night pot" provided in the room for such circumstances, and instead, decided to dash down the corridor, perchance forgetting, in your hurry, a roll of toilet paper, not to worry, as Misha Petrovsky had already foreseen such an embarrassment, and had tucked a bundle of newspapers discreetly at the foot of the toilet bowl. In calmer times, these papers could be pleasurably read. In times of crisis they were a perfect solution. A newspaper sheet crumpled and roughened fastidiously by hand, became soft and pliable and could do the job as well as any "baby-soft" commercial product.

So, well provided for in every respect, we passed our days, as the French say, "*san souci.*" Mother and I swam daily in the sea and basked in the sun, but our most enjoyable pastimes were the rides in the horse-drawn carriage late in the afternoon along the esplanade. What was most memorable for me were our excursions to the Laoshan Mountains near Tsingtao. It took two hours in a car to traverse the rough, unpaved road and to finally reach the center of those mountains.

On either side of the road as we drove along, were broad fields of shoulder-height gaolan plants, swaying their ripe brown tassels like waves on the ocean. Some fields were of golden maize. These plants had large pointed leaves with their seeds clustered on spear-like stems. We also drove through Chinese villages of mud-brick huts with straw roofs. In their central squares stood gristmills with blindfolded donkeys, tied to levers which pulled round and round a stone wheels grinding the grain to pulp. As we drove closer to the mountain range we passed family burial plots. Here we caught glimpses of grave mounds in the shadow of century-old oaks, maples and cedar trees.

I especially enjoyed our picnics near a churning brook where it was cool and where I could wade in the crystal clear waters. After a short respite, we finally, after many jolts, joggles and bounces, reached the cul-de-sac at the foot of the mountains where the road swerved abruptly to the right to zigzag up and up to the top of the first range, where we stopped, not only to rest our overheated engine, but also to admire the view.

Before us was a bowl-shaped valley with hamlets and giant step-like man-made terraces, where peasants grew their vegetables and grain. Serpent-like, the road down meandered toward the middle, a parking place in front of a group of red-tiled buildings, the Laoshan Hotel, our destination.

As we descended into this valley, the road became precariously steep. Pebbles and dirt flew left and right from under our car's wheels. If it had not been for the large flat stones embedded here and there, which gave us traction, I doubt that any motor vehicle could have negotiated this primitive roadway.

Nonetheless, slowly, carefully, occasionally burning the linings of our brakes, our chauffeur conveyed us to the parking lot of the hotel.

From here, three-foot-wide paths led up and down the mountains to the Buddhist temples, Taoist monasteries, and waterfalls for which the Laoshan Mountains had been famous from time immemorial.

21

Buddhist and Taoist Temples of Laoshan

From the earliest times, the Laoshan Mountains ("old mountains" in Chinese) had been a place for pilgrimage. Visitors and religious pilgrims sought among these lovely mountains not only their salutary pine-scented air, the breathing of which, it was believed, cured pulmonary diseases, but also the pure waters of the mountain streams and rivulets, which were known to be beneficial for the kidneys. What attracted people most of all to this region, however, were the Taoist and Buddhist temples.

In peaceful rural settings, far from the cares and raucousness of the world, a pilgrim could find serenity and spiritual strength. If they were Taoists, they communed with nature, contemplating upon the Tao, the Way, the concept of Allness, as taught by the great ancient mystic, Lao-tzu. Should they be followers of Buddha, they burned incense before the gold effigy of the Blessed One and meditated upon the transitory nature of human existence, with its sorrows and hardships, all lessons to be learned on the wheel of Samsara, the wheel of repeated reincarnations.

To inspire these pilgrim seekers to meditation and to make it easier for them to uplift their thoughts, the Buddhists, and especially the Taoists, sought to build their temples and monasteries in particularly beautiful locations, and each center of worship tried to have a special attraction.

In Laoshan, some of these temples and monasteries cling to lofty mountaintops overlooking vast valleys. Others are placed in deep ravines or groves of giant gingko trees, famous for their age. Still others are situated on precipitous cliffs overlooking waterfalls. Many face the open sea, with sand beaches at their feet. Wherever these retreats are, the pilgrim, after threading countless miles, can rest comfortably in a pavilion within the enclosed compound.

If the pilgrim is a Buddhist, he rises at dawn at the sound of the iron gong to participate in the daily ritual with the monks in the candle-illuminated temple hall. In cadence with the pealing of the bells in the hand of the Abbot, he makes his genuflections before the intricately carved and gilded image of Buddha on the altar, while inhaling the trance-inducing smoke from the bronze tripod incense burners.

If he is a Taoist, he will be awakened by the deep resonance of a great ancient bronze bell hit with a muffled mallet. He, too, will inhale incense before stepping out of the temple enclosure to find a quiet place where he can withdraw into deep meditation in his quest of oneness with the Tao.

22

The Monastery
of Delightful Vision

Father and I visited one of these monasteries. It was not famous for its surroundings, but it was renowned for the spectacular size and beauty of two peony bushes. The Taoist Abbot of this monastery was Father's friend.

We traveled in sedan chairs. Our carriers took us up a steep path, around a bend of a steep mountain, and then onto a winding trail through a sprawling valley. After an hour and a half we finally reached a narrow gorge where, to the left of us, half hidden amid a stand of acacia trees, we saw a high dark red wall with a round opening called the Moon Gate. This was the entrance to the Monastery of Delightful Vision famous for its peonies.

The month was July. The peonies bloomed in late May, so we were not able to admire the exceptional flowers, only the height of the bushes on each side of the entrance to the inner garden. They were as high as the wall. There was a curious story about these peony bushes. The Abbot assured my Father that it was true, and this is the story he told us.

Many years ago a monk by the name of Hsiao Ting, Little Ting, entered this Monastery of Delightful Vision as a novice. Among his scant possessions he had brought with him two small peony seedlings which, with the permission of the Abbot, he had planted on either side of the Moon Gate. Here Hsiao Ting watched over them tenderly. Every morning he would clip off a dead leaf or a withering branch and every morning he would carefully pour a teacupful of yellow liquid mixed with rain water from a vat around the plants. The bushes luxuriated. The peony blooms were spectacular. Because of their size and beauty, the monastery became famous. The donations from the pilgrims and visitors, who came to stay and admire the peonies, were considerable.

Years passed. Hsiao Ting, by then called Lao Ting, Old Ting, was given the important duty of striking the temple bell each morning at dawn. Lao Ting struck with his wooden mallet, the great bell hanging in the pavilion near the temple hall, and the deep sonorous sound echoed from mountain to mountain, across one valley to another. The farmers in their villages, hearing the bell, knew that it was time for them to be in their fields. The monks in other monasteries of the Laoshan Mountains, listening to the echoes, hurried to their temple halls to pray and meditate.

So it went for a long time. After striking the bell, Lao Ting always stopped and took out of his voluminous blue robes a small bottle of yellow liquid, poured a little of the liquid into a teacup, mixed it with rain water, and poured the mixture at the base of the peony plants. The remaining liquid in the bottle, Lao Ting would drink himself. The ritual continued for years.

Then, one day, Lao Ting died. It might have been from the natural causes of old age. It also might have been, as some monks suspected, from partaking of more and more of the yellow liquid both morning and evening. Whatever the reasons were, Lao Ting was dead and the monks buried him in the monastery burial yard in the shade of a gnarled pine tree. Another monk took over Lao Ting's duty of striking the great bell at dawn.

But now a strange thing began to happen. The branches of the peony bushes drooped. They lost leaves. The plants were obviously withering away. In the month of May, the peony flowers were few and looked pitifully small. The pilgrims and visitors to the Monastery of Delightful Vision did not stay long. The monastery was losing its popularity and income.

Greatly perplexed, the Abbot called a meeting in the temple hall. He placed the problem of the peony bushes before the monks and requested suggestions as to how to remedy the situation. The monks, sitting in rows before the Abbot, were silent. They lowered their heads. No one spoke. After a while, the Abbot had decided to dismiss everyone, when a young novice, who had arrived only recently, raised his hand.

"You have something to say?" asked the Abbot, surprised at the temerity of the new man.

"Your Holiness, if I may venture to express an opinion?" the young monk said politely, his head bowed low in an attitude of humility.

The Abbot waved with his wide sleeve. It was a sign for the novice to speak and that he would listen.

The young novice rose and bowed low several times. Then he said, "When the Venerable Lao Ting was alive, I was always the first to enter the temple hall ever since I arrived here. As I waited for others to come, I could see the Venerable Lao Ting in the pavilion striking the bell. I also saw that each time the Venerable Lao Ting rested, he would imbibe a little of a yellow liquid from a bottle. He would also pour a little of this liquid mixed with rain water from the vat and sprinkle this around the plants in question. I was wondering..."

"Yes? Yes?" the Abbot exclaimed.

"It may be that the plants are pining away for this mixture."

"WHAT NONSENSE!" shouted the Abbot. "That yellowish liquid is rice wine. It is fiery spirits!"

"AAAAH!!" the monks exclaimed, faking surprise. Some hid their faces behind their sleeves. But the Abbot was wise. He had known all along that Lao Ting was quite attached to the wine. He had also known that some of the other monks were, too. The austere discipline of the life in a Taoist monastery was difficult for a man. Wine might be the least of evils. So he had tolerated Lao Ting's weakness. Yet the seriousness of the situation demanded decisive action, thought the Abbot. "One cannot lose by trying," he said to himself.

"From now on, let us give the peony plants some of the rice wine mixed with water each morning," he said to the others.

The monks applauded heartily.

From that day on the young novice was given the duty of sprinkling a small cup of the wine mixed with rain water on the plants. And lo and behold! The peonies lifted their branches. They began sprouting buds. Soon the bushes were as luxuriant as before. In May when the visitors and pilgrims arrived, they were not disappointed. They stayed many days, breathing in the delicate scent of the flowers and admiring their magnificent, lacy, soft-pink and white blossoms.

As Father and I were carried away, in our sedan chairs, from the Monastery of Delightful Vision, Father and I looked back. The Abbot was standing within the frame of the round gate. In his flowing blue robe, with a silken black headband and his long moustache and beard falling down to his chest, he looked very distinguished. As Father lifted up his hat in a gesture of farewell, the Abbot bowed with his hands clasped in a gesture of respect.

23

Summers in Laoshan

With every passing year the Laoshan Mountains beckoned my family more and more. We stopped going to The Sea Villa in Tsingtao and instead would rent a small Chinese house in the mountains where we would enjoy our summers, living primitively.

As there was no electricity, we had candlelight. We went to bed as soon as darkness fell and rose at daybreak with the crowing of the roosters. There was no running water in the house, so I showered standing in an iron tub while my Mother, perched on a wooden stool, poured warm water over me from a pitcher.

Since there was no gas for cooking, Mother prepared our meals over a charcoal burner, vigorously fanning it with one hand to keep up the flames, while stirring in the pot with the other. There were no laundries. As a result, a Chinese peasant woman would take our clothes to a brook, and after dunking them into the water, she rubbed them thoroughly with a large dark-yellow piece of soap, before placing the whole lot in a pile on a flat rock, where she began to beat it with a rolling pin. Why the fabrics did not turn to pulp was a wonderment, but, remarkably, this drastic measure produced the cleanest dresses, shirts, and underwear I had ever seen.

Yes, we lacked all the amenities that the modern world considers necessary for happiness. Nevertheless, we were content, enjoying the beauty of the surroundings and the peace that enveloped us.

There were a few others who also savored this manner of living. One of these was Stepan Lebedeff. He visited Father frequently, though I suspected that it might have been Mother's cooking that attracted him more than the intellectually stimulating conversation with Father.

Stepan Lebedeff was in his late forties, with sparse brown hair and sharp eyes that darted to and fro. The most unusual feature about him was his manner of walking, a sort of skip-and-jump gait due to a partial paralysis of his left leg. This handicap, however, did not prevent him from going up and down the mountain paths as fast as any young goat. Stepan was an interesting man with an air of mystery about him and Father enjoyed his visits. The mystery was how he managed to subsist in Laoshan only on the proceeds of the sale of milk from his two old goats as he claimed.

There were rumors that his subsistence came from other sources, namely, the Chinese Nationalist Guerrillas, prevalent in that district. It was rumored that he was employed by them as an expert in manufacturing explosives and hand grenades. This story might have been true, for this was 1934–1935, and trouble was brewing with the Japanese.

Stepan would disappear for several days at a time. He never explained to anyone where he went... One day he left and never returned. His German shepherd dog, tied to a tree, attracted neighbors with his howling. The neighbors found Stepan's cabin deserted, but on his table, stood two half-filled cups of tea. A Chinese peasant told Father that he had seen Stepan with a man in uniform...

For days my Father waited for Stepan to return. He was convinced that Stepan was too smart a man not to survive. But, alas, Father was wrong. Stepan never returned.

Pavel Ivanovich Botkin, a bowlegged, potbellied former sergeant of the Russian Imperial Cossack Regiment, was another of Father's friends who lived in Laoshan. Pavel Ivanovich and Father used to recall the days of the Russo-Japanese War in 1904 in Manchuria.

"Yes, indeed, that was the time when I galloped on my bay horse in the grand attack against the Japanese redoubt," I heard Pavel Ivanovich tell Father as they sat sipping tea on our front terrace overlooking the valley. I could see that Pavel Ivanovich's eyes were blurred with tears as he waved his hand in the direction of several cabins barely visible in the distance. "Now look what kind of life I lead!" He wiped a tear with the back of his hand.

The cabins, to which Pavel Ivanovich was drawing attention, were a summer camp he owned and managed. It was a modest establishment for modest Russian guests who came to Laoshan in the summers. Sorting them according to sexes, Pavel Ivanovich packed them three or four in one cabin. His accommodations were limited. For nature's relief, everyone had to run clear across a field to a four-hole privy erected behind tall bushes. To wash, everyone went to a matted enclosure with an ingenious original contraption for showering: a bucket tied with a rope to a lever which dipped into a cistern of rain water.

For all these inconveniences, Pavel Ivanovich compensated his guests with his food. He knew that as long as a Russian stomach was delighted with what went into it, other discomforts would be of no consequence. His emphasis was on the Russian dishes: *pelmeny*, *kulibaky*, *pirozhky*, *pirogy*, etc., etc., etc. And, indeed, Pavel Ivanovich was correct. His summer camp teemed with guests, testifying to the business acumen of its proprietor. He may not have been galloping on a bay horse in full attack on the battlefield, but his profession now was not only safer but also much more lucrative. It also testified to the Russian adaptability and stamina. Like so many other Russian emigrants in China, Pavel Ivanovich survived and prospered.

24

Doctor Bergman's Sanatorium

Besides the Taoist and Buddhist temples in the Laoshan Mountains, there was also Dr. Bergman's Sanatorium. It had a fine reputation for expert care, comfortable rooms and, above all, excellent cuisine, which, together with the pure mountain air, was considered essential for curing ailments.

I was fourteen when our good Dr. Kuznitsoff urged my parents to send me to this institution. He became alarmed at my sudden loss of weight and my unhealthy, lethargic appearance. He feared that I might succumb to tuberculosis, so prevalent in those days. Therefore, that summer I was packed up and shipped to Tsingtao, where Dr. Bergman's representative met me and delivered me to the tender care of Frau Bergman, the manager of the sanatorium. My sojourn there for three months left several vivid memories.

The sanatorium comprised a group of whitewashed wooden cottages built on the side of a mountain slope, overlooking a small rivulet. Frau Bergman, the wife of Dr. Bergman, managed it splendidly. With her fiery red hair and her respect-inspiring dimensions, she was an imposing figure at the head of our long dining table. From here she kept a sharp lookout for any transgressions in the consumption of her food. Woe to anyone who pushed aside any vegetables or mashed potatoes!

"*Mein Liebchen*," Frau Bergman would say, pointing her finger in the direction of the culprit. "Das ist gut fur yoo! Yoo moost have zie carbohydrates!" The tone of her voice left no doubt that there was only one option, which was to stuff the substance into your mouth and swallow. Willy-nilly, we would do just that.

On the whole, the food was worthy of its reputation. All was prepared and planned with attention to a balance and consistency that would have fattened Mahatma Gandhi himself. My own objective was certainly reached during the three months of my stay. The tightness of my skirts testified to it!

Among the other guests at the sanatorium, who had also come because of health problems, was a charming young blue-eyed, flaxen-haired Russian woman with a son four years old. In contrast to his fair-skinned mother, the boy had the darkest brown hair, a tan skin, and the blackest eyes so typical of a southern Italian. For some reason, the other guests seemed to shy away from her; so she adopted me as her companion and we spent many pleasant hours frolicking in the rivulet or romping along the mountain paths.

Normally, a very fair-complected mother with a son so Latin in appearance might have been considered normal if the father of the child was an Italian or Spaniard. However, Vera's husband, Dr. Wilhelm, a prominent Shanghai businessman, was the personification of his Nordic ancestry, very blond and blue eyed. Unfortunately, this condition was Vera's problem, and the reason her husband had divorced her, and why she was convalescing in the sanatorium.

Much later, my Father, who knew Dr. Wilhelm well, related to me a conversation he had had with him before the divorce took place.

"If only the child had been blond, then I could have accepted Vera's infidelity," Dr. Wilhelm had confided to Father at one of their meetings. "But look at him—a true Italian."

"So forgive Vera," Father counseled. "You did admit that you have neglected her because of your business. If every husband or every wife, who had been deceived, applied for a divorce, how many intact families would we have?" Father was very tolerant in his views toward human weaknesses. "Besides, you love Vera," Father added, trying to convince the man.

"I know! I know! But the boy will be there haunting me with his Italian handsomeness! *Ach du lieber Gott.* If only he was blond!!" Dr. Wilhelm lamented.

"I realized that it was useless trying to reason with him. His pride took precedence over generosity of spirit," Father concluded and sighed.

It was a sad story. Frequently left alone by her much-too-busy husband, Vera would go down to the various Consulate and other social gatherings. At one of these parties she met a handsome Italian naval officer. With his charm and knowledge of women, he swept her off her feet. There were several brief encounters.

Soon after, the Italian officer's cruiser left Shanghai, and with it left the officer. The handsome little boy, however, was born in due time, a tragic memento of several hours of weakness.

Several years passed, when one day I ran into Vera in Shanghai, shopping on Avenue Joffre. She stopped to chat with me, but I noticed that her vivaciousness was gone. She was elegantly dressed, but there was a cloud of sadness about her. After that meeting I never saw her again and what happened to her I do not know.

Going back to my stay at Dr. Bergman's Sanatorium, I recall several teenaged boys and girls whose parents had cottages in the mountains.

Two of the girls were German sisters, Hannah and Gertrude. I always admired the colorful cotton tunics they wore over their white lace blouses. But, especially, I remember Peter Peterhansel, a boy of sixteen, the son of the owner of the biggest German haberdashery store in Tsingtao.

Oh, how my heart used to beat when Peter looked in my direction with a meaningful smile! With what exhilaration I sang in chorus with several other boys and girls a German song, *"En einem kühlen Grunde der geht ein Mühlenrad, mein Leibchen ist verschwunden, das dort gewohnet hat..."* while he held my hand. How I looked forward to my secret meetings with Peter in the gazebo overlooking the rivulet, and we watched as the dark purple shadows of the night crept up to swallow the golden sunset on the mountain peaks across the valley. My heart would pound with excitement as I hoped Peter would kiss me...but, alas, he was either too proper or too shy...

Our romance and evening meetings must have been noticed and reported to Peter's parents, because Peter left Laoshan, unexpectedly.

Hannah, one of the German girls, noticing that I was upset, tried to console me. "You see, Peter is needed in his father's store," she explained.

Before I left for Shanghai, I wanted to say goodbye to Peter. Hannah took me to the Peterhansel store. It was an impressive red-brick building on the corner of Main Street, with wide show windows full of mannequins adorned in fashionable dresses and hats.

As we entered, Peter greeted us cordially. He was as good looking as ever. His light blond hair was brushed smoothly back with a brilliantine cream and his gray suit fit him perfectly. He looked at me and smiled, but I saw no hidden meaning in his smile. What I read in his manner was a desire to sell us something. Not to disappoint him, I bought a cheap scarf. It was all I could afford.

Returning from Dr. Bergman's Sanatorium, 1934

25

We Visit California

A very important event for our family took place in the year 1935. My parents and I visited the United States, where Father lectured at the University of California at Berkeley.

The British Colonial employment provided for its civil servants a leave of absence for six months with full pay every five years, should they desire to go back to England or travel elsewhere. The passage, for the whole family, was also paid.

In the Spring of 1935, Father became eligible for this benefit. Mother and I were more than excited at the prospect of a long, interesting trip. Father chose the United States, a country that had always held an attraction for him, probably because several of his childhood friends from Russia had immigrated there and, through their steady correspondence, kept telling him what a place of opportunity it was.

Father's publisher, Mr. Davis, the chief editor of *The Herald Shanghai*, looked at this situation as a chance to promote in the United States Father's books, **New Lamps for Old**, published in 1930; **Shanghai: Its Mixed Court and Council**, published in 1925; and **Shanghai: Its Municipality and the Chinese**, published in 1927. At this time, as foreigners had many interests in China, such books had worldwide distribution. In addition, the University of California at Berkeley was renowned for its prestigious Department of Asian Studies, and Mr. Davis felt that Father, as an authority on China, would be more than welcome to lecture there.

He was correct. After writing to the Dean of the Department of Asian Studies, he received by return mail an invitation for Father. So, it was decided that we would go to California. Arrangements were made for us to sail for San Francisco in the early Spring on the *U.S. Sherman*, a small American cargo vessel.

Mother and I could hardly wait for the day of our departure. Mother ordered several new dresses for herself and for me from our Russian seamstress, and Father, always fastidious about his appearance, had his regular Chinese tailor custom make a tweed jacket to go with a pair of gray flannel trousers. As Father had Chinese citizenship, given to him by General Chang Kai Shek, we had no trouble procuring the necessary tourist visas, which were otherwise difficult to obtain for Russian emigrants, who were considered stateless.

At last the day arrived, and that afternoon Father, Mother and I went aboard the *U.S. Sherman*, a small but sturdy-looking ship with only one outstanding feature, a tremendous black and white smokestack. As the anchor was raised and the gangplank pulled away from the ship, it gave an appropriately sonorous toot to announce our departure.

The *U.S. Sherman* was not a fast-moving ship; its maximum speed was about thirteen knots. Stopping for a day in Nagoshima, Japan, we picked up additional cargo, and were expected to reach San Francisco on calm seas in a week or ten days.

After arranging our luggage in our small, but comfortable, three-bunk cabin, we heard the chimes announcing our first evening meal. In the dining room, the steward conducted us to the Captain's table. This honor pleased Father immeasurably. The cuisine on the *Sherman* lacked neither variety nor gastronomic excellence. During our trip, among other dishes, we had pheasant, different kinds of fish, paté de fois gras, and even frog legs. All attention was centered on pleasing the passengers.

For entertainment, in the salon, we had a selection of card games and dominos, while on deck there was shuffleboard. Our passage across the placid East China Sea to Japan permitted us to walk on deck or lie basking in the sun on chaise lounges. Once in a while we saw dolphins jump playfully in and out of the water, racing our ship. At other times, a school of flying fish would suddenly leap in unison into the air, and after traversing quite a distance the little creatures would dive back. Spectacular, also, were the sunsets, with fiery gold flashes coming from behind billowing clouds.

At night I remember looking up into the deep indigo expanse of sky studded with thousands of twinkling stars and it reminded me of the times, when I was a little girl, traveling with my parents from Shanghai to Tsingtao, lying bundled on a cot in the stern of a Japanese "maru," and how, even then, I was aware of how microscopic was our ship on the boundless sea around us, totally at the mercy of the weather. Fortunately, our voyage to Nagoshima continued to be pleasurably calm.

We reached port according to schedule and went ashore. The town had no particular tourist attractions. It was a little center for small ships to stop at and pick up Japanese merchandise for different parts of the world. At that time, in 1935, Japan was not yet the giant of manufacturing and distribution it was to become. We found, however, one interesting feature in Nagoshima.

It was the street of shops selling exclusively second-hand, hand-woven silk geisha kimonos with obis (belts), head ornaments, fans and umbrellas used by geishas in the Japanese tea houses. These goods were artfully hand-woven and hand-painted objects, interwoven with gold or silver thread, which the geishas had traded in for new clothing. As it was essential for them to have different costumes when they danced, sang, and served as hostesses while entertaining groups of Japanese men out on the town, a custom common in Japan where men had the privilege of escaping from the monotony of family life and loveless marriages, frequently arranged by parents with practical goals in mind.

Mother purchased two kimonos for herself, a black one with white and silver bamboo painted along the hem line and on the wide sleeves. Mine was soft blue with cherry blossoms. She also bought two obis to go with our kimonos.

Leaving Nagoshima, *U.S. Sherman* sailed southward, around the small green island of Tanega Shima, and then directly eastward across the Pacific. Aboard, we continued to enjoy our cruise. When the chimes announced our meals, we hastened to the dining room. We played various games in the salon, and in the evening, watched the stars as we promenaded along the decks. Thus the first two days passed "sans souci."

On the third day of our passage from Japan, the placid waters of the Pacific commenced to heave and our ship started to roll a little, while, straight ahead of our bow, an unusual configuration of menacing clouds was rising. No one, however, paid much notice to this. The chimes announced lunch, and Mother, Father and I made our way down the corridor and up the stairs to the dining room. Now and again, because of the increasing movement of our ship, Father had to be supported to keep from losing his balance. Nevertheless, we reached our table in good time.

To our considerable puzzlement, we saw that strange, barrier-like wooden boards protruding several inches above the surface, encircled the table tops.

"What is this?" Father inquired, turning to our Captain, at the head of our table.

"Oh! A small precaution should the dishes slide," he answered, seemingly unconcerned, just as we felt our ship incline quite a bit to starboard. The Captain adroitly lifted his bowl, preventing his soup from spilling, while our own bowls slid to the right, with appropriate results.

"You see how it works?" the Captain laughed. But I noticed that the laugh seemed a little forced and, shortly after, he left us. In his haste he even forgot to excuse himself.

His urgency left us feeling very uncomfortable, particularly as sailors rushed in to lock the windows, and we heard the clangor of the portholes as they slammed them shut.

"I think you'd better help me back to the cabin," Father said, bracing himself to arise.

With the assistance of the steward, Mother and I got Father back to the cabin. Raising another board to the other side of Father's bunk, the steward left us.

This precautionary measure was just in time, as the ship suddenly heaved upward, trembled, and rolled to port. I managed to grasp at the bunk post, not to be thrown against the door.

"May Heaven help us!" Father exclaimed, making several quick signs of the cross.

"Saint Serafim, please watch over us!" Mother's voice rose in supplication.

Leaving my parents to their prayers, I slipped out of the cabin. As the doors to the decks were locked, I slowly made my way through the corridors, up the stairs, to the glassed-in deck facing the bow of the ship.

I will never forget what a terrifying experience it was to stand there with only a sheet of glass protecting me from the steady barrage of foam from the threatening waves that came toward the ship like mountains. It seemed that any minute we would be swallowed by the sea. But the *U.S. Sherman* was a sturdy vessel. Tightly closed against the waters, it bobbed like a cork and rode the crests of the thunderous waves.

The storm lasted for several hours. Eventually, we passed through it into good weather. Father was convinced that it was a sheer miracle that kept our ship from capsizing. Perhaps. We were, however, swept off course, and lost time. One of the engines also needed repair.

Overdue by several days, the *U.S. Sherman* did reach the Golden Gate Bridge at the entrance to the Bay of San Francisco. We sailed past the small island of Alcatraz with its fortress-like prison, and moored late in the afternoon at one of the wharves of the city. As soon as the gangplank closed the gap between the ship and land, a bevy of newspaper reporters and immigration officials with their briefcases rushed aboard.

While my parents went to process the visas, I stood on deck with my binoculars, observing our surroundings.

"Ah! That's perfect. Hold it right there," someone said to me.

"Who are you?" I asked.

"I am a reporter from the *San Francisco Chronicle*. Please look through the binoculars again. It will be such a lovely picture in tomorrow's newspaper," he told me.

Flattered, I naturally posed. His camera clicked. Then he proceeded to ask me various questions. Who I was and whence I came? Why I was traveling?

I answered all his questions. He thanked me and disappeared.

When I told Father that a picture of me had been taken for the *San Francisco Chronicle*, he was furious.

"You should have sent him to me. It would have been good publicity," he told me.

Father was even more upset the next morning when he opened the newspaper. There I was on the front page, peering through my binoculars. The caption under my picture said: "Muse Kotenev, only fifteen years of age, and already a historian."

"How ridiculous!" Father raised his voice angrily. He picked up the hotel telephone and called the *San Francisco Chronicle*'s Editor-in-Chief.

"Sir, are you aware of what your paper has on the front page? My fifteen-year-old daughter's picture with the caption that she is a historian. What nonsense is this?"

"Mr. Kotenev," the Editor laughed, "don't take this too seriously. In America, we thrive on sensations. The newspaper's life span is only a few hours, and we write for the mentality of twelve year olds."

Father was astounded by such an answer.

This was our introduction to the New World.

Another amazing episode of our acquaintance with a different culture happened on the night of our arrival, when we finally made it to the hotel.

It was ten by the time we settled in our room and we were very hungry. The bellhop had just brought in our luggage and Father inquired if the restaurant was open.

"No, sir, but I can get something for you from the diner," he said.

"Ah, splendid. Do they have sandwiches?"

"Why, of course, sir."

"Well, how many do you think we should order?" Father asked my Mother.

"I think a dozen with ham or cheese would be sufficient," she answered.

"A dozen sandwiches, please," Father told the bellhop. "And a pot of hot tea."

"A DOZEN?" The bellhop's mouth dropped open.

"Sure. Why not?" Father answered.

"Are you sure you can eat a dozen?" the bellhop asked again.

"Yes, yes, and please hurry," Father repeated, a little annoyed with the bellhop's behavior. "What an impertinent creature!" Father remarked as the man left the room. "Certainly different from our polite Chinese boys. And why should he question us about how many sandwiches we can eat?"

We soon found out why he had. There was a knock on the door and into the room stepped the bellhop, carrying a great big box with four-inch-thick sandwiches of hefty slices of ham and cheese between monstrous slices of pumpernickel bread, long pieces of pickled cucumbers, and no end of coleslaw in cartons.

"My God!" Father exclaimed. "You did not understand us!"

"Sir, you said a dozen. This is a dozen."

"But, but...I did not mean the size for elephants."

"Sir, the sandwiches are the usual size we eat. The diners are known for them," the bellhop explained, as he handed Father the bill: U.S. $12.00.

"Oh! My!" Father gasped, converting in his mind the U.S. $12 into Chinese currency. "It is astronomical!" But he realized the mistake was his. In China, the restaurants served small, thinly sliced bread sandwiches. We later found out that in the United States they called them "finger sandwiches" and that they were usually only served at ladies' teas and cocktail parties.

At the University of California at Berkeley, Father's lectures in Sproul Hall were successful. The number of students attending was more than satisfactory and the review in the University magazine, *Spider*, was favorable. The Dean was pleased and Father was pleased.

We found Father's old friends from Russia quite changed from the old days in Russia. They, too, had had to adjust to the New World. To survive, many had to work in the blue-collar sector. Forgetting their former positions in pre-Revolutionary Russian high society, they now worked as elevator operators, doormen in hotels, and waiters in restaurants. Though expediency had forced them to take these lowly jobs, Father was glad to see that they had all preserved their self-respect and dignity, and that everyone was doing well.

The end of our visit to the United States started full of excitement. The stevedores' strike prevented our ship from mooring in San Francisco. It had to be diverted far up north to a small port in the State of Oregon. How to get there? That was the perplexing question, as our finances were at a low ebb.

"Not to worry," one of Father's Russian friends told us. "I will drive you there. Just pay for the gasoline and my food and lodging along the way."

Father agreed. And what a blessing in disguise it turned out to be. What an opportunity to see the beauty of America!

We drove along the coast as far as Portland, stopping at night in quaint motels with scenic views of breakers beating against the rugged cliffs. We marveled at the ancient giants, the Sequoia trees, and drove through the lovely sun-filled Moon Valley of Jack London's stories. Finally, we reached our point of departure, the tiny port of Westport, from which our ship took us back home to Shanghai.

In China again, we were happy to be in Shanghai, back to eating our small, delicate sandwiches, and back to reading the Russian and British newspapers that were published for adults.

Muse with Parents in California, 1935

26

The Year 1937

The year was 1937, and full of events in our family. My Father's last book, **The Chinese Soldier**, was published in English, and soon after, was translated into Chinese. The subject of the book was the martial history of China, the lives of famous Chinese generals and heroes, and the philosophy of the Chinese toward war. The Nationalist government found it important and included it as a textbook in all Chinese public schools. Sixty thousand copies were printed by the Commercial Press in Shanghai. Everything seemed very promising for Father.

As for myself, I was looking forward to the time when, according to tradition, I would have my first evening gown and, because I was seventeen, I would be presented to the world, the Shanghai Russians.

Mother ordered from a seamstress a gown of white chiffon in the style of the Directoire, just like the one Napoleon's Josephine had worn. I also had pinned to my waist a corsage of lavender silk orchids. Looking at myself in a long mirror, I was pleased with what I saw. I was a tall slim girl; my dark auburn hair had a glint of gold in it and was arranged in waves which fell to my shoulders. My face, though not classical in beauty, was nevertheless, I felt, appealing, with a slender neck and eyebrows in the shape of the wings of a bird in flight, and I had large, alert blue eyes.

"Enough of that! You're pretty!" Mother motioned toward the door. She herself was not going with us.

"Not bad, not bad at all!" said my Father, holding his monocle to his left eye as he braced himself to rise.

"Now don't forget to hold your back straight and head up," admonished my Mother, as Father and I were climbing into the taxi on our way to the Former Russian Officer's Club, where I was to be presented to the local Russian society.

The sound of the orchestra playing a waltz, "On the Slopes of Manchuria," greeted us as our taxi delivered us to the entrance of a large Victorian mansion at the end of a long driveway. It was nine in the evening and the ball was in full swing.

"My daughter, Muse," Father presented me to the president of the club, a stately elderly gentleman with a bushy Franz-Joseph-of-Austria mustache.

"At your service!" The president of the club clicked his heels adroitly, bowing slightly in my direction. In an elegant old-world gesture, he extended his arm in the direction of the dining room, inviting us to follow him. I helped Father across the highly polished floor of the ballroom and through a wide arch into the walnut-paneled dining room.

The president led us to one of the long tables covered with a white tablecloth and an elaborate arrangement of chrysanthemums in a crystal vase in the center. As etiquette required, we were ceremoniously introduced to each lady and gentleman seated at the table.

There were Lieutenant Colonel So-and-so, Madame Elena Mihailovna or Maria Fedorovna This-or-that, General of the Imperial Russian Cavalry of the Ural Division, Mihail Fedoseivich, etc., etc., on and on. Everyone greeted me cordially. The ladies extended their hands. The gentlemen rose and bowed. I thought the introductions would never end.

Fate and the Russian Revolution had thrown all these people together far from their homeland. Now, dressed in their best finery, they clung to their former glory, forgetting some of their present lowly positions as janitors of hotels, salesmen, clerks, jailkeepers or policemen—jobs that they took to survive. Here, in the Former Russian Officer's Club, before the portrait of Tsar Nicholas II, hanging above the fireplace, they were again Russian nobility twirling in waltzes, gliding to polonaises, and skipping elegantly to mazurkas and polkas.

"Father, where are the eligible young bachelors you talked about?" I asked, looking around, seeing only gray hair and wrinkled faces.

"Be patient," Father answered, as he drained a small glass of vodka and bit into a hard-boiled egg with a pickled herring.

Eventually a tall young man, with curly hair, did approach me. He bowed elegantly and invited me to dance. My heart was beating intensely as we stepped onto the floor to dance a polka.

The young man danced very well, and we performed our steps in perfect timing with the music. What remained in my memory about this dance, however, was garlic. Yes, the smell of garlic. My gallant young man must have eaten something with a goodly amount of this ingredient before his arrival at the Club. Each time he turned his head and spoke to me at this close range, the smell of garlic on his breath overwhelmed me.

So, there I was in my white chiffon Directoire dress, just like Napoleon's Josephine used to have, with a corsage of specially made orchids pinned to my high waist, and gracefully stepping to a light polka, enveloped in a cloud of garlic. Fortunately, the music stopped and the young man escorted me back to my seat. When he approached me again, I politely but firmly declined the honor.

The rest of the evening I danced with the elderly officers. They were the best dancers I had ever encountered. As it was considered a prerequisite in the old days in Russia for every officer to dance well, they all had dancing lessons as cadets. Holding their ladies at a little distance, these gentlemen performed with distinction all the demanding steps of the old-world ballroom dances.

The Russian waltz, where one turned continuously, they danced like veritable dervishes—one, two, three, one, two, three, one, two, three, without stopping. It was a marvel how they preserved their balance when the orchestra suddenly stopped.

Father made several other attempts to introduce me to eligible bachelors. At one soirée I met Andrew Panitowsky, the son of a former Russian bank official. He lived with his widowed mother. Andrew's manners were impeccable, which counted highly with my Father. Andrew escorted me several Sundays to Jessfield Park, and we promenaded along the meandering paths and watched the swans gliding in the pond. But somehow the spark was absent.

Andrew and his mother returned to Russia when the Soviet government started to encourage the return of emigrants. Many did. What happened to these Russians remained a mystery because very few of them wrote to their friends in China, and what they did write was very vague, and not very reassuring.

Muse at age 17

27

Madame Tokmakoff

The day of my Father's retirement finally arrived. Father was fifty-five years old, the age limit in the British Colonial Service. Having received a good severance pay from the Shanghai Municipal Council, he was free to realize his dream of moving permanently to the Laoshan Mountains and to spend the last days of his life in the peaceful surroundings of nature, just as the Chinese officials and scholars in the olden days used to do.

In Laoshan, Father planned to build a house not only large enough for us, but also spacious enough to have paying weekend guests. He hoped that the proceeds from these visitors, plus the royalties from the recently published Chinese book, **The Chinese Soldier**, would provide a comfortable living.

When I, a little worried about our future isolation, asked Father, "What about my own future?" Father answered me without wavering: "Trust in life. It will show the way."

That autumn, my parents left for Tsingtao. They took with them our four Lhasa Apso dogs, the progeny of Mimi, our exotic fish in a tank, and the four golden finches, and, of course, all our furnishings. Grandmother moved in with Uncle Vsevolod, while I was left in Shanghai for a short time in the care of Elizaveta

Mihailovna Tokmakoff, the widow of a wealthy tea merchant, whom Father had known since his Peking days in 1902.

Madame Tokmakoff, as everyone called her in Shanghai, was a remarkable lady. Though by now of very modest means earned by renting a room or two, she, nevertheless, continued to maintain an illusionary ambience of prosperity. From early morning she was fastidiously dressed, groomed and bejeweled, with long strings of pearls wound around her neck, large diamonds glistening on her fingers, and earrings of intricate design—all fake, theatrical embellishments—the diamond-beveled glass fitted into her old settings instead of the real diamonds, which had been sold long ago.

Though not a beautiful woman—she was very thin, with small eyes, a large mouth, and very pronounced cheekbones—she did have charm, particularly when she spoke. Not only was her speech witty, but she also had a way of moving her slender hands to punctuate her thoughts. With her costume diamonds glistening, it was quite effective.

Madame Tokmakoff also liked to entertain. Her parties were unique. I remember one of them, the celebration of her sixty-fifth birthday.

Several hours before the arrival of the invited guests, all friends from former days, Madame Tokmakoff spread her best Venetian-lace tablecloth on the dining table. She placed a silver candelabra in the middle and surrounded it with her best china, silver, crystal bowls and Sèvres platters. On the server stood buckets with ice for wines. Everything was in place. Everything was shining. Everything was sparkling. The only things that were missing were the contents. None of the dishes had food.

I looked into the kitchen. There was no food. Our cook-boy, the servant, was calmly wiping glasses, while in the living room, Madame Tokmakoff, all dressed up for the occasion, was sitting on her yellow damask Louis XV chair. I looked at the clock. My goodness! Just an hour was left before the festivities were to begin.

"Elizaveta Mihailovna, where is the food and wine?" I asked.

"Don't worry, Cherie," she replied. "All will be here in time."

"But the time is now!" I exclaimed.

Madame Tokmakoff waved her slender hands in the air and shrugged her skinny shoulders, visible through the black chiffon blouse. "All will be here."

And, sure enough, there was the sound of the bell at the entrance door. The cook-boy rushed to open it. In stepped delivery men with packages and containers of roast chickens, fish dishes, pies, caviar, salads, bottles of vodka, wine, champagne, baskets with breads, fruit and pastries, all gifts of her thoughtful guests, who, knowing Madame Tokmakoff's financial predicament, had made sure that nothing would be lacking at her sixty-fifth birthday party.

That evening, wine and vodka flowed in torrents as toast after toast was drunk in remembrance of the "good old days." Numerous speeches honoring the hostess were given, while the hostess meanwhile sat on her Louis XV chair like a queen, bowing and waving her slender hands.

At midnight the guests dispersed, satisfied not only with their own generosity, but also with having shared in loving camaraderie an evening with friends from the old days in Russia.

28

An Unexpected Assignment

While staying with Madame Tokmakoff, I received a letter from Father. He had purchased a large piece of land in Laoshan, and had found a building contractor, who had started the construction of our house, the Rock Mansions. Now Father needed plumbing equipment, pipes and fixtures, for four bathrooms. I was to purchase everything for him secondhand, but in good condition, and at the best prices possible, in the warehouses of Shanghai. Attached to the letter was a draft on a bank and a detailed list of the length and gauge of pipes and other necessary items. In addition, I was to have everything crated and bring the crates with me on the ship on which I would be sailing to Tsingtao.

I was aghast! What did I know about plumbing equipment—a girl of seventeen? The assignment frightened me, yet it was a challenge. I could clearly imagine my Father's eyes twinkling with mirth as he was sending this vote of confidence.

So, I took a deep breath and turned for assistance to the only man I knew I could trust, a friend of Father's, Vadim Vadimovich Lasoff, whom I suspected could not distinguish a kitchen sink from a wash basin. As a former lawyer, I hoped he could be helpful in some way or another.

Two days later we took a pedicab into China Town, south of Shanghai International Concession, where I was told all the large plumbing warehouses were located. We found them. Having found them, however, we also found, to our consternation, an overwhelming variety from which to select—five-foot bathtubs, six-foot bathtubs, wide bathtubs, deep tubs, shallow tubs. It would have made even an experienced plumber's head giddy.

With difficulty and much tribulation, I finally made my selections and filled Father's list. Now it came to payment. At this point I was overjoyed to discover that I had not made a mistake in asking Vadim Vadimovich to come with me.

"You must offer less than half the price asked or the merchant will not want to do business with you," he told me in a low voice. "I have lived long enough in China to know all their tricks. A sale is a game of wit. To arrive at the proper price is an art. Both parties must feel benefited by the transaction."

Vadim Vadimovich, bless his soul, proved very astute in this bargaining game. With his long, naturally pale, expressionless face, he showed no emotion. He made his way toward the door several times as though he intended to leave. The merchant went way down in his price, and we did well with Father's money. The merchant also threw into the deal crating and delivery to the ship on the day specified.

When we were leaving, something bothered me a little. As I looked back, the merchant's bows seemed much too deep and I thought his grin much too wide. Perhaps after all, Vadim Vadimovich's astuteness had been insufficient. Ah, well…What consoled me was the thought that the Chinese merchants had thousands of years of business practice behind them. Who were we to compete with such oriental finesse?

On the day I was leaving for Tsingtao, the crates were delivered to the ship. After some intensive negotiations with the purser and a little money placed into his cupped left hand, I finally persuaded him to secure my unusual baggage on the bow of the vessel.

In due time, everything arrived safely in Tsingtao, where Father met me in grand style in a newly purchased dark-blue four-door sedan driven by a chauffeur. After arranging proper transportation for the crates, we drove off to Laoshan.

29

The Swiss Chalet

While building "Rock Mansions," my parents rented a quaint Swiss chalet. It stood halfway up the mountain slope directly overlooking the main valley of Laoshan. Its picturesque Tyrolian architecture lent a touch of Switzerland to the view. From the small balcony on its second floor the vista was breathtaking. I loved to watch the shadows take various shapes as the clouds hid the sun. Now I would recognize a dragon, then a monstrous bird or a weird-looking animal. My imagination must have been stirred by the strange atmosphere in the chalet itself.

The rooms were comfortably furnished by Mrs. Bernhard, the owner of the house. The walls had well-polished paneling of pine. In the living room, as one entered, a well-designed fireplace of red brick, with a cuckoo clock hung above it, made a pleasing picture. Yet, something started to bother me as I stepped inside. On closer scrutiny, a curious detail became apparent. Except for the entrance door hinges and the hands on the clock, there was no other metal in the room. All tables had three legs and were round. The armchairs were all held together with pegs. A steep staircase led up to a spacious landing which, for some reason, I was afraid to cross.

At night, I would awaken and hear the downstairs' clock going TICK, TICK, TICK, and on the half hour, CUCKOO! CUCKOO! CUCKOO! sharp and clear. The sounds sent shivers through me and I would hide under my covers.

No doubt my nervousness was caused by events in our family. While we were living in the Chalet, my Father, my idol, whose every word I took as the very truth itself, and whom, like a knight in King Arthur's Court, I believed was without fear and above reproach, I discovered was a mortal, a very foolish mortal, whose folly led to serious consequences in my family.

In the famous Russian opera *Eugene Onegin*, the elderly husband of the young heroine sings a doleful aria. Some of the words are: "To love all ages bend their knees." At the age of fifty-five, at that time considered venerable, Father fell passionately in love with a pretty brunette of twenty-five. She was staying in the hotel below our Swiss chalet.

At first, neither Mother nor I paid any attention to Father's sudden interest in nature. Every afternoon he would call for his sedan chair carriers in order to be carried, so he explained, up the mountain to observe the rural vista.

After several days, however, Mother became suspicious. Normally, to become suspicious, Mother needed little incentive. But now Father's behavior would have aroused wonder in anyone. As a result, one afternoon she followed him at a safe distance. Imagine her consternation when the chair bearers, instead of turning to the right and heading up the mountain trail, turned to the left, descending down to the center of the valley and stopping at the hotel. She watched Father enter.

My Mother was not a woman of control. She rushed into the situation full steam ahead. In the hotel she listened at several doors until she found one through which she heard Father's voice.

BANG! BANG! BANG! went her fists against the closed door. The door opened and there stood the young brunette, sparsely covered with her dressing gown. Behind her, Mother could see Father, also somewhat scantily clad.

"Oooih! Oooih!" Mother shrieked in anguish. Then, after calling all evil down upon the pretty brunette, Mother vented upon Father an array of colorful Russian expressions, with which the Russian language abounds. The commotion drew the other guests of the hotel into the corridor. They escorted Mother out of the building.

Dragging herself back to our chalet, Mother climbed up to the attic, pulled out her suitcase, threw a few items of her clothing into it, and finally collapsed in a chair awaiting Father's return.

He arrived shortly after. From their heated discussion, I gathered that Mother was leaving us.

Father knew that it was useless to try to calm her down. He had to have felt guilty. In silence, he wrote her a generous check. With this in hand, Mother ordered our chauffeur to drive her to Tsingtao.

I stood at the door as Mother walked by me without saying goodbye. I was shattered, mute. "No, no!" I kept saying to myself. "It cannot be true. No, no!" My head started to shake and I could not stop it. My head continued to shake for several weeks until, with sedation under a doctor's care, it finally stopped.

In Laoshan, the brunette, discovering that Father did not have much, and with Mother's departure, even less, she, too, promptly embarked on a steamer for Shanghai. One afternoon when Father arrived at the hotel, the doorman handed him a note. In it was a cryptic message which read, "I am returning to a friend I have in Shanghai."

It was quite a blow to Father's pride and it pained me to see him so humiliated. I tried to console him, but what could I say? We both realized that his actions were imprudent and impulsive.

Time heals all wounds, however, and so it did with Father.

One morning at breakfast, he turned to me with a funny smile. "You know, it is better to have loved and lost than never to have loved at all." He also quoted me something from the Bible about cymbals striking in the desert, and he laughed because he could not remember the exact quotation. I, too, laughed, glad that he was feeling better.

In Shanghai, Mother did not get along with Madame Tokmakoff, with whom she was staying. They were both miserable. Mother was completely unable to sustain herself without Father's presence. She spoke no English and had no profession to fall back on. After several months, Father received a desperate letter from Madame Tokmakoff. She begged him to take Mother back.

By now, his limited finances were greatly diminished not only by what he had given Mother, but also by the construction of Rock Mansions. I thought, too, that he missed her. After all, they had been many years together and Mother had been a faithful wife.

Putting his pride aside, Father wrote her a letter replete with apologies. Mother, naturally, forgave him and returned. She was a kind and loyal woman, despite her mental illness. When Father married her, he took her for better or for worse. Through all the trials and tribulations of their long years of marriage, they had stood by each other 'til death parted them...or, maybe, united them forever.

30

The Building
of Rock Mansions

Having purchased a ten-acre lot on the side of a mountain, a lovely site overlooking a rivulet and a vista of a gorge, the next step was to find a contractor, which was accomplished with the help of the headman of the neighboring village of Pei Chui Shui. Father hired two brothers, Sun Hsienshun and Tah Tuza, with a crew of masons, carpenters, and their helpers.

The older of the brothers was Tah Tuza, or Big Belly, as everyone called him for obvious reasons. Ever with a smile on his moon-shaped face, he moved slowly and thought even more slowly. His younger brother, Sun Hsienshun, or Master Sun, was the complete opposite. He was lean, fidgety, and ingenious at speedily solving problems, and these problems did crop up due to the political situation in China at that time.

My Mother took an immediate dislike to Sun Hsienshun. She nicknamed him Satan Satanovitch, a Russian appellation of that sinister figure blamed for much of the evil in this world. There was, indeed, something about the appearance of Sun Hsienshun to inspire such a cognomen. In his long black gown, with his saffron-colored complexion, peering at you through slitted eyes, he aroused one's apprehension.

Mother's feminine intuition had sensed something unusual about the man. And there was. One day the headman of Pei Chui Shui revealed to Father in a confidential whisper that Sun Hsienshun was a soothsayer. He used the **I Ching**, the "Book of Changes," an ancient oracle, to foretell the future. His proficiency was greatly respected.

Father accepted this news with tongue in cheek. But Russians are notoriously superstitious. Therefore, Father did not brush off this information. What the man's side occupation was, was none of his business. What worried Father more was Sun Hsienshun's ability as the supervisor of construction. That was the area where he found something disturbing.

No sooner would he pay Sun Hsienshun for the work accomplished thus far, than Sun Hsienshun would disappear for several days and the workers would not come to work. When Sun Hsienshun reappeared, his tiny eyes seemed bleary and he looked unkempt. He also had a very strange, pungent odor about him. After several such disappearances, Father, in desperation, called Tah Tuza.

Tah Tuza smiled from ear to ear. He rubbed his belly and shuffled from foot to foot, obviously embarrassed, but he would not clarify the situation. So, Father sent for the headman of the village of Pei Chui Shui.

"Why, Honorable Sir, did you not know that Sun Hsienshun smokes opium?" The headman opened wide his eyes in amazement. "Why, the whole world knows that."

What a dilemma! Father began paying the workers himself. But there developed a new hitch. The carpenters, masons, and their assistants started to make costly mistakes. They depended for their future work on Sun Hsienshun. They had to cooperate with him.

Eventually, seeing that the construction of the house was at a standstill, Father again called Tah Tuza. Tah Tuza promised to speak with his little brother, as he called him, but he needed a small advance. What could Father do? He gave it to him.

Lo and behold, the next morning, the sun had barely risen, when the sound of the masons' mallets striking the blocks of granite reverberated through the valley. The Zip, Zip, Zip of the carpenters as they planed the boards and the ZOOM-ZOOM, ZOOM-ZOOM of their assistants sawing the logs, was like music to my Father's ears. When he arrived in his sedan chair, Tah Tuza greeted Father with a low bow. In the distance Father could see Satan Satanovitch, busily supervising the placement of a long granite slab as part of the foundation.

"Soon we will need windows, doors and roofing materials," Father said to Tah Tuza, speaking through an interpreter. "How are we going to transport everything from Tsingtao? I hear bad news about the road."

"Not to worry, Master," the interpreter translated Tah Tuza's reply. "We carry everything."

"WHAT?! Carry?! What do you mean?" Father thought he had misunderstood.

"Yes, Master. We carry on back and walk on feet," Tah Tuza replied, looking pleased.

"But how much will it cost?"

"Oh, a little. Not to worry. My little brother will hire coolies."

To carry on foot all the items that were needed for the house seemed to Father tantamount to insanity. Not only did he fear the extreme cost of transporting everything in this manner, but also the damage that might be done to the glass on the way. Yet there was no other way, and the arrangements had to be made. The Chinese Nationalist guerrillas had torn up the road to Tsingtao.

Thus, our doors, windows, and four large glass panes for our great-room picture window were carried, step by step, on the backs of coolies, the thirty-six miles from Tsingtao. Only in China was this possible. It took several days, and Tah Tuza was right. There was no need to worry. Everything arrived safely. Not one window glass was broken.

This work achieved, another problem arose. Roof rafters, plywood, and roof tile were needed.

"Not to worry," Tah Tuza assured Father. "My little brother will arrange everything."

And Satan Satanovitch, that is, Sun Hsienshun, did arrange it. Pine trees were cut down for rafters and bunches of straw were tied in long bundles and placed between the pine branches. The branches, placed tightly side by side, were covered with a layer of clay right from our own land. When it dried, it became a perfect surface on which to lay the tiles, which had been purchased in the nearby town. As long as I was there, I did not remember our roof leaking.

For the finished details, Father eventually had to hire someone else. He found Stanislav Potenko, a young, good-looking, enterprising Polish man, who spoke Chinese well. He doubled as our chauffeur, flirted with me incessantly, adding to Father's apprehensions, but proved himself useful. In no time, with a small crew of craftsmen, he finished our Rock Mansions, Father's splendid creation.

One hundred and twenty-nine solid granite steps, meandering around huge rocks, first led up to a small terrace, my rose garden, then to the main terrace with trees, and finally, still higher, to the terrace before the arched entranced to the house. The house itself was gothic in style.

Rock Mansions had a high gabled roof and a buttress on either side. It was splendidly located, and the granite walls were visible from afar. White as sugar, the walls, standing against the dark green of the pine trees towering above the brown of the thatched-roofed village of Pei Chui Shui.

Father, also, had a tall flagpole set up. When the days were breezy, our white flag, with the nobility crown and my initials in the middle, would flutter.

"This is our banner," Father would say, looking with pride at the flag. "We Kotenevs do not cringe or lower our standards, whatever difficulties life might bring."

Every morning he would be carried down to raise the flag and every evening, weather permitting, he would again be helped to lower it. With this daily ritual he was throwing a gauntlet of challenge to life.

This was the end of the year 1937. Into Tsingtao Harbor sailed the Japanese fleet. The Japanese forces also had occupied Shanghai. The Commercial Press, the publishers of Father's book in Chinese, was burnt along with the warehouses in the southern section during the fighting between the Chinese troops defending Shanghai and the attacking Japanese. The first publication of sixty thousand copies was lost.

The Laoshan Mountains, in the meantime, became a place for Chiang Kai Shek's straggling soldiers. Joining with the local peasants, they formed guerilla bands and dug up the roads. Not that our Shantung Laoshan district had any strategic value. It did not. The Japanese only occasionally visited it.

A hundred Japanese soldiers would come from time to time and stay a day or two. In the central Laoshan plaza, they would set up camp, polish their machine guns and rifles, and then would leave. The local Chinese understood the message, "Behave or else!" The Japanese meant it. Order prevailed because the Japanese reprisals, carried out in the full Samurai spirit, were merciless.

Rock Mansions

Rock Mansions
View from the Main Hall

31

Life at Rock Mansions

"Life will provide! Trust it!" Father declared despite the bad news that his books had been burnt in Shanghai, and of the escalation of hostilities between the Japanese and the Nationalists.

With his last dollars, Father purchased additional furniture from Laoshan residents who were leaving. Having arranged the rooms, Father announced, "Now we are ready for guests!"

"But, Father, how will they get here with the road from Tsingtao torn up?" I asked.

"Never you mind. Trust life!" he replied, and sent a messenger to Tsingtao to place an announcement in the local English paper that Rock Mansions in Laoshan was open for guests.

"But, Father, who will venture thirty-six miles on foot or in a sedan chair?"

"No buts, please!" Father said sternly, as he sat by our picture window in the great room. "This is the time to hold onto one's faith. Miracles do happen!" And he placed his monocle to his left eye as he looked through the window at the gorge, as if expecting something.

The next few days passed quietly; then, lo and behold, a week later, we received a letter by runner. It was from the German Consul residing in Tsingtao. He was inquiring if we could accommodate a party of seven for a weekend. Father immediately wrote back that indeed we could.

We already had a cook. Now we hired Lee, a man to serve at table, and Hsiao Hwai, a woman to clean the rooms and do laundry. Most important, we hired four peasants to carry water from the river to be poured into five barrels on the second floor of the house for washing and drinking. My duty was to greet the guests and see that everything went well.

Two weeks later our first party of guests arrived. They had ridden by car to Licun, a small market center. From there they had hired sedan chairs. After six hours they reached Rock Mansions. Despite the grueling journey, everyone was in great spirits and ready for the next day's picnic in the mountains.

This group of stalwart people comprised the Consul and his spouse; a French couple; Hans Leuen, a representative of the German medical firm Schering, and his wife Inna; and an Irishman, Vincent Dalton, who was the Director of the Postal Service in Tsingtao. Like all postal services in China at that time, it was under British management.

Everyone in the party was an avid hiker and the next morning they undertook an excursion to our famous waterfall several miles into the gorge. We prepared for them box lunches of chicken salad sandwiches and slices of goat cheese, homemade by my Mother, and fresh peaches from our own peach tree which we had found growing on our land.

In the evening, Father made sure that our great room was ablaze with candlelight from the wrought-iron chandelier overhead and several candelabras. To add to the festive atmosphere he had an immense log burning in our very large fireplace.

I remember that dinner was served on our best lace tablecloth and with the white and blue willowware china. Our Number-One-Boy, Lee, in his spotless white jacket, served the dinner. The menu was appropriate to the occasion and everyone seemed to be satisfied when they retired to their rooms.

Vincent Dalton and I remained. We were sitting on the sofa. I was keenly aware that he had one eye on the burning log in the fireplace and the other on me. It made me feel uncomfortable because it was my duty to blow out the candles, and I had to wait for the last guest to go to bed. After a while, Dalton got up, stretched himself, and, having excused himself, he, too, retired. I blew out the candles, secured the log in the fireplace, and went to my room, tired, yet satisfied that all went so well that day.

32

Vincent Dalton

Vincent Dalton was a remarkable man. He was remarkable not for his good looks—because, in appearance, he was most unprepossessing: short in stature, about 5'4" tall, and with a nose much too large for his pockmarked reddish face—but for his personality. When he spoke, his blue eyes sparkling with that incomparable Irish humor, displaying his prodigious knowledge and fluency in several languages, he captivated his audience.

Everyone listening to him forgot his physical unattractiveness. I, a girl of seventeen, was naturally entranced by the stories he told with so much wit. No doubt, a young, pretty girl, looking at him with undisguised admiration, attracted him, a man of forty. The consequence was that after that first visit to Rock Mansions, he made reservations for a small party to arrive two weeks later.

Father was ecstatic. At last his plans were paying off and he would be able to pay the peasants some of his debts for provisions.

Mother looked at me with suspicion, but said nothing. As for myself, my heart pattered a little. At least I would not be bored and have to walk alone with my little black dog, Futi. I knew that there would be long excursions and picnics, and I hoped that our guests would invite me to go along with them.

On the Friday specified, Dalton arrived with his guests. His friends were a young Italian naval commander, Count Montedoro, and a lovely Italian woman, Itala Chieri, one of two beautiful sisters well known in Shanghai social circles.

My parents outdid themselves in preparations. The food was excellent, and, of course, the candles and the large log burning in the granite fireplace added to the romantic ambiance.

As a consequence of our efforts, we soon read in the *Tsingtao Daily News* an announcement of the engagement of Miss Itala Chieri to Commander Montedoro.

Father swore that it was our candles that finally had achieved in Laoshan what had not been accomplished in Shanghai. He might have been correct, for it was well known that, despite the Chieri sisters' beauty, they had not succeeded in their quest for desirable husbands. "Yes, our candles did it!!" Father insisted.

I must confess that Itala looked especially dazzling that evening at Rock Mansions. She took her place at just the right angle to the candelabra, a little higher on the arm of the sofa, so that the light of the candle flames had a strikingly glowing effect on her auburn hair, and her almond-shaped black eyes shone full of mystery. The Italian Count did not have a chance.

Picture an immense room, fire cinders crackling in the grand granite fireplace to the left, the stars twinkling far beyond the vast glass window, and Itala in the foreground, sitting like a goddess bathed dramatically in candlelight. Who could resist such an alluring sight? It would have melted an Eskimo's heart, not to mention a full-blooded, passionate Latin in the prime of manhood. My Father, who never lost his sense of romance, was in a state of euphoria at the thought that all his artistic touches were already bearing such ripe fruit.

The candles, the burning log in the fireplace, and the starry sky seen though the large picture window had its effect on our other visitor, Vincent Dalton. He tarried with me in the living room, long after our Italian guests had retired.

Occasionally, he would get up to move the log in the fireplace with the poker and then resume his place at the other end of the sofa from me. Occasionally, he would steal a glance in my direction. Though not a word was spoken, it was clear that there was something on his mind as he turned away with a sigh. Feeling uneasy, I kept quiet and was relieved when he suddenly arose, said goodnight, and quickly left the great room.

The floor plan of Rock Mansions was designed in the shape of a four-pointed star. Each wing had two bedrooms with a bathroom in between. My room was in the back wing of the house off the great room. Vincent Dalton's room was in the same wing.

Having extinguished the candles and assured myself that the fire in the fireplace was safe, I went to my room. The day had been full of activities. I was tired and before I knew it I fell asleep.

How long I had slept I was not sure, but suddenly I became conscious that someone was turning the handle of my door. I had not locked it. There was no reason for such precautions.

I heard the door creak open and there was the muffled sound of steps on the wooden floor. Someone was feeling the end of my bed. I froze in terror as, in the next moment, I felt my covers pulled off and a warm body pressing against mine. I tried to push my intruder away, but the weight of his body was too heavy for me. I was held in a tight grip while, with his legs, my own legs were forced apart.

I was about to scream when a man's voice whispered, "Hush!" into my ear, and a hand covered my mouth. "Hush!" he repeated, with menace in his tone. I felt sharp pain as he penetrated me with force. There were several fast thrusts and then he groaned. It was all over. For a few seconds, he lay on top of me, breathing heavily, then slowly he withdrew. I tried to reach for the matches on my bedside table.

"Don't move or I will...," I recognized the slight Oxford accent. It was Dalton's.

For several more minutes Dalton lay next to me. Then, quietly, he made his way to the door. I heard the click as he closed the door behind him.

I sobbed, burying my face into my pillow, as the full realization of what had happened came to me. "God, please, God, help me!" I prayed.

That was the beginning of events helpful to the subsistence of our family, but which led to traumatic events for me.

From that time on Dalton became a regular visitor. Every other week he would arrive, bringing with him several guests.

My Father might have suspected what was happening, but he asked no questions. I, too, kept quiet. Dalton had made it quite clear what he expected of me, and there was no alternative. The income from Dalton's visits to Rock Mansions was vital to our survival.

33

The Kushnareff Family

The sunset colors reflecting on the mountain range across the valley from our front terrace were magnificent. Gold to orange, and then, as the last rays of the sun hit the peaks, the colors changed from blue to purple and finally to indigo, as night descended. I was aware of the beauty of the mountains, but I was also aware of our isolation and my loneliness.

"Oh, God! Oh, God! Don't let me die here!" I prayed. "I am only eighteen! I want to live!"

More than ever I was conscious of my family's plight. We were stranded, prisoners within these lovely surroundings. Living in a mansion, yet existing on a gruel of millet when there were no guests, and guests ventured less and less into this region, which by now was deserted by all the other residents except ourselves. Only Dalton, with his friends, our mainstay, continued to come once every two or three weeks. I dreaded these visits.

What I looked forward to were the rare times when Father would send me to Tsingtao on errands. Then I could stay with our good friends, the Kushnareff family, who adhered to the old traditional hospitality, and where I was welcomed with love and understanding by Tatiana Mihailovna, the matriarch. She ruled in a large white house amid a grove of old Linden trees. Here everything was as it used to be long ago in Russia.

Walking through their wide stained-glass entrance doors, you stepped back into a time one read about in the Russian classics—Turgeneff's **Father's and Sons**, Tolstoy's **War and Peace**, or Gogol's **Dead Souls**. It was the world of the old Russian gentry, owners of the vast estates where lives were lived with all the idiosyncrasies and strange habits that wealth and isolation bred.

Though the Kushnareffs were now living in Tsingtao, Nikolai Stepanovitch Kushnareff, a former "sable fur king," whose home, far to the north in Siberia on the River Lena, had been a replica of a Venetian palace, a whim of his grandfather. Now, though somewhat modified in size and grandeur, his residence resembled his past.

To the right of the red-carpeted vestibule, a heavy oaken door opened to the Master's study, a spacious high-ceilinged room with two walls crammed with books. Against the wall, painted hooker green, stood a huge couch upholstered in black leather. Here Nikolai Stepanovitch liked to rest after a midday meal and look at a large portrait of his father. Across the room, in front of wide windows with white lace curtains, was a great desk with carved lion-claw feet. On this desk a green gooseneck lamp burnt to all hours of the night. Nikolai Stepanovitch kept late hours checking his figures in his accounting books. The study was his private domain and no one dared to enter his sanctum sanctorum without his special invitation.

To the right of the vestibule was the parlor. It, too, reminded one of the past. In white slipcovers the loveseats, chairs, and stools stood like soldiers around the walls. Straight across from the entrance, through a vast archway, was the dining room, with dark oak paneling. The dining table had five extra leaves to accommodate a dozen or more invited, or casual, visitors who, whether they wanted to or not, had to stay and partake of Nikolai Stepanovitch's hospitality.

The table, covered with a white linen tablecloth hanging down to the floor, was heavy with silverware, crystal and costly dinnerware. At the head of it, Nikolai Stepanovitch presided like a potentate, his heavy black beard resting on a large napkin meticulously tucked under his cravat.

The dining room in the Kushnareffs' home was a temple, and foods and beverages served here were a celebration of a cult. Nikolai Stepanovitch lived to eat, rather than ate to live. Endowed with an excellent digestive system, he indulged his gargantuan appetite.

The fish, the veal, the goose, the duck, the chicken, and the vegetables were perfect. If roasted, Nikolai Stepanovitch required the color of the fowl skin to be just a perfect golden brown. If it was fish, salmon, sole or sturgeon, they were displayed in just the right fashion, and the sauces and garnishing of dishes had no flaws. One look at a platter and your taste buds would be activated.

I particularly liked the desserts. What tarts and cakes! They melted in my mouth! After months of enforced Lent in Laoshan, I naturally overindulged in these dainties, with sad consequences to my stomach, which was not accustomed to rich food. The enjoyment of the moment, however, was worth the later discomforts. No doubt I was not the only one of the guests experiencing these problems. Not to take a second or third helping was considered by Nikolai Stepanovitch a personal affront.

Lunch had hardly been finished when, with his mouth still full, he would turn to his wife. "Tatiana Mihailovna, my dear, what are your plans for this evening? I believe I had a sumptuous saddle of beef sent from the farm." Nikolai Stepanovitch addressed his wife, always, in the formal fashion his father once used with his mother.

"Niki," Tatiana Mihailovna would answer more familiarly, "that is exactly what I intended to serve."

"Splendid, splendid," and Nikolai Stepanovitch would reach for another piece of pie. "Don't forget, Dear, the mashed turnip and the mint jelly. Of course, serve the 1932 Medoc and be sure to cool the bottle."

The Kushnareffs were fortunate to have retained the financial means that surrounded them with comfort. This affluence was due to the perspicacity of Tatiana Mihailovna.

When the Russian Revolution broke out in 1917, the Kushnareffs, because of their sable fur business, had connections in New York. They also had a sizeable bank account in the United States. Nikolai Stepanovitch promptly made his way in that direction. In New York, forgetting the reality at home, he lived in the grand manner of a wealthy Russian merchant in the best hotels, enjoyed lavish meals in the finest restaurants in the company of questionable characters who clustered around him like moths around a light, and lavished presents on women.

Before he knew it, his bank account had dwindled to nothing. Because of the political upheavals, no furs were available from Russia. His New York connections, who had been so eager to meet him for dinner at the Waldorf Astoria, now suddenly became very busy. With polite excuses, their secretaries made it clear that their employers were not available. In a panic, Nikolai Stepanovitch cabled his wife, who had been left to her own devices in providing for two elder sisters-in-law living under the same roof and in keeping the large household going.

It was a larger task than one might think Tatiana Mihailovna, a frail woman with myopic vision, could handle. But handle it she did, and most wisely and decisively. Under her frail and not too attractive appearance, she possessed the will of her stalwart ancestors, who had trekked from Russia thousands of miles on uncharted terrain, to settle in Siberia. There, with unimaginable toil, they cleared land, built cities, and prospered.

Tatiana Mihailovna sold what she could, packed several of the most valuable sable skins into bags, gathered her jewelry, and, with the two elderly sisters-in-law, took the first boat that sailed down the Lena River in the Spring when it became navigable. They managed to reach China, where Tatiana Mihailovna decided to settle in Tsingtao, then under the control of the Germans.

Sable skins were always rare and valuable, and the skins that Tatiana Mihailovna brought had particularly thick piles with gray hair that showed the maturity of the animals, a most desirable attribute for the connoisseur. She sold the skins at very high prices. With the money, she bought the house under the Linden trees, and a milk farm. She also sent her prodigal husband enough money to return to the Orient.

Nikolai Stepanovitch might have been accustomed to lavish spending, but he was not without the useful qualities of his ancestors. One of these qualities was perseverance. Taking up the management of the farm, he built it in time, into a prosperous business.

His cows were maintained in the best of condition. As at home, where nothing was spared on food, so on the farm; Nikolai Stepanovitch did not stint on the fodder. He loved his cows dearly.

Every cow had a name: Mashenka, Irinushka, Lizenka, and so on. Every morning, Nikolai Stepanovitch, while making his rounds between the stalls, would gently pat and whisper an endearing word or two to each animal. Sometimes they rewarded him with a low "MOOOO," which brought tears of gratification to his eyes. Under his gruff, demanding manner lurked a tender heart.

Whether it was their master's loving words or the fodder he provided, the milk on the Kushnareff farm was rich with cream, and the cottage cheese and yogurt were the best.

Russians loved milk products. Yogurt was considered salutary for any ailment. Kushnareff's farm became a traditional place of meeting at five o'clock. During the spring and summer tourist months, one had to stand in a long line to get a seat at the table on the farm's screened porch.

Whenever I was in Tsingtao, I walked to the farm where, as a guest of the family, I was served cottage cheese topped with sour cream and a glass of milk, heavy with froth, showing its recent milking.

I enjoyed visiting the farm and I remembered the porch with a view of the beach. There was always a fragrance of newly cut hay from the farm's enclosure and there was the sound of the splashing surf against the sands. A bevy of gulls glided in circles above as they searched for a school of small fish. How serene, how peaceful the world seemed to me then, sitting at the table surrounded by others who were, like myself, contentedly scooping out of their dishes yogurt, cottage cheese, and sour cream.

My other enjoyments in Tsingtao were the invitations I received from some of the Europeans who, in company with Dalton, had visited our Rock Mansions in Laoshan. My friendship with Elena, the oldest daughter of the Kushnareffs, was also a delight. She was an expert interpreter of dreams and a fortuneteller with cards. Elena was also a pianist. Her rendition of "Liebenslieder," songs of love, by Brahms and Schumann, or the "Hungarian Rhapsodies" by Liszt were superb. I was always enthralled by the quickness of her long slender fingers on the keyboard.

She infused the music with her own longing for love and marriage, for she was already thirty-six, an age at that time when one was considered to be an "old maid!" Her sensitive performance seemed to transform her pale complexion and her unattractive high Buriat cheekbones and small slanted eyes. Swaying her body in tempo with the melody, she became gracefulness itself. I could listen to her for hours.

Unfortunately, after several days of good food in the pleasant company of friends, and after completing my Father's errands, I returned to Laoshan.

With my bundles and baskets I took a rattletrap bus that rattled as far as the small town of Licun, where I was met by a peasant with a donkey. Astride the animal I rode for six hours, my posterior keeping time, all the way, with the animal's hoof beats. Up! Down! Up! Down! Up! Down! The consequence of this syncopation, as anyone who has ever experienced this pleasure knows, was most painful. I was ever so happy to see, at last, Rock Mansions in the distance, and eventually to arrive, where I was helped off my donkey and assisted into the house. I was back to the beauties of Laoshan, and back to its monotonous existence...

Thus I had returned once in 1939, prepared for the long days and even longer nights. Except that this time something else was transpiring, not in the immediate surroundings, but in me. I gradually became aware of changes in my body. My breasts had started to acquire a fullness. But what perplexed me most was nausea in the morning and the absence of my normal monthly feminine occurrences...I sensed that not all was as it should be. I had my suspicions. What was I to do?!

Knowing what an emotional eruption it would cause my Mother if I consulted her, I waited for an opportune moment when she was away from Father, to talk to him. After several days I found him alone, sitting on our front terrace. I took the seat next to him.

Father listened to me with lowered eyes. He knitted his brow and his voice sounded strained as he replied: "Of course, this is a woman's business. But..."—he cleared his throat—"under the circumstances it may be prudent to keep all of this between ourselves."

Then, after a pause and clearing his throat, he continued, his voice almost a whisper, betraying his anguish, "You must see a doctor immediately. We must be certain what it is. I will arrange a sedan chair. Go to Tatiana Mihailovna. She will know what to do."

I got up from the chair and was about to step through the door when Father suddenly asked, "Is it...is it Dalton?"

I nodded my head.

Tatiana Mihailovna Kushnareff received me, as usual, with all the warmth and kindness of which her big, kind heart was capable. After hearing why I had returned so soon after my previous visit, she clasped me in a warm embrace. "God is not without mercy! He forgives and helps us poor misguided mortals!" she exclaimed with great fervor. "Now don't you worry, dearie! I will send word to Dr. Helmuth to see you. It may be nothing."

Tatiana Mihailovna took command. It was reassuring to me. Yet, deep inside a small voice kept saying, "It is not nothing, not nothing. Shame. Shame. What are you going to do if it is a baby?..."

At the appointed hour, Dr. Helmuth, a German gynecologist, received me at his office. He examined me thoroughly.

"Hmmm, hmmm, so-o-o," he said, lifting his eyebrows.

"So...what?" I asked anxiously.

"So...der iz no doubt. You are pregnant."

I caught my breath. Everything around me suddenly grew dark. The question, What will I do? What will I do? kept echoing in my head. Dr. Helmuth sat calmly observing me. He must have understood my predicament, for in a very gentle manner he asked, "Iz der possibility of marriage?" I shook my head. Dalton had a wife in Ireland.

"*Ach, du liebe* [oh, my dear]. Vat can I say? You must speak to your Vader. In China there is no law about it. Abortion is possible. *Aber* [but], very soon, very soon. You are more dan two months."

How I got back to the Kushnareffs' house, I do not remember. I must have looked frightful because Tatiana Mihailovna took me by my hand and, without a word, led me up the stairs to the room I shared with Elena. After undressing me she ordered me to bed while she went to get me a bowl of chicken broth.

"Drink this," she said gently but firmly. "Rest now. We will talk later." After assuring herself that I was well covered, she pulled together the curtains on the two windows, lit a small table lamp on the vanity table across the room from me, and left. I heard the click of the lock on the door. Tatiana Mihailovna made sure I would not be disturbed.

"Oh, God! Help me!" I prayed. I felt utterly crushed by Dr. Helmuth's diagnosis. The hot chicken broth, however, was somewhat calming and the blankets felt good. After a while I dozed off. When I opened my eyes it was evening. There were no streaks of light from behind the curtains, and I could hear Elena playing "Liebestraum" on the piano.

I had just pushed away my covers to get up when the door slowly opened and Tatiana Mihailovna looked in. "Ah! Good! You're awake! I brought you something to eat. Veal with potato salad. Our cook Mishka is a wizard when it comes to salads, you know." She approached me with a tray. Having first propped up my pillows and having placed the tray on my knees, she made herself comfortable at the foot of my bed. With difficulty, but so as not to disappoint her, I took several bites of veal and some salad.

"Well, what did the Doctor say?" Tatiana Mihailovna came to the point.

I told her.

"Write a note to Dalton immediately. He must take responsibility for the costs."

"But what if…" I began to express my fears.

"No buts. Whatever happened, happened. You are too young to burden yourself with motherhood," Tatiana Mihailovna interrupted me. "You have your whole life ahead of you. Now, here is paper and pen." She took a pad out of the desk drawer. "Mishka will deliver it. I will instruct him not to come back without an answer."

I wrote the note. Mishka sped away with it. Within an hour I received a cryptic message: "Don't tarry. I shall pay whatever is necessary." He had signed the note with his initials, "V.D."

I was crushed by the impersonal tone of the answer, but Tatiana Mihailovna was satisfied. She arranged the rest.

Dr. Helmuth performed the operation efficiently. To be sure of my well being, he kept me in the hospital several days. Tatiana Mihailovna picked me up and I stayed in bed at the Kushnareffs' for several days, during which time everyone tactfully avoided asking what was the matter with me. Nevertheless, I felt terribly guilty and ashamed and embarrassed.

When I finally returned to Laoshan my mother embraced me silently with tears in her eyes. Father hugged me and, as I bent over him, he whispered, "Hold your head high! Steel is tempered under pressure." Though he expected me to be brave, I also could see that he was very troubled and avoided looking into my eyes.

Dalton was true to his word. He paid all the expenses of my sojourn in the hospital. It also ended his interest in Rock Mansions. He and his groups of friends stopped coming to Laoshan.

34

Difficult Times
at Rock Mansions

The absence of income from the weekend guests made our life difficult. We were back to millet gruel for breakfast, lunch, and dinner. I could hardly stand the sight of the yellowish mush in my soup plate, but I ate it.

Mother increased the number of prayer sessions before the icon of our patron Saint Serafim of Sarof. Whatever salad oil we had in the bottle was assigned to the little lamp which burnt day and night in front of his effigy.

Our three servants, who had not seen wages for several months, looked grim, but they remained loyal and did not leave. What else could the poor men have done? There were no other employers left in the Laoshan Mountains. So, they ate the millet with us.

Our creditors, the peasants who had supplied the food when we had had our visitors, came regularly to see if things had changed and to see if, perchance they could collect on Father's promissory notes. For hours they sat on their haunches outside the kitchen door and waved the little square white papers in the air, while philosophizing with our cook about the precarious times. They shook their heads sadly but did not press us for payment. Patience and understanding were great virtues with the Chinese, who had suffered much throughout the millennia of their turbulent history. It had taught them prudence, too. In our case, no more provisions arrived until some money materialized. Our fare continued to be millet gruel. It was a very sad state of affairs, with no relief in sight.

The war continued. Our roads were worse than ever and impassable except to the most hardy. In addition, there was the presence of the Chinese National guerrillas. While they did not bother us, as Father had their ammunition and guns hidden in our cellar for safekeeping from the occasional visits by the Japanese troops, the rumor of their activities in our mountains added fear to anyone in Tsingtao who might have wanted to come to Rock Mansions. Our situation was desperate.

Father was the only one who kept his morale. Every morning he raised our flag and, helped by Lee, he sat on the front terrace facing the eastern mountain range. From here he continuously watched over the roofs of Pei Chui Shui village below us, where he could see the beginning of the trail leading to the central valley of Laoshan. Thus he sat and waited. Days passed. No one except the peasants, like dark specters, could be seen walking on the trail.

"Father, maybe we should consider moving to Tsingtao. We can sell some of Mother's golden rings and chains," I ventured to suggest to him one morning.

"No, we stay here!" Father looked at me sternly. "God is not without mercy," he said as he placed his monocle to his left eye to see better into the distance.

"Father, our sack of millet is nearly empty and the oil that Mother burns in the lamp is almost gone. What are we going to do?"

"Trust in God!" was Father's curt reply.

It is hopeless, I thought, and turned to walk into the house, when suddenly I heard Father excitedly exclaim, "LOOK, LOOK, A MESSENGER!"

I looked in the direction he was pointing. Yes, there was a figure moving on the trail. "Oh, Father, don't get too excited. It might be only a peasant," I said, trying to calm him so he would not be too disappointed.

"No, no, it is a messenger! I know!" Father insisted.

He was correct. It was a messenger from the German Consul in Tsingtao informing Father that on a certain day a Herr Rittmueller was coming to stay at Rock Mansions for several months. We were to prepare a suite of rooms for him.

The news infused everyone with energy. Our serving boy, Lee, normally a little on the lazy side, now rushed to sweep the hundred and twenty-nine steps that meandered between the rocks from the trail below up to the house. Mother hastened to add the remaining oil into the lamp before our patron saint. The cook sent his son to our creditors with a list of provisions. Now, our solvency being assured, there was no question of their delivery. Everyone at Rock Mansions came alive. Everyone was smiling and laughing, especially Father. He looked triumphant.

"Didn't I tell you? Didn't I tell you?" he kept repeating, with a mischievous glint in his eyes.

Herr Rittmueller arrived by sedan chair on the day specified. He was escorted by several German gentlemen and the Consul himself, for Herr Rittmueller was an important person. He was the president of the Deutsche Bank, a stately edifice on the "Bund," the road that ran along the Wang Pu River in Shanghai, where all the eminent European businesses were located.

The German Consul explained to Father that, alas, Herr Rittmueller, a brilliant man in his time, was now suffering from a progressive deterioration of his mind. His doctors had recommended a quiet place, good mountain air, and care. Therefore, Rock Mansions, with its reputation for excellency, was chosen. This note of praise pleased my Father immensely.

We gave Herr Rittmueller all the care and quiet possible. He stayed with us for three months. He was a charming man, tall, stately in his manner, and with his gray hair, small well-trimmed mustache, and impeccable clothes. He was the personification of a gentleman of high class.

In the morning, when he came out of his rooms, he always bowed ceremoniously to Mother, and he never forgot to thank Lee in his fluent Chinese.

It was sad to watch this attractive middle-aged man gradually deteriorate. As time passed his eyes became more and more expressionless and the movements of his body resembled an automaton. At last, it was obvious that he needed more attention than my Mother and Lee could give him.

With sadness, not because we were losing a well-paying guest, but because we had great respect for him, Father notified the German Consul of the situation. Herr Rittmueller was picked up and taken to Tsingtao, where he died several months later.

Our lives at Rock Mansions returned again to depression. I walked with my little back dog, Futi, when weather permitted, and in the evening, attended vespers at the Catholic nunnery in the central valley. What a monotonous, demoralizing routine it was, until one evening, who should arrive, but my friend Elena Kushnareff. She had braved the roads and had come to stay with us.

"I needed a change of scenery and some excitement," Elena said, laughing as she emerged from the sedan chair on our upper terrace. I could not have been happier to see her.

Now I had a companion. The summer days continued to be balmy and beautiful. Elena and I went for long walks with picnic baskets to the Taoist monasteries. We swam in the rivulet in the valley below Rock Mansions. After attending the vesper service at the Catholic convent, we returned for tea in our great room, where Father would already be waiting for us. He sat in his green armchair on the right-hand side of the picture window. Behind him was the grand panorama of the western range of mountains, with the rivulet, below in the valley, swirling its way around boulders.

One afternoon, as we were sitting thus, Lee brought us tea with Russian pancakes that Mother had made. Elena and I were sitting on the sofa across from Father. Through the window I could see the mist arising from the cool waters below. The mountains were changing colors, from the bright green of day to various sunset shades of yellow and finally to blue.

We were sipping our tea in silence. I was content to sit quietly and let the shadows gather about us, although the prolonged quietness and subdued light must have made Elena restless. She began fidgeting with her napkin and several times cleared her throat. I sensed that something was on her mind. I was about to ask what it was, when she suddenly turned to Father.

"Anatoly Mihailovitch, I have been thinking about Muse. Really, she should be living in town. It is not good for her, a young girl, to be so isolated here in Laoshan. There is not a chance for her to meet anyone she might like, and certainly not a chance for her to get married."

I looked at Father. I was curious as to what he would say. Father continued puffing on his cigarette. Elena, thinking that he had not heard her, was about to repeat what she had said when Father stopped her. In a low, pensive voice, without taking his eyes off the scenery beyond our window, he said, "You know, my life has been very eventful. I have experienced and seen much in the world and I have come to the conclusion that our thrashing about trying to achieve this and that, forcing events to happen, is useless. Yet, if we place our trust in life, our Destiny, God, however you want to put it, it will lead us. If it is the destiny of Muse to meet her future husband, it is even possible she will meet him on our narrow trail, right where the little 'Miao' stands near the village of Pei Chui Shui."

Oh, my, I thought. Father certainly has quite an imagination. It certainly would be miraculous to meet someone at this troublesome time and of all places near the temple, the "Miao", on the bend of our trail. I looked at Elena. She had difficulty suppressing her amusement.

"Yes," Father continued after a brief moment, "I think it will happen, if it is your destiny, Muse." He turned to me and smiled, as he helped with his hands to recross his paralyzed legs and lit another cigarette.

"Why, certainly!" I exclaimed. Elena laughed with me. Father did not laugh. He inhaled deeply on his cigarette and then slowly, pensively exhaled a cloud of smoke. His face had a curious, sphinx-like expression. "Spinoza, the Jewish philosopher, wrote that man is like the stone that is flying through the air thinking that it is travelling of its own accord. But it was a hand that had tossed it into the air. The hand that tosses us, too, is the hand of God."

Father concluded our conversation. The rest of the evening Father was pensive and silent.

35

The "Miao"

Elena remained with us a while longer. Late July approached and the weather continued to be splendid, perfect for long walks during the day and cooler towards evening. Before one knew it, August was here. The mountains started to take on autumn colors; here a yellow bush, there an orange one. At this time Laoshan was even more breathtaking, with splashes of reds on the trees, making the sunsets unforgettable in their picturesque splendor.

At Rock Mansions, the mood was not as ebullient. Several weeks had passed since Herr Rittmueller's departure and not one inquiry had been received. What money we had was fast melting. I could see that Father was really worried. So was I.. I knew that the snows of the winter would cut us off completely for several months from Tsingtao. Then what?

Father, his coat collar turned up, cap on his head, continued to keep his watch on the front terrace. One afternoon, at last, he was rewarded by the sight on the trail of the postman. The postman brought, among other mail, a telegram from Shanghai. It read, "Request a room and bath for two weeks STOP Arriving 10th August STOP Recommendation of Herr Rittmueller." Signed, Karl Spanier.

This was August 9th. The household was thrown into a panic. The cook's son was sent with the last of our cash to the nearest town to purchase a shoulder of pork and other necessities. Mother hastened to prepare the front rooms with the best view of the mountains and a private bathroom.

"Elena, the man must be out of his mind to come to this wilderness at this time of the year," I whispered. Elena nodded in agreement.

The 10th of August came and went. No one arrived. Father waited until dark on the terrace. Finally, Mother, near hysteria, persuaded him to come into the house.

Several days passed with no further news from our awaited guest. Then one afternoon, Elena and I decided to go to the convent. The day was windy and the leaves, torn by the gusts of wind, were flying in all directions. We pulled our shawls tighter and increased our pace. The trail led us through the village of Pei Chui Shui. The air in the narrow valley we had to traverse was thick with yellow dust. We hurried on through the deserted square of the village, with its sunbaked circular clay platform and the millstone.

Soon we reached the other side of the village. From here we could see the little "Miao," the roadside temple with the statuette of the guardian god. Its yellow glazed sloping roof stood out against the dark brown surface of the mountain slope. The trail ran along beside it. Who should be standing across the trail but a donkey with his peasant master. For some reason known only to the beast, it would not move, despite the cajoling and blows of the peasant. We could not move either, for to the left was a steep drop to the river.

So there we stood. A couple of minutes passed with no change. Some more minutes passed. The donkey stubbornly resisted moving. I was beginning to fear that we would be late for vespers when I felt Elena pulling my sleeve.

"Look!" She pointed in the direction where the trail bent to the right. Two Chinese coolies had appeared, each with a large suitcase on his back. Behind them a gentleman, dapper in a beige sports suit, was swinging a cane as he walked.

As soon as the coolies approached the "Miao," the donkey moved on, and was soon out of sight in the village.

"You must be Herr Spanier," I addressed the gentleman when he had approached us.

"Yes, I am sorry I am later than my reservations called for. I was detained in Shanghai," he replied with a slight German accent. "Frau Rittmueller, my mother-in-law, spoke very highly of her husband's stay with you."

"We are expecting you," I replied. "Please continue on this path. The men know the way." I waved my hand in the direction of Rock Mansions, visible above the roofs of Pei Chui Shui.

Karl Spanier nodded and as he passed me, I noticed that he glanced sideways at me with some interest.

"My, that is a handsome man," Elena remarked as we walked toward the convent. "He looks fortyish, and yet his prematurely gray hair only adds to his distinguished appearance."

I did not answer. I was thinking.

The Miao

36

Mao Tse-tung's Visit

Soon after Spanier's arrival, Elena returned to Tsingtao. Her departure left me alone with our guest. In Laoshan, entertainment was limited to hiking, eating, sleeping, and again hiking, eating, and sleeping. So, Spanier and I did the first. We took long walks to the Taoist and Buddhist temples, visited the waterfalls, and even undertook a day-long journey to the mountain monastery overlooking the Yellow Sea. Another excursion, which I suggested to Spanier, was especially memorable. It was to the other side of the eastern mountain range, a place I had not visited.

We started early one morning. The day promised to be beautiful. We walked first to the center of Laoshan where the hotel formerly stood, and where cars used to stop. From here we crossed the shallows of the rivulet and started to climb the path up. We had no difficulty negotiating this path, as it was well trodden, although the higher we climbed the more difficult it became. Bramble bushes crowded our way and the ground was skiddy. Loose stones underfoot also added to our discomfort. The difficult, steep ascent started to tire us.

We were halfway up the ridge when Spanier decided to rest. From where we had stopped we could see the white granite walls of Rock Mansions, against the browns and russets and the dark greens of the pines, and its red-tiled roof with the sun shining on it. The sky above it seemed bluer than I had ever seen before. For a few minutes I stood transfixed by the lovely autumn panorama.

"It will be a long walk back. We should be on our way, if we want to return in time for tea," Spanier nudged me.

He was correct. If we were to go over this mountain and return around the other side, I knew it would take us several hours. We continued our climb. Up, up we went. The crest had just come into sight when suddenly I heard *"Bu yao dong! Bu yao dong!"* We looked up and there stood a man in uniform, barring our way. Hand grenades hung on his belt and he had a band with ammunition across his shoulder. He was pointing a machine gun at us.

Keeping his presence of mind, Spanier bowed politely and smiled. I did the same, yet, naturally, I was feeling very uneasy. The soldier was obviously not one of our Laoshan guerrillas, judging by the newness of his uniform and how well he was armed.

In a very polite tone, Spanier, familiar as he was with Chinese ways, asked the man what was the matter. The soldier did not answer. He just continued to point the gun at us, motioning with it for us to proceed in front of him.

"He must be from the South, a Cantonese. He does not understand my Northern dialect," Spanier whispered to me.

Impatient that we just stood there, the soldier nudged Spanier with the barrel of his machine gun.

"Ho, ho [good]," Spanier smiled politely as he helped me up the path. We were over the crest in no time and fast descending into the next valley. It was densely wooded with pines. As we continued making our way around the trees, I began hearing voices, and soon we found ourselves in a clearing crowded with armed soldiers. They greeted us with laughter. Some even jeered.

"Not a friendly bunch," Spanier remarked. I could see that he was very uneasy. To all his questions as to where we were going, the soldier only waved his gun, indicating to us to go on. Soon we were approaching a small village surrounded by tall acacia trees. We passed through the village square and into a narrow passageway where the soldier stopped in front of a gate and motioned for us to wait while he disappeared into the courtyard beyond. Several minutes passed before he returned, but this time he bowed politely, inviting us to follow him through the gate into the house.

Stepping from the bright light outside into the interior blinded me for several seconds. When my eyes became accustomed to the semi-darkness of the room, I saw a group of men in uniforms standing around an earthen platform, the village khang-bed, on which reclined a heavyset man holding a cup of tea in his hand. He was important, because the men around him showed every sign of deference in the way they spoke to him.

The man on the khang scrutinized us for a second or two, and then, with a half smile on his broad face, he turned and said something to a tall, fine-looking young man. He was a scribe, judging by the leather bag with paper, brushes and other writing paraphernalia, that hung on his shoulder.

"My chief wants to know if you are from Pei Chui Shui," the scribe inquired.

"Yes, we are," Spanier replied, surprised at having been addressed in English.

The scribe interpreted what Spanier had said to his chief, who again said something in Chinese.

"You may have seen Chinese soldiers near your house?" the scribe asked.

Sensing that there might be more to the question than a casual interest, Spanier replied with great caution. "Rock Mansions, where we live, stands between two trails. It is difficult to see who is passing."

The scribe translated it to the man on the khang, who laughed loudly, "*Ho! Ho!* [Good! Good!]" he praised Spanier's diplomacy. I began feeling most uncomfortable, thinking of the local guerrilas' guns and ammunition hidden in our house. These men were certainly not our guerrillas, or the man would not be inquiring about our area. Thus, I feared that we might have fallen into most undesirable company, to say the least. Meanwhile, the scribe continued translating what his chief was saying.

"Can you prepare a banquet for seven officers, tomorrow at noon? My Chief will pay for it. Is it possible?" The scribe was addressing me.

"I am sure it can be arranged. My Father will be honored to serve your very honorable chief," I replied in the best Chinese form that I could muster.

The scribe translated it to the chief, who said, "*Ho, ting ho!* [Good, very good!]" On this amicable note our conversation ended.

The scribe escorted us to the entrance of the house, from where the first soldier led us out of the village and to a path that eventually brought us to the main road and back to our own valley.

When I told Father about our adventure and the request of the officer, he shook his head with misgivings. "These are not the Nationalists. I wonder if it is not the Communist Fifth Chinese Army led by Mao Tse-tung."

37

The Banquet

Two days later, at noon, a group of six officers and their chief, whom Father suspected was Mao Tse-tung, arrived.

With serious faces, they entered our great room as Father greeted them. Their chief, wearing a simple khaki uniform and a small cap on his head, bowed ceremoniously to Father without even a smile on his broad face. The officers, a little at a distance from him, passed by Father, each with a quick salute. The scribe was with them, but he stayed in the entrance as a guard.

Our dining table, covered with a white tablecloth, was ready for them and as soon as everyone silently took his place, Lee proceeded to serve the food.

The meal was sumptuous. Our cook, Old Po, made sure that he procured the best he could find at Litzung, making a special trip. Of course, there was the roast duck, a large platter with fish in a savory brown sauce, beef with mushrooms and bamboo shoots, and a large tureen of steaming white rice. Also a tray of various nuts, sweets, and sweetmeats.

I could see that the dishes were met with satisfaction, as the belching was loud after the food was consumed. Lee also served wine, and soon the group became less restrained and more jovial as they urged each other to drink more and more.

Spanier had gone to his room. I sat on a stool outside our picture window, on the terrace overlooking the rivulet. I could not explain it, but a strange feeling that all was not well started to possess me. From where I sat I could see the valley below us and the trail meandering across the rivulet toward the waterfall, the dead-end of the valley. And this view, for some reason, was what was disturbing me. All I could think of was what would happen should the Japanese arrive at this moment. The officers would be trapped and there would be reprisals for us.

I thought I heard something. I listened again. All was quiet except for the murmur of waters below.

I was greatly relieved when, at two o'clock, the banquet ended. The chief officer paid the bill, and, as his rank and importance prescribed, he also left a generous tip for Lee and the cook. I escorted them to our front door and, as Chinese etiquette required, down to the end of the terrace to the granite steps, and I watched as the officers, a little unsure of their steps from the wine, disappeared behind one of our large rocks. Soon their voices faded away. Now it was time for me to help Lee with the dishes and tidy the great room.

Having collected the dishes from the dining table on trays, Lee and I were on our way to the kitchen when suddenly we heard shouting and gunshots. I opened the entrance door. There was no mistaking that the noise was coming from Pei Chui Shui village and someone was running down the opposite slope screaming and firing into the air with his pistol.

Then came a sound I had never heard before: TAT-TAT-TAT, TAT-TAT-TAT! Machine guns flashed into my mind. I looked at Lee. He stood pale with fear.

"*Nipon jen!* [Japanese men!]" he whispered.

I was horrified! Now the raucous noise came clearly from below our house. What if Lee was correct and it was the Japanese? I rushed to look out of our living-room picture window. Spanier was already there. He, too, had heard the commotion.

What we saw below made us shudder. A group of Japanese soldiers with machine guns and rifles were pursuing the Chinese soldiers. Among them I recognized some of the officers who had just dined at our house. As the Chinese fled up the mountain, some were scrambling to the right into the river to hide behind rocks from the Japanese bullets. It was horrifying to see that some of the Chinese were falling dead; others, wounded, bleeding, were trying to crawl away. Most awful of all was how the Japanese dispatched the wounded with bayonets.

Curiously, however, the Japanese did not pursue anyone up the trail in the waterfall direction. They also ignored the many who were climbing to the left. Instead

I heard a loud command. The Japanese shouldered their rifles and machine guns, and, in perfect order, marched back, past our house, and were gone.

"Strange tactics," Spanier observed. "The Chinese were perfect targets. They could have killed everyone."

Later that evening at dinner, when we had all somewhat regained our composure, I asked Father what he thought of the whole affair.

"I suspect that there were either too few Japanese or that there was more to it than meets the eye," Father replied thoughtfully. "The Orientals often defy logic. Their ways are not our ways, especially when it comes to the game of war. They may have wanted to scare more than damage. We will find out soon enough."

"I was glad that the Japanese bypassed us. But I fear reprisals for our banquet," I said.

"The Japanese know all about us. They also respect me as an officer who had been wounded by them in the Russian-Japanese War, and their code of Samurai honor, to some extent, protects me. Let us drink to our luck that our windows were not broken by stray bullets." Trying to uplift our spirits, Father raised his glass of vodka.

"Let us also drink to the timely departure of our guests at the banquet," Spanier added as he raised his own glass. Everyone laughed, glad that all had ended so fortunately for us and that several minutes had separated us from what might have been a disaster if the party of officers had remained longer.

"It was the angels who shielded us," Mother observed, making a sign of the cross.

"Perhaps it is our Saint Serafim of Sarof, who was our protector," said Father, as he, too, made a sign of the cross. Though a man of legal training, with an analytical bend of mind, he had never lost his reliance on and belief in supernatural powers. In this respect my Father was always a true, superstitious Russian. At this moment, however, who could have proven him incorrect?

The candles in the silver candelabra in the center of the table and the burning logs in the fireplace filled the room with golden light. Outside our picture window I could see the stars twinkling in the dark sky. We were finishing our dessert, bread pudding with stewed fruits. Father had called for another cup of coffee and a glass of brandy, while conversing with Spanier, when I happened to look in the direction of the entrance hall.

To my surprise, I saw our cook standing there. He was frantically gesticulating, trying to catch my attention. In his soiled apron, he did not dare to enter the room. Father, too, must have noticed him, as he ordered Lee to find out what was the matter. By the expression on the cook's face and Lee's sighs, we could see that something serious had happened. Finally, Lee came back, looking worried.

"Master! We are in trouble. A very unfortunate complication," he sighed, wringing his hands.

"Yes, yes, what is it?" Father asked impatiently.

"One Chinese, the scribe, is wounded. He is downstairs."

"Oh, my God!" Father turned to me. "Go see what must be done!"

I ran to the kitchen, and sure enough, there lay the scribe, soaking wet, shaking from cold, and moaning. Blood was oozing through the fingers he held to his side.

My first thought was to hide him. With the help of the cook and Lee and our two sedan carriers, we carried him to the far end of the pantry next to the kitchen, a safe room with no windows where my parents had hidden the guerrillas' ammunition under a pile of rags. Then I rushed back for blankets.

"Wrap him well," Father instructed, and sent word to the Abbot in the Taoist temple. "He will know whom to notify. Meanwhile, what medicine do we have?" We had none.

"I have aspirin," Spanier offered.

"Better something than nothing. Go give him two tablets," Father told me. This I did, and also sent one of the carriers to the Taoist temple.

The Abbot must have gotten in touch with the Fifth Army, because the next morning several soldiers with a litter carried the scribe away.

We also found out what had happened.

It was Mao Tse-tung and his staff that had dined in our house, and while they were being served, some of the Fifth Army soldiers, feeling secure, were bathing in the rivulet below the village of Pei Chui Shui. Only one sentry was posted on the mountain ridge above. They did not have a prearranged signal in the event of danger.

Meanwhile, the local guerrillas, who had been pushed out of their territory by the newcomers, were upset. So, in a true, practical Oriental manner, they had sent word to the Japanese, informing them of the whereabouts of the recently arrived soldiers of Mao Tse-tung.

The Japanese apparently did not intend to have a major confrontation in such difficult terrain, yet they could not ignore the presence of the Fifth Army. As Father correctly surmised, their intention was to frighten more than harm, and that was exactly what they did.

When the Japanese convoy made their surprise visit, the sentry on the mountain had no signal to give his men. All he could do was shout and shoot his pistol. By the time the bathing soldiers realized what was happening, the Japanese were at their side.

After this episode the Fifth Army left Laoshan. It moved farther northward to the more open lands of the Shantung peninsula. The local guerrillas returned and continued to live off the peasants as they had done before.

Several years later when I was in Shanghai, Father wrote to me that the young scribe had paid them a visit. He had come with a basket of eggs as a gift to me for helping him.

38

Karl Spanier

During the remaining days of Karl's stay with us, we went for walks in the mountains. In the evening, we sat in front of the fire in our great room. These moments were especially dear to me as by now I was in love with this worldly, elegant man. I felt that Spanier, too, was sharing my feelings.

My unfortunate experience with Dalton had not dampened my healthy, youthful optimism and the desire to love and be loved. I also believed that I could trust Karl. The age difference of twenty years did not bother me. My own Mother was much younger than my Father. Besides, I knew that in Europe wives younger than their husbands were a common occurrence, and I was hoping that our relationship would develop into something serious. The strange synchronism of our meeting in front of the little Miao, just like Father had predicted, made me think that it might be destiny, after all, and that a happy future was awaiting me.

The last days with Karl flew by much too swiftly. The morning of his departure arrived. I watched him go down our one hundred and twenty-nine steps followed by two coolies carrying his baggage, and watched him disappear around the bend toward the village of Pei Chui Shui.

A terrible emptiness overwhelmed me. I walked sadly back to the house and stepped into the great room. The fireplace was now cold, filled with ashes. Beyond our picture window, the trail, winding to the waterfall seemed to me like a road to nowhere...

The autumn days that followed dragged by tediously for me. I took my little Futi for walks, each time returning home, expecting to find a letter from Karl. There was none. Several weeks passed and still no word. I began fearing that he had forgotten me. I said to myself, "Who are you? Only a poor girl with one pair of shoes and those worn thin. Why would a sophisticated gentleman like Karl Spanier think of you when he can have his pick of many beautiful women in Shanghai?"

I would have fallen into despair if it had not been for my dear Father, who kept my spirits up by quoting various old native aphorisms. One of these that I remember, I found to be rather of questionable consolation. He would say, "Do not fear, every dirt finds its trash." Another, more appropriate to the occasion, and one that became a favorite of mine throughout my eventful life, was from Klausevitz, a German Military tactician. "Battle lost, nothing lost; morale lost, everything lost." I tried hard to keep my morale. It was not easy, but then one day, we saw on the trail the silhouette of the mailman. Among the letters was one for me from Karl.

In a properly friendly tone, he wrote about his life in Shanghai. He also mentioned his little daughter Ilona, a girl of two years, and noted that his mother-in-law, Mrs. Rittmueller, the widow of Herr Rittmueller who had stayed with us in Laoshan, had moved into his apartment to take care of her granddaughter. This particular detail filled me with foreboding; however, I quickly brushed it aside. I was elated to have received a letter from Karl. It had reassured me of his interest.

I answered him in the same friendly manner and soon there was a regular correspondence between us, which continued until the middle of that summer when we received a telegram from him requesting that a room be prepared, as he was coming to stay with us for several weeks.

Father was all smiles. "Remember, dear, what I told you and Elena in the great room?"

"Oh, Father!" I exclaimed. But deep in my heart I wanted to believe that he was correct in his prophecy. Yet, it seemed too fantastic.

Mother, as always, shook her head dubiously. "Now, now, don't anticipate too much," she warned me and sighed.

"Treat Karl Spanier cordially but a little at a distance," Father continued. "It does not behoove a lady to be too forward, you know. Always keep your self-respect and also keep in mind that a woman becomes more desirable for a man if there is a little resistance on her part." There was a mischievous glint of conspiracy in Father's eyes as he was inhaling and slowly blowing the cigarette smoke into the air.

We prepared the West wing for Karl. It had a bedroom and a sitting room. Lee swept, dusted and thoroughly scrubbed the private bathroom. I placed a vase with wild flowers on the dressing table in the bedroom. All was ready for Karl's arrival and on the day specified in the telegram, I saw Karl and his coolie, toting a large trunk, arrived at our front terrace.

In his dapper light beige sports suit and with his prematurely gray hair brushed back, he looked extremely handsome. I wanted to run down to embrace him but stopped, recalling Father's instructions. Restraining myself, I walked toward him and casually stretched out my hand to greet him. For a second I thought I saw a shadow of disappointment pass across his face, as in his eyes I read his own eagerness to see me.

I often wondered how two persons so disparate in age, education and background could have been so attracted to each other. My own feelings could have been prompted by my loneliness. But Karl, a handsome man with a fine job, living in a large city...why would he choose a young, unsophisticated girl like myself? Probably, that was exactly the reason. Spanier's former wife, who had deserted him as soon as her little girl was born, was sophisticated and beautiful. Her desertion must have been devastating to him. A proud man would not accept such a rejection easily.

My sincere ardor and admiration for him, the warmth and the sense of belonging that we both felt, must have been reassuring. It also redeemed his sense of worth. He needed someone to love him. Soon after his arrival, he expressed his serious intentions to Father. Father was not surprised. A few days earlier he had had a dream in which he saw me ride away on the back of a white elephant. Father had interpreted it correctly, and, of course, he gave his consent to our marriage.

I was overjoyed! A true miracle had happened! There was only one detail to be overcome. This was in the year 1940, and Hitler was in power. Karl, a German, had to have the approval of the German Consulate, which would be given only upon proof that I was not Jewish.

Father was not worried. I had the birth certificate issued at my birth by the British Consulate in Vladivostok. We could not foresee any difficulties in establishing my non-Semitic origin; we were Russian, Slavs. I also had a German Grandmother. Besides, Father was well known in the international legal circles of Shanghai, as well as abroad, being the author of several books on international law and Chinese history, for which he had been given an honorary Chinese citizenship by Chiang Kai Shek.

Nevertheless, Karl thought that it might be helpful if I followed him to Shanghai and was with him at the Consulate when he requested the permit. So, with my parents' permission, I packed my few belongings in a small valise and early one morning, waving to them a tearful goodbye, I was carried in a sedan chair to Licun. There I took the bus to Tsingtao. One of the Japanese ships was in the harbor awaiting passengers for Shanghai. I was one of them.

After an uneventful journey of twenty-four hours on a calm sea, the ship moored at the Wang Pu Wharf. Karl was there to meet me.

39

Miss Blanchard's Boarding House

Karl had arranged a room for me in a small, reputable boarding house owned and managed by Mademoiselle Blanchard. Although it left a great deal to be desired, it had to suffice. Living quarters in Shanghai in 1940 were difficult to find.

The city was occupied by the Japanese, and, strangely enough, that fact was what made Shanghai so desirable to live in. Shanghai was a center of law and order. There was still another reason why it attracted people, especially the rich Chinese, who congregated there. Shanghai was safe from bombing. The many real estate properties owned by foreigners in the International and French Concessions protected the city against destruction.

At night we heard the sirens shriek and we heard the propellers of Allied airplanes overhead. But they were on their way elsewhere. Once or twice a bomb had been dropped on the outskirts of the city. Everyone was sure that it had been dropped by mistake. As a result, at this time, no one worried about the Great War waging elsewhere.

Shanghai had provisions for five years. There was no lack of anything. Hogs, cattle, and produce were brought in regularly by chartered ships, which were arranged for by some of the most respectable religious organizations, not with benevolent intentions, but for sheer profit on the black market.

The Japanese military trucks and convoys passed along the streets. They bothered no one and nobody gave them a second glance. The foreigners who were in Shanghai—not including the British or the Americans, who were in camps—but the German citizens, Russian emigrants, and the French went about their business of living as usual. I, too, moved into my boarding house, oblivious to what was happening in the rest of the world, preoccupied only with my own worries.

My room, on the second floor of a dark gray row-house, was certainly not a place to uplift anyone's spirits. An iron bed with a hard horse-hair mattress, a small chest of drawers, a night stand with a small lamp, and two chairs were the furnishings. Out of the single window facing the north, I looked into the backyard and kitchen of the house thirty feet away. I did not know who occupied that dwelling, but judging by the odors, that defied description, coming from its kitchen, the occupants had to have been extraordinary. At first the smells did not bother me, but later they presented quite a problem.

Mademoiselle Blanchard, the owner of the establishment, was a "blue-stocking" personified. Hair pulled in a tight knot, always dressed in dark, high-necked dresses; the only curve which showed was the left-hand corner of her mouth, slightly turned down in a frozen expression of disapproval. By the manner in which she addressed me at dinner, it was obvious that she was highly critical of my situation and Karl's frequent presence.

Having taken the double rent for room and board, however, she made it clear that she was bravely overlooking my questionable morality. The other residents, all single ladies of indeterminate ages, were just as cordial. One consolation for me was that the food was modest, but decent, and rather palatable, which we owed to Mademoiselle's inborn French partiality to tasty dishes. This cuisine compensated for other privations while I was constantly anticipating that any day would bring the necessary papers from the German Consulate. When Karl and I were married, I would naturally move into his lovely apartment overlooking a stately boulevard of trees, the Avenue Joffre.

Day after day I waited. Week after week passed. Still there was no news from the German Consulate. Meanwhile, unforeseen circumstances started to intrude into the situation.

The cooking smells from the kitchen across the lane bothered me more than ever. Mornings I felt nauseated, and later, in a most unladylike fashion, I threw up several quite palatable dinners.

"It is time for you to visit the doctor," I told myself and made an appointment with a French doctor.

He examined me thoroughly, shook his head ominously, and pronounced, in the most lyrical French, "Mademoiselle, vous êtes enceinte!" (In more prosaic-sounding English, it meant: "Miss, you are pregnant!") I had suspected it all along, yet the pronouncement, spoken even in the beautiful French, fell on my ears like a bombshell.

I asked myself, "What am I going to tell Karl? What are we going to do?" Yet tell him I had to. I did, that same evening.

"Wunderbar!" he exclaimed. "I love children!"

"But, but...what is so wonderful?" I asked incredulously.

"Why, Liebchen, now we can get married!" he smiled in a funny sort of way.

"MARRIED?!"

"Hush, not so loud. Yes, married!"

"You have heard from the German Consulate?"

"No."

"Then how can we marry. They may find that one of my great-great-great-grandfathers or -mothers had a drop or two or Jewish blood. Then what?!"

"Then nothing! We still will marry!" Spanier's eyes twinkled. "I have found out that you, as a Chinese citizen because of your Father's honorary citizenship, can marry according to Chinese law. As long as it is done in the proper manner, it will be accepted by all nations."

"What about your firm?" I worried.

"There is nothing they can do. We are in China. The only inconvenience is that you will not have a German passport for a while, and I am afraid we will have to live apart for a short time."

Karl explained that he had long suspected my condition and had sought advice from a lawyer, who told him that a marriage between a foreigner and a Chinese, performed according to Chinese tradition, in a public place with witnesses, and an official to certify the signatures on the marriage document, was legal. Now all that remained was to find two witnesses, a restaurant, and draw up the contract in Chinese.

Karl and I decided to go ahead with this plan.

40

The Chinese Marriage Ceremony

Karl chose the Fair Wind Restaurant for our wedding "tiffen," or lunch, as we called the midday meal in the colonies. The restaurant was conveniently located and its name conveyed good luck. Besides, it was renowned for its good food and a rich decor.

Like all Chinese restaurants, it lacked no detail to attract the "Chi," the benevolent energy that conducts good luck into our lives according to "Feng Shui," the ancient Chinese hieromancy.

In the entrance of the restaurant stood a large aquarium where several exotic butterfly-tailed fish swam among quaint rocks in a simulated sea bottom. Over the cash register hung red ribbons with a mirror to frighten away evil spirits who, moving in a straight line, would meet their own reflections. Beyond the ornate archway, the entrance to the main dining room, the walls had phoenix and dragons in flight. But most important, for our special occasion, were the bowls filled with huge fresh peaches on teakwood stands near our table. They were symbols of longevity and marital bliss. Indeed, the setting for our ceremony was insuring the happiest of futures.

On the dot of twelve o'clock I entered, dressed in a demure cream-colored dress with a corsage of roses, symbolic of love. The lawyer, Dr. Franz, in an appropriate black pin-striped suit, met us at the archway. My two witnesses, Marian Schwikovsky and another friend, Ludmilla Saloff, were already standing near the round table covered with a white tablecloth.

The tiffen was sumptuous. Every dish arrived on a silver platter elaborately garnished with vegetables cunningly shaped like flowers, birds and insects. After the variety of sweetmeats came the egg rolls and stuffed black Chinese mushrooms. The steamed minced pork in whole eggshells was followed by fish and shrimp dishes. Finally, the Peking duck, the specialty of the house, was carried in with all due pomp; that is, the large pewter platter had on it the semblance of a duck. These were crisp grilled slices of duck skin arranged in the shape of the bird. One ate only the skins, wrapped in paper-thin pancakes. The meat of the bird was considered fit only for the servants who, presumably, were awaiting their masters outside. Naturally, we had wine, and everyone lifted their cups, wishing Karl and me much happiness.

At last the time arrived for the signing of the contract. With dignity appropriate to his official capacity, Dr. Franz unfurled the carefully folded yellow parchment, decorated with paintings of leaves and flowers, and bearing several square vermilion and black seals. We all signed our names in the designated places. Dr. Franz signed and placed his own seal below the others.

"Herr und Frau Spanier, may I be the first to congratulate you and wish you many happy years of marital joy!" Dr. Franz kissed my hand in the proper European fashion which a gentleman uses as a sign of respect for a married lady.

The "Frau" (Mrs.) sounded so comforting. Standing hand in hand with Karl was also reassuring. Now, I thought, I will not have to avoid the curious glances of acquaintances when we are in theaters and restaurants. Yes, soon I will be living like the other young married women of my age. How wonderful it will be!

Alas, I was not aware then of the old saying, "Man proposes, but God disposes." Maybe it was just as well...

Muse and Karl Spanier - 1942

41

I Return to Tsingtao

To my chagrin, I still had to return to Miss Blanchard, who, noticing my wedding ring, now became a little more cordial. The wedding ring made her even more compassionate of my predicament.

"Ah! Voilà les hommes!" (Ah! Behold the men!) And, indeed, my situation was rather peculiar—married and yet not married. I was not living in my husband's residence not only in order to evade the German Consulate, but also because of a still more formidable obstruction, namely Mrs. Rittmueller, Karl's former mother-in-law.

As the widow of a former bank president, she carried weight in social circles. Karl tried to avoid the harm that her long sharp tongue could inflict on me. To prevent any gossip and unpleasantness, Karl and I decided that it would be advisable for me to return to Tsingtao for the last months before my confinement. In Tsingtao, I had friends and my parents were not far away in Laoshan. There was also no shortage of housing. So, with the next Japanese ship that was sailing, I left Shanghai.

In Tsingtao I rented a lovely furnished bungalow with a spacious garden. It was near the beach where the large summer homes were located. Some of these houses were occupied by German families; many others by wealthy Chinese. It was considered a safe area to live in.

I was also pleased to find an excellent servant. Liu was his name. He had rung my doorbell and asked if I needed a good cook-boy. He showed me an excellent letter of recommendation from his former German employer. It stated that Liu was a good cook and a very honest domestic who could be trusted to perform his duties to perfection. I could not believe my luck. There was only one rather peculiar thing that puzzled me for a second or two. The first was, how did Liu know that I needed a servant? But this I brushed aside, knowing that in China news gets around by the "pontoufle" (slipper) post very fast. The second was that Liu looked completely out of character for the job. He was tall, had handsome features, held himself proudly and had a jacket of expensive silk.

Liu noticed the doubts in my eyes. He immediately assumed a more subservient stance and in a voice of supplication assured me that he really was in desperate need of work. I forgot my doubts and hired him. Our agreement was $15.00 Mexican (Chinese currency) a month, plus food, and he would stay as my guard in the little white house for servants behind the vegetable garden. There, he would be within call in case of need.

Liu proved himself to be all that his previous employer had stated. He was meticulous in keeping the house and, as a cook, he could have surpassed the chef in the Grand Cathay Hotel in Shanghai. When my Father or Mother visited me, Liu outdid himself. Father, who was partial to good food, could not believe that this was a simple cook-boy.

"Are you sure he is telling you the truth about himself?" Father whispered to me after one of the dinners he had served that was fit for a king.

"Oh! Father! Even if he is not telling me the truth. What can he be? He obviously needed the job or he would not be here."

"Yes, why with you? That is the question." Father frowned.

"Who knows?" I answered, but I, too, began wondering.

Time passed. I walked, read, and listened to my phonograph. One day a German neighbor, all excited, came to tell me that down the street a Chinese had been kidnapped. After a couple of weeks, I heard that still another rich Chinese had disappeared. Such news made me very uncomfortable. Not that I feared for myself— I had nothing. Nevertheless, it was disconcerting. I asked Liu if he had heard about the happenings on our street.

"No worry, Missy!" he replied as he continued stirring the contents of the pot on the cooking stove.

All was quiet for some time. Then one night I was startled by some strange noises coming from the large house on the corner next to mine. I rushed to the servant's house to call Liu. The door of the little house was unlocked. I looked in. The house was empty; but what was worse, I saw no bedding, not even a mattress on the iron bed. It was obvious that no one lived there. I stayed up the whole night worrying why Liu had left without telling me. The thought filled me with suspicion.

At daybreak, I suddenly heard steps in the kitchen. Petrified with fear, I had my hand on the entrance doorknob, and was ready to rush out for help, when in walked Liu.

"Ah! Missy, you be long ready for breakfast?" he asked nonchalantly.

"Liu! What are you doing here?"

He looked at me strangely. "What you say, Missy?"

"You no sleep in house! I ran to fetch you last night. Many bad things happen! Two men kidnapped!"

"Ah! This!" Liu looked at me for a minute in silence, as if he was considering something. Then in a low, conspiratorial voice he continued, "It belong my big brothers who do this...You all right," he dropped over his shoulder as he stepped back into the kitchen.

I leaned against the wall of my entryway to brace myself.

"No worry, Missy!" Liu repeated as he emerged with a pot of coffee. "Have cup coffee!" He placed the cup on the dining table. "I bring breakfast."

So this was why he took the job with me! Liu was a scout for a gang of kidnappers!! Knowing the truth made me feel better. I understood that I was safe as long as I kept Liu's secret.

There were a couple of more kidnappings after that. But I slept soundly—knowing that, as part of the conspiracy, I was well protected. Ah, such are the ways of the Orient.

42

Elena Kushnareff

While I was staying in Tsingtao awaiting my first child, sad events took place in the Kushnareff family.

In Tientsin, while on a piano concert tour, Elena met Sergei Nenuzhny. His attention, compliments, and interest swept her off her feet. Elena, to whom men never gave a second glance, was now being fawned over. Innocent of human guile, she could not resist. She fell in love with him. On her return to Tsingtao, she promptly announced to her amazed parents that Sergei had proposed, and that they were getting married.

"Who is Sergei? What is his profession?" Tatiana Mihailovna asked.

"Mother, he must be doing something to support himself," Elena replied. It had not entered her mind to ask him.

"But, Darling, you really don't know him. Don't you think we should make some inquiries about him?"

"Oh! Mother! Please remember me. What do I have in life? I'm an old maid! That's what I am! And this man loves me. He told me that he loves my sensitive soul, He could hear it in my piano performance."

When it comes to "soul," Russians are especially vulnerable and they frequently refer to it. For example, someone asks, "How are you today?" The other answers,

"Oh! My soul is troubled today." Or, "What do you think of this or that?" The answer: "You know, my soul is not inclined toward it." And so on.

Thus, with troubled souls and terrible misgivings, Tatiana Mihailovna and Nikolai Stepanovitch finally decided to acquiesce and invite Sergei to Tsingtao for a visit. He came and he stayed.

I met Sergei at the dinner party when the engagement was formally announced, and my impression of him was not too favorable. Of medium height, heavy boned, with dark curly hair, a small moustache and stubby nose, he was not attractive. He reminded me of a Cossack warrior from Siberia. Yet there was a certain appeal about him. The ladies at the dinner seemed to be quite taken by his ways and were enjoying his familiar and flirtatious manner. I wondered if Elena had noticed this. But apparently she did not. She trusted Sergei completely.

The day of the wedding was beautiful and rather warm for the late autumn. The interior of the small Russian Orthodox church was ablaze with candlelight burning before the iconostasis and the icons. The choir sang a lovely ancient Slavonic hymn as Elena entered, leaning on the arm of her father, in her white silk gown, trailing a long veil. I had to admit that the groom, all spruced up in a dark formal suit, looked very presentable as he waited for them at the altar.

After the religious ceremony we were invited to the feast. It was lavish. Nikolai Stepanovitch Kushnareff saw to it that it surpassed all expectations.

A full-sized roast piglet, with an apple it its mouth, was carried in on a huge platter. On the buffet table, was a plethora of salads, hors d'oeuvres and various Russian dishes. When it came to desserts, the Kushnareffs had to have exhausted the cookbook, such was the array of tempting delicacies from which to select.

At Russian weddings one seldom saw a wedding cake, which was more a Western European tradition. At Elena's wedding, however, the cake, too, arrived with all due ceremony. Of course, champagne poured in torrents. According to tradition, with every glass the guests shouted, "GORKA! GORKA! [Bitter! Bitter!]" The young married couple had to kiss. I always found the word "bitter" a little incongruous at a wedding, particularly when the newlyweds were expected to be looking forward to eternal happiness. Sadly enough, on this particular occasion, it foreshadowed correctly.

After the wedding feast, because of the hostilities between the Japanese and Chinese, and also because of the groom's lack of finances, the newlyweds were unable to travel on their honeymoon. Therefore, I had offered them my bungalow for a couple of weeks, where they could be alone. Meanwhile, I had moved to the Kushnareffs'. After the two weeks, Elena and Sergei resumed their residence at the

Kushnareff home. Tatiana Mihailovna and Nikolai Stepanovitch accepted what, from the very beginning, they had suspected would happen.

At first all went well. Tatiana Mihailovna managed her household efficiently and Sergei did his best not to get in her way. After some time, however, when she suggested that he try to find employment, she discovered that there was nothing that he could really do. He could not even be useful at the farm.

"Believe me, Tatiana Mihailovna, Dooshenka [my soul]," Sergei told his mother-in-law, "I am prepared to take any job. But you must understand it is very difficult to find just the right position suitable for my qualifications and training."

"Mother, please be patient with Sergeiooshka [little Sergei]," Elena interjected. "As soon as the war ends I assure you he will find just the position for himself."

Tatiana Mihailovna sighed and did not answer. What else could she have done, particularly at this time, when Elena was already pregnant. Her mother was willing to overlook anything in her anxiety to see the birth of a healthy grandchild.

Russians believe that during pregnancy, the young mother must be kept as calm and happy as possible. She must hear and see only beauty. Liquor is completely forbidden and she must never, never look at anyone with black eyes, the "evil eye." The nine months the Russians believe also are vital to the baby's health and future happiness.

Tatiana Mihailovna was more than aware of these beliefs. Besides, she was also fearful of her daughter's frail constitution. Elena was thirty-eight years old, an age considered to be beyond childbearing.

Her mother's fears were well founded. Shortly before I myself was to deliver my baby, Elena suddenly began bleeding. In a panic, the Kushnareffs rushed her to the nearest hospital. There, a Japanese doctor on duty had to perform an emergency abortion. Whether it was because of Elena's frail constitution that could not rally, or because of a careless hospital staff, Elena developed septicemia, an infection of the womb. It was fatal for her. She died in dreadful pain.

At her funeral I could not bring myself to approach her open coffin. I was told that even in death, her face was a mask of suffering.

It is difficult for me to think of Elena and her tragic, untimely end. I will always remember her as a loyal friend, always there to console me when needed. I will also remember our picnics in Laoshan, when she stayed with us, and I will think of her whenever I hear "Liebestraum" by Liszt.

An American philosopher and writer, Hubbard, once said, "If you have even one true friend in your life, your life has been worth living." Elena was such a friend. I have been fortunate to have had several such friends. And, indeed, my life has been enormously enriched by them.

At Elena's funeral, Sergei stood with his head lowered, forlorn and dejected. Very few people came up to him. I went up to shake his hand. His eyes were filled with tears as he clasped my hand in both of his. I could see that he was grieving. Poor man. Like Elena, he, too, had needed love, which Elena had given him. Whatever his motives had been in the beginning, when he had seen an opportunity with an unattractive spinster daughter with rich parents, he had to have eventually understood her kindness and appreciated it. He was no fool. To lose her was a great blow. His whole being expressed it.

"*Vsevo horoshevo* [All the best to you]," I said, hugging him.

Sergei shook his head sadly.

Much later, Tatiana Mihailovna told me that they had given him a goodly sum of money as an inheritance from Elena. They wanted to be rid of him. Sergei left Tsingtao and was never heard of again.

43

Regina Is Born and I Leave for Shanghai

Karl arrived in Tsingtao at the beginning of October to be with me when the baby was born. It was due in October and, true to calculations, on the 13th of October at ten o'clock in the evening, I was rushed to the German Faberkrankenhaus Hospital and I gave birth to Regina. Either the doctor was too slow in coming or I was too quick in giving birth, because the head nurse had to help with the delivery. The doctor was in time only to announce that it was a girl.

The baby was a healthy seven and a half pounds. We named her Regina Gertrude. As she lay in my arms she cried lustily in protest at being forced from the enveloping protection of a warm womb into the cold, cold world.

A week later, Regina and I were back home. In the meantime, my good Liu had found a nurse. Her name was Huang Hwa [Yellow Flower]. She was to come with me to Shanghai. Her husband, the cook, would follow with their young son. All that was needed to complete my happiness now was for Karl to find a suitable apartment in Shanghai, because the one he was occupying with his little daughter Ilona, the grandmother, Mrs. Rittmueller, was unwilling to vacate.

As fortune would have it, one of Karl's colleagues in his firm, Deutsche Farbenwerke, was being transferred to another city and was looking for someone to take over the lease. The apartment was a penthouse on the eleventh floor of a building owned by a Hungarian whose own residence was on the same floor. The two doors faced each other across the hall. This proximity to the landlord presented a problem, as the Hungarian was very particular about who would be allowed to take over the lease.

Karl's qualifications were perfect. For a modest payment to his colleague, "key money" as it was called, Karl was able to take possession. He immediately sent me a telegram instructing me to prepare to return to Shanghai.

With no difficulty, I purchased tickets on one of the Japanese steamers. This time I was not on the poop deck, but in first class.

With considerable sadness I bid farewell to Liu, wishing him much success in the many years to come.

"We go home to Peking. My big brothers also go," he told me, while bowing and holding his hands together, as Chinese do to show respect. I guessed that with my leaving he had to give up his scouting for potential kidnap victims in the district.

On the day designated for departure, baby Regina, Huang Hwa, and I boarded the ship. No sooner had we arranged ourselves in the cabin when there was a knock on the door. I opened it. It was the steward with three bulky orange lifejackets in his arms.

"What's this?" I asked, surprised, wondering where we were going to store the jackets.

"This is for you three," he announced as he pushed the jackets and himself into the cabin. "Here also knives." He handed me what looked like two twelve-inch-long bayonets.

I was completely taken aback. Lifejackets? Knives? Ah, protection against attacking sharks. "So many sharks?" I asked.

"No, no, not sharks. Cut off jackets," the steward explained.

"WHAT?"

"You no understand." I could see the man was getting annoyed. He sucked in air through his teeth as Japanese do when perplexed. Then he slowly continued. "You see, jackets made of kapok. In water, after time, naturally get heavy. You sink. So-o-o-o...you cut off ropes that hold jackets. See?"

Yes, I did see, and what I saw in my mind's eye was not pleasant: Our ship being torpedoed, Huang Hwa and I in life jackets, holding onto the baby, bobbing in the choppy sea, our life jackets beginning to absorb water, getting heavier and heavier, about to sink when we cut the ropes that held the jackets...

"THEN WHAT?!" I turned to the steward.

He rolled his eyes, shrugged his shoulders, and before I could stop him, he was gone.

"What a beginning of a journey," I said to myself.

Despite all precautionary measures and several drills in how to handle the lifeboats, our trip back to Shanghai was uneventful. We sailed steadily southwest at fifteen knots on a calm sea. If there were Allied submarines around, they did not make their presence known. I also doubted that our small, nondescript passenger ship would have been an important enough target. We proceeded on schedule and the first call was to the dining room. Huang Hwa stayed with the baby while I went to have my dinner.

The steward showed me to my table, where several other passengers were already seated. I do not recall them, but remaining clearly in my memory were two Japanese ladies, one older than the other, escorted by a Japanese colonel. As they entered, I was struck by their appearance. Dressed in beautiful kimonos of somber colors, they were very much taller than the average Japanese. Their stately manner of walking and fine aquiline features and sad expression were also unique. The ship's chief purser was showing them to their table with many bows and every sign of respect. In perfect silence, the Japanese ladies and the officer ate their dinner and just as silently, again escorted by the chief purser, they left.

It was obvious that the group was important. The mystery was resolved when our ship moored in Shanghai. On the wharf, I saw a large Japanese honor guard of soldiers in dress-parade uniforms standing at attention. With them were several high-ranking officers. As soon as the gangplank was lowered, the officers came aboard.

After greeting them in a most cordial and formal manner, the ship's captain led them through the main door towards the staterooms. Before long the officers returned. One of them, walking slowly, was carrying a square box wrapped in a Japanese flag. Another officer followed the first. In his outstretched hands, he was holding a samurai saber in a beautifully wrought sheath. The two Japanese ladies and their escort walked behind. As soon as they reached the gangplank, the honor guard saluted with several quick movements of their guns.

"What is happening?" I turned to a Japanese gentleman standing alongside me.

"That was a container with the ashes of a general who had been killed in action," he explained. "The two ladies are his mother and his wife. They are bringing the ashes to be flown back to Japan in a military plane."

We were forced to wait until the Japanese ladies, officers and soldiers had left the wharf. Only then were we permitted to disembark.

Before I knew it I was in Karl's arms.

"Liebling, you will love the apartment! And what a view!" he told me excitedly as he kissed me. "I cannot wait to show it to you."

"Dearest, with you I would be content even in a hovel," I laughed. It felt so good to have his arms around me.

"Let's not go to extremes," he chuckled, as he led us to his car. "Now, let's get in and be on our way."

Huang Hwa sat next to the chauffeur, and I sat with Karl in the back, with the baby in my arms. Assuring himself that we were comfortably seated, Karl gave instructions to the chauffeur: "Great Western Road Apartment."

"Yes, Master," the chauffeur said respectfully, touching his cap's black visor in a salute.

"The car and Ling are at your command," Karl said, turning to me. "After he takes me to the office in the morning, just let him know where and when you want to go."

My goodness, I thought, what a change from the donkey rides. I would be chauffeured in a black four-door sedan all my own...

"By the way," Karl interrupted my thoughts, "I have also made arrangements with the bank to send money every month to your parents. It should help them."

I had to make an effort not to burst into tears. Karl's thoughtful generosity overwhelmed me.

"Thank you, Dearest," I whispered.

It took quite some time to reach our apartment on Great Western Road. It was the continuation of Bubbling Well Road, the road that ran from east to west and was the main Shanghai thoroughfare.

Negotiating the streets in China had always been quite an undertaking, requiring from a driver not only steady nerves, but quick muscular reflexes and very powerful vocal cords. The Chinese pedestrians, rickshaw pullers, pedicab drivers, and other chauffeurs of the various vehicles that thronged the Chinese roadways were, by nature, fatalists. The word, "danger," meant nothing to them. If they were Buddhist, it even seemed that they invited their end in anticipation of a better life in the next reincarnation.

Nonetheless, in this laborious life they wanted to get to their destination as fast as possible, which meant, in a straight line, right down the middle of the street. So, the driver has no other recourse but to toot, and toot, and toot, and to shout and shout, whatever colorful expressions the moment inspired. Then, of course, he had to press on the brakes incessantly. And that was the way Ling, our chauffeur, conveyed us that day.

First, we passed through the south end of Shanghai, where the wharves were located. This area was reserved originally for industry, and it was dismal. Now, however, on every side, I saw remarkable changes. Everywhere were prosperous-looking shops, small busy factories, restaurants, and tidy living quarters.

The transformation had been accomplished by the Jewish émigrés escaping Hitler. They had arrived by the shipload in Shanghai, one of the few cities willing to offer them refuge.

Although stripped of every valuable possession, a few of them had ingeniously managed to hide a diamond or two, or a few gold objects sewn into the linings or hems of their sparse clothing. On the other hand, what they had brought with them, more valuable than possession, was their stamina, their professions, and their talents for enterprise.

They had turned this dirty, rundown district into a thriving center of manufacturing. From here came beautifully knitted women's wear, which we bought in the elegant Shanghai shops, and marvelous sausages and other comestibles of German cooking, which we sought in the delicatessens. What excellent restaurants they had opened! Except for a very few Russian restaurants, such a variety of special foods had not been available before.

As we left this thriving district, Ling had to drive over a bridge that spanned a wide canal, an ancient passage for sampans, of different sizes, transporting merchandise into the interior of China. The bridge we crossed brought us to the Bund, the most elegant and affluent European section of Shanghai. The wide, four-lane road, skirting the Wang Pu River, had all the important banks and businesses.

Driving by these impressive structures, I looked to the left where the Bund Garden was located. I remembered how, as a little girl, I used to promenade here with my Grandmother, and how we stood for hours watching the life of the riverboat people and how, at low tide, they dug for eels in the river mud. Within minutes of this garden, the Nanking Road started. At this intersection stood two buildings, the Palace Hotel, on one side, and the Sassoon House on the other. How often we could be found sitting at a table before the tall arched windows of the Palace Hotel at four o'clock, the traditional tea time.

Here we sipped the "spot of tea" and consumed, by the dozens, the delicious miniature sandwiches. On the other side of the street, the "rich and powerful" were alighting from their limousines at the entrance of the Sassoon House, towering over the Bund, a most prestigious edifice erected by one of the richest families from Arabia, the Sassoons. They, with the Hardoons and many others, had made millions selling opium during the time European powers were encroaching upon China.

As we drove up Nanking Road, we passed Wing On Department Store, where Mr. Wu's Number-One-Wife used to take me shopping. Soon Ling was driving by the Racecourse where, on Sundays, Mr. Boerstling had indulged his weakness for horse racing…or something. As we continued, we drove by what used to be Mr. Wu's residence, now most unattractive rows of gray townhouses. Then came the six-foot-high wall of the Hardoon Estate. A little farther, on the left-hand side, was the Shanghai Cemetery. The Buddhist Temple was directly across the street from it.

At long last we reached the intersection where Great Western Road started.

"There! See that brick building? That's our apartment house! Our penthouse is facing this way." Karl pointed excitedly to a tall brick building far on the horizon, which, like a spire, rose above the gray roofs of the Chinese houses. "I know you will like it," he assured me.

44

109 Great Western Road

How could I not like it?—a penthouse on the eleventh floor of an important-looking building, with a breathtaking view of Shanghai from all windows. As I entered, at the end of the vestibule, I saw an atrium full of lovely plants. From here a flight of seven steps led me up to an L-shaped living room. To the left was the dining room, with a terrace beyond it. Straight ahead, divided with rich velvet brown portieres, was Karl's study. The carved desk of light wood and a pair of strikingly beautiful Chinese cabinets caught my attention.

"What lovely finish, and how well they are carved," I said, feeling with my hand the smooth surface of the rocks and the cherry branches carved on the doors.

"Yes, they are several hundred years old. I bought them in the interior of China, while working in Chungking," Karl explained. "But let us not tarry here. I have something else to show you."

He led me to the bedroom. "Look, that is the room I had enclosed." Karl pointed to the eastern corner of the apartment. "It was another terrace but now it will be the nursery for Regina."

I was delighted with what I saw: a cozy, medium-sized room with lace curtains on the windows and a wicker bassinet with embroidered covers, all of it ready for the baby.

"Oh, Karl! How very thoughtful of you. I love everything about this place," I said, my eyes filling with tears of joy.

"Good! I knew it would meet with your approval." Karl put his arms around me.

"Wait, that is not all. There is something for you in that blue box." Karl pointed to the dressing table. "Go look, while I show Huang Hwa to her quarters."

I opened the box covered with blue satin. In it was a check for several hundred dollars and a note saying, "Your monthly allowance for 'pin money' Love, Karl."

As I took the check out of the box, I remembered how my own Father also gave "pin money" to my Mother when he was in Shanghai. Mother told me that it was customary for a man, as the head of the family, to give an allowance to his wife.

Holding the note and check I felt so very rich.

"What miracles are happening in my life," I said to myself as I hugged Karl tenderly.

Soon after my arrival in Shanghai, Huang Hwa's husband and her little son joined our household. Karl also hired Ting, an older Chinese servant, who was to be our Number-One-Boy. His duties were to clean the apartment and to serve at table. With Ting, our complement of help became three, considered to be the proper number necessary to live comfortably, and our life style certainly reflected this.

Oblivious of the war raging in Europe and in the Pacific, we began living in a most elegant manner.

Our evening meals had candles on the table, and Ting served us in white gloves. The food came in gold-edged French Limoges dishes with the wine and water in cut crystal glasses. The menu, the planning of which was my only housewifely duty, was composed of four courses: hors d'oeuvres, soup, entrée, dessert, and ending with cheese and fruits.

As a lady of substance, I naturally had my hairdresser, manicurist, and a masseuse come regularly to the house, while my generous "pin money" permitted me to purchase fashionable clothes.

As Karl was meticulous in his appearance and I was dressed according to the latest fashion, I felt that we certainly made a striking pair when we attended a concert or opera, or some other event.

In a cosmopolitan city like Shanghai, there was no lack of entertainment. We had the best musicians, singers, dancers and actors, many of whom had escaped from the

Russian Revolution, while many others were world-renowned performers who came on tour. Music was Karl's and my particular love. Karl was quite well versed in it, and I, as a child, had been introduced to music by my Grandmother and had regularly attended concerts. Consequently, I, too, knew the famous composers and their works.

Karl and I set aside Sunday afternoons for the performances of the Philharmonic Orchestra, under the baton of Maestro Paci. We attended, too, ballet and drama. These events were important social gatherings. Everyone made their appearance as chic as possible, in formal attire.

We also found time for trips into the countryside. I loved these walks. They reminded me of Laoshan. On some lovely spring or autumn days, Ling would drive us to an area outside the city from where we would walk along the pathways in the fields.

After finding just the right spot on a knoll overlooking a picturesque Chinese village, or some shady nook under a majestic tree in an old Chinese family burial compound, we would open our picnic basket, take out the sandwiches, wine and fruit that our cook had prepared for us, and proceed to enjoy our repast.

Sometimes, when Karl was free, we would take our little Regina in a pram to Jessfield Park, a large English public garden where lush green lawns, clipped and tended for many years, felt like a carpet under our feet. There we walked along the banks of several ponds and watched the sky and the gliding clouds reflecting in the waters. In a rustic pavilion there was also a restaurant where we could order a light lunch of a tossed fruit or vegetable salad.

Excursions like these were quite a habit with the Europeans in Shanghai. On autumn, spring, summer, or even cold winter days, whole families promenaded in the parks. Eventually, when the Chinese were permitted by the English authorities in Shanghai to participate, they, too, could be seen, sometimes, with whole households of parents, sons, daughters, and grandparents, along with a slew of servants and a bevy of children.

No one enjoys nature as do the Orientals. Their reverence and love of it is reflected in their every form of art, from Chinaware to wood carvings and paintings. How delightful are their paintings of lonely scholars meditating amid precipitous mountain peaks or single fishermen in boats with mist-enveloped mountains in the distance.

The Chinese gardens are always as natural as possible. Unlike the Europeans, who cluster plants for effect in their formal gardens, the Chinese like their gardens to appear as though no human hand has touched them. Many such famous gardens have been recorded for posterity to remember, while the memory of their gardeners is also revered.

45

A Strange Occurrence

Karl and I had been married for two years when, one evening in late autumn, something most unexplainable happened. We were sitting in front of our fireplace watching the flickering flames. Hearing the wind shaking our windows, I called Ting to pull the curtains together for warmth.

We had finished our coffee and were listening to a record on our phonograph. The music, the fire, and Karl, next to me on the sofa, made me feel especially happy. The past two years had been like out of a storybook. In this state of contentment, I had leaned my head back on the sofa pillow, when, suddenly, everything around me was transformed.

I was not in the living room with Karl sitting by the fireside, but was standing on the corner of a road. To the right of me was a tall white building. Across from me on the other side of the road was the sea and the beach, with angry waves splashing and beating against the sands. At my side were two little girls in white blouses and green skirts. I was holding them by their hands. As I looked around, a terrible sadness and a dreadful feeling of loneliness swept over me.

How long this bewitchment lasted I did not know, maybe a minute or two. Suddenly, from a distance, I heard Karl's voice asking, "Muse, Muse, are you all right?" And I was back on the sofa.

"Yes, Dear, why?" I tried to sound calm.

"Your eyes had such a strange look in them."

"I must have dozed off," I laughed. For some inexplicable reason, I could not bring myself to tell him what I had just experienced, or dreamt, or had a vision of. "All is all right," I repeated, brushing away my apprehension. "All is all right," I assured myself."

46

My Longest Walk

As the days passed, I brushed away what misgivings I had about my strange experience, and, as our life continued to flow in the same pleasant manner, I forgot all about it. Besides, both Karl and I were especially happy as another addition to our family was expected in the beginning of April.

April arrived. One week passed, then another, and still another, with no signs of approaching birth. My doctor, Nina Antonoff, an attractive, middle-aged woman with many years in obstetrics, became worried. She told me to go to the Country Hospital, a fine medical center not far from our apartment.

"We must not wait much longer. I will have to induce labor," she explained.

That same afternoon the nurse gave me what seemed to be a dose of castor oil large enough for a Percheron mare. The remedy was certainly potent and everything proceeded accordingly, although it did not entirely satisfy my fastidious doctor. After listening with her stethoscope a couple of times and tapping on my stomach, Dr. Antonoff wrinkled her forehead.

"Musa Anatolievna [the respectful Russian way of addressing a person]," she said, "you will walk to the delivery room."

I caught my breath, because of a sharp pain that I felt at that moment. "WALK? But, but, I feel it coming already!"

"Not strong enough. Walk!" the doctor instructed. "That will do it."

"How far?!" I visualized miles and miles of corridors.

"Just a few steps straight up this corridor, and then go left down the corridor you will come to. At the next corridor, turn right and there at the end you will be at the Delivery Room."

"You think I can make it?" I whimpered, clutching my abdomen.

"KONESHNO! [Of course!]"

"But the pain is increasing!!"

"Good. We have no time to lose. Nurse, help her," Dr. Antonoff ordered the nurse who was standing by, as she herself hurriedly left the room.

The nurse quickly helped me out of the bed, into a dressing gown, and out into the corridor.

"Let's go!" she ordered.

Down the long white passageway I proceed as fast as I could. But soon I had to stop. The pain was sharp. I felt like my innards were about to fall out. I crossed my legs.

"Go on!" said the nurse.

I shuffled very slowly down the second corridor, stopping again and again.

"Oh, God! I will never make it!" I moaned, clinging to the nurse's arm.

"Lady, you MUST! Just a few more steps. A few more steps," she urged. The corridors seemed endless, but finally I turned into the last corridor, and there at the end I saw the double glass door.

"Praise be the Lord!" I said to myself. I felt myself being picked up.

After that, all I remember was that I was on something high. My spasms were coming faster and faster. Now the pain was so excruciating that I could not help scream as a Russian would: "OOOOOIEH!!"

"SHUT UP!" was my doctor's fast and short response. Then I blacked out.

The walk was effective, as the good doctor had anticipated, for the baby arrived quickly. After several minutes, I regained consciousness. I heard my doctor say, "Ha, a healthy little baby girl." She placed the moist little body on my abdomen.

What an unusual way to force a reluctant soul into this world, I could not help thinking, as I happily embraced our little Agnes Carola. I was also relieved that the longest walk of my life was over.

The day was April 25, 1944.

Contrary to the present-day practice of letting the young mother go home very soon after having given birth, at the time my Agnes Carola was born, I was kept in the hospital for a week. Twice a day, Dr. Antonoff would visit, and Karl came as often as he could. One afternoon their visits happened to coincide.

After an exchange of the usual pleasantries, Karl left, while Dr. Antonoff remained. She made some notes on the chart at the foot of my bed and then, casually, asked, "Is your husband's health good?"

"Why, yes," I replied, a little puzzled by her question. "Why do you ask?"

"No reason in particular." She changed the subject. "You will be going home tomorrow."

The happy thought that I would be leaving the hospital put Dr. Antonoff's disturbing question out of my mind completely. The next morning I went home.

As I entered our apartment, it was a joy to see my atrium, bathed in sunlight and bright with the colors of yellow daffodils, red and purple tulips, and white narcissus, all in pots which Ting had distributed among the green house plants. In the center of the dining table he also had a beautiful bouquet of lilacs. What a thoughtful and kind servant of the old school Ting was!

Little Regina, who was just learning to walk, ran to greet me. The cook, too, came out of the kitchen to make his bow. Everyone was smiling and, of course, little Agnes Carola received all due attention. Huang Hwa immediately wanted to cradle her in her arms.

That evening our dinner was especially sumptuous, with a whole roast duck served with decorative garnishes on a large platter. It was our cook's idea to have my homecoming celebrated appropriately.

The days that followed went by, as everyone who has ever had a baby knows, according to the feeding schedule. Karl attended to his business from nine to five at his offices in the Shanghai business district close to the Bund. Thus, our life proceeded in the normal, happy fashion.

Then one night, after I had fed the baby, Karl and I went to bed. I was soon fast asleep. How long I slept, I was not sure, because all I remember was that suddenly, something awakened me. I thought I heard a strange noise. I listened. It was a muffled, rasping sound coming from the bathroom.

I remember stretching out my arm to awaken Karl, but he was not next to me. Now the sound became louder. It sounded like someone was suffocating.

"Karl!" I called, as I sprang out of bed, fearful that something terrible was happening. I opened the bathroom door and switched on the light, and there was Karl, clinging to the window sill. He had opened the window to have more air and was gasping, unable to breathe. I stood on the threshold in utter bewilderment, not knowing what to do.

Some time passed before Karl's breathing became easier. Noticing that I was there, he gave me an embarrassed smile.

"It is all right, Liebling. I can breathe now." He stumbled into the bedroom. I helped him into bed and propped him up with several pillows. Exhausted by his ordeal, Karl fell fast asleep. But for me, that night dragged on and on. Full of anxiety, I kept listening to his every movement, to every rustle of the sheet.

At break of day, after having fed Agnes Carola, I went quietly back into our bedroom. I was startled to find Karl shaving in the bathroom.

"You are not planning to go to the office?" I asked, astonished to see him up so early after the previous night's attack.

"Sure. Tell Ting I will have two soft-boiled eggs and one piece of toast this morning, and please don't worry!" He patted me on the cheek.

"Shouldn't you speak to your doctor first?" I suggested. "Maybe you should stay home today." I could not tell him that he looked exceedingly drawn and pale.

"I will get in touch with him this afternoon." Karl's voice had an impatient note in it. "I will be all right."

That morning I tried to distract myself. I took an especially long time to plan the day's menu with the cook and to make a list of additional purchases at the market. At eleven, I again breast-fed my baby and had my own lunch. I was about to take a nap, when Ting knocked on the door. I saw that he was worried.

"Missy, the House Master want see you."

"House Master?" I wondered what he meant. Ting spoke what we, in China, called Pidgin English. It took time to get the knack of it.

"Master of House," Ting corrected.

"Ah, you mean the owner of the building?" Ting nodded his head affirmatively.

Wondering what had brought about the Hungarian's visit, I went to greet him in the vestibule. But before I could even extend my hand, he interrupted me.

"Frau Spanier, I have just received a telephone call from Herr Spanier's office. I am sorry to inform you that your husband was taken to the hospital."

I caught my breath. "Which hospital?!" was all I could say.

"To the Shanghai General Hospital."

"Is it his heart?!"

"Yes. Dr. Straube has been notified." With these words the Hungarian bowed and left.

Alone in the vestibule, I stood stunned, staring at the atrium. I was only dimly aware of the colorful flowers, which I had always enjoyed.

"Ting, if Ling is not back, fetch me a pedicab," I called finally, knowing that Ting must be near and on the alert.

"Yes, Missy, call pedicab—Ling not here," I heard him answer from around the corner.

The Shanghai General Hospital was on the way to the Bund, not far from the Race Course on Bubbling Well Road. In a pedicab, an ingenious arrangement of a double seat on a three-wheeled bicycle propelled by a man peddling at a fast pace, I arrived at the hospital within half an hour. I found Karl breathing with the help of an oxygen tank. He was dreadfully pale and his sunken eyes had dark rings around them.

"Ah, Liebling, it will pass," Karl smiled faintly, trying to be brave.

"Of course, of course," I assured him.

"Dr. Straube told me I can go home, provided I have help in the house. He is arranging for two nurses."

After several days two nurses were found, one for the day shift, and one for the night. We placed a bed for Karl in his study. It was the brightest corner of the apartment where he could sit in front of the windows.

As soon as the room was ready for Karl, I hastened to the hospital. Karl and his day nurse were expecting me.

The doorman found for us two pedicabs, the reliable conveyance in those days when motorcars were unavailable due to war and the absence of gasoline.

Aware of how it was important for Karl to get home as fast as possible, I promised the two drivers additional tips for speed. Then, after helping Karl into the first vehicle with the nurse and a portable oxygen tank, I climbed into the second cab.

Our drivers—young, strong and adept at negotiating the congested Shanghai streets—started off. We were driving on the Bubbling Well Road. Here the throng of rickshaws, bicyclists, wheelbarrows, and electric trolleys increased.

I was beside myself with worry about Karl in the other pedicab. However, soon enough we were passing the Buddhist temple just before turning onto our Wei Hai Wei Road. How they maneuvered through the dense traffic seemed miraculous. Before I knew it, I saw the roofline and the upper stories of our apartment building, and shortly thereafter our pedicabs stopped at our imposing glass entrance doors. I breathed a sigh of relief, seeing that Karl was all right. The nurse, I noticed, looked worried.

"We had to use the oxygen along the way," she whispered to me as Karl, ahead of us, stepped into the elevator.

"Oh, Liebling! How happy I am to be home." Karl smiled when we entered our penthouse. "How lovely those plants are," he said, pointing to the begonias in full bloom in our atrium, which I had purposely placed there to greet him.

Assuring myself that Karl was comfortable in his study, my next thought was to see Dr. Straube. We needed instructions on Karl's diet. I also was anxious to know exactly Karl's condition and how we were to care for him.

Dr. Straube's office was not too far from where we lived. He received me cordially. After inviting me to sit down in a chair, he took his own seat behind his desk.

"Dr. Straube, I have brought my husband home this afternoon. Please tell me what I should do and…I also want to know…how serious is his condition?"

For a minute, Dr. Straube was silent. He lowered his head and stroked his well-trimmed graying beard as if he were trying to find the right words. Then he slowly looked up at me. "Frau Spanier, your husband is terminally ill. His heart is terribly enlarged. The angina attacks will become more frequent. And he can die suddenly."

"Isn't there anything that can be done to help him?" I asked, terrified at the thought of Karl's suffering.

"No, Frau Spanier, at present there are no known means, only the medication I have prescribed. The pills will prolong his life a little. I am sorry." With these words, he stood up, indicating that he had nothing else to say.

I staggered out of the doctor's office. Like an automaton, I returned home.

"Ah! Liebling, you are back. What did the good doctor tell you?"

I kissed him tenderly, trying my best not to show how upset I was. "He told me you will be all right," I lied, hoping that he would not guess the truth. Fortunately, just then the nurse entered with a tray, Karl's dinner.

Thus began that painful period of knowing that there was no hope and that the end was soon to come, despite the doctor's efforts to stave it off with medication and oxygen.

Realizing that he had little time left, Karl called for Dr. Wilhelm, his friend and lawyer. In accordance with German law, he had to write his will by hand.

Meanwhile, reminding myself several times a day that my life as well as my children's had to continue, I did my best to perform my motherly and housewifely duties. I even took little Regina and Agnes Carola to Jessfield Park. But these were sad, sad walks. The memories of the times when Karl had accompanied me on the same paths, were very painful.

At the apartment, the nurses ministered as best they could. Within a couple of weeks, the attacks occurred every twenty minutes. I lived in constant terror, expecting that each attack would be the last. Yet Karl clung to life; though, with more and more pain and difficulty.

Finally, one morning when Dr. Straube arrived, I asked to speak to him privately. So as not to be overheard, we went into the little washroom in our vestibule.

"Doctor, how long will this continue?" I asked.

"As long as he takes the medication," Dr. Straube answered in a low, sad voice.

"His suffering is terrible."

Dr. Straube only waved his hands in a gesture of helplessness.

"Is there no hope?"

"None. We have no means to correct his enlarged heart."

Why prolong this torture? Why prolong this torture? I grasped my head with both hands as the question kept hammering at me.

The doctor must have sensed my turmoil, for after a brief silence, he added, almost in a whisper, "As a doctor, I cannot do otherwise. It is my duty to keep him alive. If I stop the medication, he will die within hours."

At that moment, I knew that I had to make that decision for the doctor—and for Karl. I could not bear to see Karl going on and on in such a senseless, cruel way.

"Please stop the medication. I will take it upon my conscience," I forced myself to say, convinced that it was the only humane way.

Dr. Straube bowed his head.

The next morning at seven the nurse awakened me. "Come quickly, your husband is dying."

When I reached Karl's bed, he was already gone. All I could do was hold onto his slowly cooling hands. It was July 7, 1944.

The nurse told me much later that Karl's last words were "Poor Muza."

47

The Funeral Parlor

A courteous gray-haired gentleman with an appropriately sad expression on his face, wearing a formal tailcoat and striped trousers, greeted me at the entrance of the funeral parlor. After I told him who I was, he bowed ceremoniously, and, with a silent gesture of his hand, invited me to follow him. We proceeded through several corridors, with crystal chandeliers overhead and luxurious oriental carpets underfoot, past several rooms where I could see coffins surrounded with lighted candles. At last we reached the room where Karl's body had been prepared for visitation.

Uncertain of what to expect, I approached Karl's coffin slowly. Peering down into it, I was taken aback at how changed he looked. In the light of the candles of the four surrounding torchieres, I was looking at a waxen mask. The friendly features that I remembered now were sharp, unpleasant, a vague semblance of the man I had known and loved. In front of me, a shell, dressed in a dark suit with hands folded on the chest, lay retouched with cosmetics and powder.

Suddenly I was aware that this same fate awaited all of us. The thought frightened me. The sorrow and the realization of the loss of my beloved became even more intense.

I could not remain any longer in this luxurious house of the dead. I fled as quickly as I could, down the corridors and out into the street, out into the world of the living, where the cacophony of tooting horns, shouting pedestrians, and screeching car brakes, somehow, at that moment, were strangely reassuring.

"Ling, take me home," I told our chauffeur.

In due time Ling delivered me to our residence and the elevator took me up to our eleventh-floor apartment. Ting opened the door.

"Gentleman to see you, Missy," he announced.

Dr. Wilhelm, a tall, stately looking man with slightly graying auburn hair, was awaiting me in the living room. He had brought Karl's will with him and wanted to acquaint me with what lay before me.

After reading the document aloud, in lengthy legal terms, which bequeathed to the third generation what sounded like a sizeable inheritance, Dr. Wilhelm cleared his throat and coughed several times.

"Frau Spanier," he said, wrinkling his brow, "I regret to tell you that, despite what I have read, after investigating, I have found that your husband's estate is very limited. The contents of the apartment, of course, are yours, and the cash balance in the bank, which amounts to $350 "Mexican" dollars (as the Chinese "Yuan" currency was called). In addition, you will be receiving a pension from the firm. I must inform you, however, that you will not be able to continue living in the manner you are accustomed to."

"But the will sounds like there must be some money somewhere," I said incredulously.

"If there is, it can only be in a secret account in Switzerland, where, during the war, many Germans deposited their money for safety. I do intend to make inquiries."

"But, Dr. Wilhelm, the $350 will not even pay for the cremation and funeral expenses."

"The firm will be paying for that, as well as the eventual delivery of the urn to Germany, in accordance with your husband's desire." Then, abruptly, Dr. Wilhelm asked my permission to leave. I nodded. There was nothing else to say.

He hurriedly placed the papers into his briefcase and just as hurriedly, was walking toward the entrance, when he stopped for a brief moment. "Oh, by the way," he said, "there is a lady who might be interested in your apartment. She is able to pay 'key money' for the lease."

"But, Doctor, where will I find another place to live at this time?"

"I am afraid you will have to. I wish you all the best," he answered as he shook my hand without meeting my eyes. As Karl's friend, I understood that he must have been disconcerted. As I closed the door behind him, I felt like an abyss had just opened before me. Slowly, like an automaton, I walked past the atrium, up the seven steps to the living room...

"Mama! Mama!" I heard Regina calling, as she ran toward me with her arms outstretched, her little face smiling. She brought me back to my surroundings. I caught her up in my arms, pressing her tenderly to me, yet full of anxiety about the predicament I was facing.

"What are we going to do?! What are we going to do?!" The question kept nagging at me.

Then, from somewhere deep inside of me, came the answer, "Trust life." Those were my Father's words. How often he had thus admonished me in moments of hardship. At this moment, they inspired hope in me.

"We will manage," I whispered into Regina's ear. She giggled, nestling her head on my shoulder.

"Missy, time to feed the baby," I heard Huang Hwa tell me.

"Yes, let's go," I answered.

Huang Hwa brought me my baby wrapped in a light pink coverlet. As I took my little girl into my arms, she grasped my nipple hungrily and began sucking; but, instead of gulping down the milk as she normally did, she started to whimper. I knew something was wrong and soon realized that she was not getting anything. My breasts were empty!

"Huang Hwa, Huang Hwa," I called in dismay. She came running.

"Quick, prepare the baby's bottle!"

Huang Hwa disappeared into the kitchen and promptly returned with the bottle of formula which we kept in reserve.

"Maybe you drink rice water," she suggested. "It help Chinese ladies."

"Prepare whatever you want. I will drink it," I answered.

She boiled rice and water into a tasteless watery substance for me. Several times a day I drank it, but there were no results.

"Maybe oatmeal gruel and plenty ice cream help," Huang Hwa decided.

So I added oatmeal mush to my daily diet and gallons of ice cream. Nothing happened. My anxiety for the future and the bewilderment of Karl's sudden death had physically affected me; so my little Agnes Carola had to be fed with the bottles of formula from then on. This added to my worry, as I was aware of how important it was to breast feed a baby as long as possible.

These days would have been even more difficult for me had it not been for my Grandmother. She came to stay with me and her unflinching belief that her granddaughter would be able to overcome any difficulties kept my dwindling spirits alive.

Several other kind individuals also helped. Kurt and Inna Leuen, whom I knew from the Laoshan days; Deannie Fessler, a lovely American lady, whose husband was Karl's colleague; and Hans Mosberg, a business acquaintance of Karl's, stayed in constant touch with me.

The solicitude of these friends and their advice pulled me through that trying period.

Karl's funeral took place at the Shanghai Lutheran Church. It was filled to capacity with people whose faces were mostly unfamiliar to me.

Vaguely, as though in a fog, I remember sitting in the front pew during the service. Kurt and Inna Leuen were on either side of me.

In front of the altar, on a table covered with a white lace cloth, stood the urn with Karl's ashes. I heard the organ playing and the air was filled with the fragrance of many flowers. I was terribly sad, yet I was unable to cry.

I also dimly recall the corpulent figure of the minister in his flowing black robe, speaking from the podium. He spoke of Karl's contribution to the German colony in Shanghai, and of his many years of service with the Farbwerke Hoechst, and when he finally ended his eulogy, Inna nudged me and whispered, "Muza, time to take the urn and follow the minister."

As if in a trance, I stood up and went to pick up the urn. It was heavy, but I was able to carry it through a door to the left of the altar into a spacious room where the walls were subdivided into niches. After climbing a ladder, I placed Karl's remains into one of these niches. Here, together with the urns of other Germans, Karl's urn would remain until it was sent to Germany.

Later, I stood at the church's massive portals, shaking hands with a long line of people, who seemed to look at me with pity. No doubt, I must have appeared to be the picture of a poor young widow left with two tiny children and facing a very uncertain future at this climactic point in time when World War II was coming to an end.

Although our short-wave radios were blacked out with static by the Japanese, preventing us from receiving news from the United States, news, nevertheless, slipped through. The situation looked bad for Germany, and was not good for the Japanese in the Pacific. Every German national was concerned about what reprisals the war's end would bring.

Thank goodness I was too young, too inexperienced, and too preoccupied with my own immediate problems to worry about the consequences global affairs might bring into my own life. Father, however, was attuned to what was happening and, in an effort to boost my morale, he wrote to me from Laoshan.

"My dear daughter," he wrote, "remember that steel is forged under pressure. Only to the strong do the trials come. Go forward bravely, trusting life and your destiny, and like an officer in battle formation, keep your morale and the morale of those who depend on you. 'Though a battle is lost, with morale sustained, nothing is lost.'"

Willy-nilly, I went forward. What else could I do?

After the funeral, on that memorable day in July 1994, I went back to my apartment to try to solve the problems as they might occur.

My first act was to make arrangements for my four servants. I also sold my car, as fuel was, by now, hard to get. Ling, the chauffeur, was not a problem. He went with the new owner of the car. For Huang Hwa, her husband, my cook, and their little son, I purchased tickets on a ship to Tsingtao, their home. With great sadness I parted with Huang Hwa, a good, intelligent woman who had become, during these few years, more than a nanny to my children. She had become my friend.

Now only Ting remained, but due to his age and his increasing loss of sight, which I suspected because he left large areas undusted, I feared that he would have difficulty finding another job. There was, however, one chance for him. There might be someone who needed a servant with recommendations from the previous employer. So I placed an ad in the local paper. It read: "Former owner guarantees the services and honesty of a reliable servant." And I gave the telephone number of my landlord.

Several days later I had a call from a lady who spoke with a French accent. Her first question was "How old is the man?"

"Well, it is hard to say," I answered cautiously. "You know the Chinese do not show their age until they are very old."

"*Eh, bien*, approximately?" she pressed me.

"Probably between fifty and fifty-five," I lied, knowing that Ting was much, much older.

"Oh, *mon Dieu!* So young?" the lady exclaimed.

I was stunned. At that time I considered fifty-five to be quite elderly! "Well, maybe he is a little older," I said, to keep the conversation going and not to lose a job for Ting.

"How much older?" There was a hopeful note in her voice.

"Maybe sixty or so…"

"No! No! Still too young," she sighed.

Good heavens! What is this? I thought, and decided to pose a direct question. "Madame, what sort of a man are you looking for?"

"*Eh, bien*, you see, *je suis une Supérieure* of a convent, a school for girls. We need a gatekeeper. Well, you know, a safe one. You understand?" She cleared her throat.

"May I ask if it is, by any chance, the Sacred Heart Convent?"

"*Mais oui*, the Sacred Heart. How did you know?"

"Many years ago I used to be one of the pupils. My name was Muse Kotenev."

"Oh, Muse! I remember you. I am Mother Foy, your catechism teacher."

"Why, you are the teacher who told me that only Catholics will go to heaven." I could not help chuckling.

"Hah! In those days we were certain of it." She laughed.

With old connections established, I felt that it was time to tell the truth. "Mother Foy, I have to confess that Ting is really quite old, more than seventy, and his eyesight is not too good."

"*Mais, c'est bien!* Splendid! Tell him to come to see me at once."

Needless to say, Mother Foy liked Ting and he got the job. Several days later Ting brought me a bouquet of flowers to thank me. He became a loyal guard of the convent gates and, because of his old age and failing eyesight, Mother Foy felt confident of the virtue of her nuns and pupils. I was happy that everything worked out so very well.

In the meantime, my Hungarian landlord, aware of my reduced circumstances, was busy on my behalf. He found a rich German widow who offered to pay me U.S. $3,000 as key money. In those days it was a considerable sum of money, though far below what our luxurious penthouse would have brought if I had had the time to wait for another buyer. But being already behind in my rent and having found, by chance, a place to move into without having to pay key money, I did not tarry.

I packed my personal belongings, stored them with my furniture in the garage downstairs, and moved with my children to what I hoped would be very temporary quarters: a small ten-by-twelve-foot bedroom with a walk-through to the kitchen, and a bathroom, with a single window overlooking a dismal yard. What a change from my eleventh-floor apartment with the panoramic view of Shanghai on all sides!

My landlady, a red-haired, middle-aged woman, rented this room in desperation. Her recently deceased husband had left her with bad gambling debts and no money. She worked six days a week as a cashier in a coffee shop, but her salary was far too insufficient. Thus, our needs met. For me, this was a timely solution for a place to move to. For my landlady, it was additional income to pay her husband's obligations.

Though I was cramped and uncomfortable, and though my landlady had to sleep on a decrepit sofa in her front living-dining area, we nonetheless managed. Her absence during most of the day helped. It permitted me to spill over into to her side during the day, and when she returned from work, late in the evening, my children were already asleep. As a result, she was able to rest.

In this manner, we lived for several long months, until I found a better place. At least, I perceived it to be a better place, although my friends did not share my opinion.

"Muza, you must be crazy even to consider such a move!" Inna Leuen said, grasping her curly blond head in both hands.

"But this Verdun Terrace town house is comfortable, with two bedrooms on the second floor, and a small garden in front," I tried to convince her.

"How can you think of taking your children to such a location?" Kurt interrupted, as he adjusted his glasses. "Don't you know that Verdun Terrace, on the other side of the wall of the French Club, is now the most dangerous place in the French Concession?"

"Are you sure?" I asked. "I have heard rumors, but are they true?"

"There is no doubt! Haven't you seen the constant comings and goings of the Japanese military trucks?" Inna looked at me as if she were seeing an extraterrestrial.

"Why don't you just tell her what it is," Kurt interrupted her.

Inna raised her voice. "Muza, everyone knows that it is a big Japanese ammunition dump."

"Yes, smack in the middle of the residential district," Kurt added.

"The key money is only $300 U.S. Where can I get such a cute little house for so low a price?" I insisted illogically.

"Naturally, you can't. The reason is that no one in his right mind would pay even that much for it, especially with the Allied planes flying daily over Shanghai. What a target it might be." Kurt's voice sounded utterly frustrated.

"But I cannot stay forever where I am now. Besides, it may seem ridiculous, but don't we have a saying, 'God works in mysterious ways his wonders to perform'?"

For a few moments Inna and Kurt looked at me in silence. They shook their heads in disbelief.

"Well?" I asked.

"Well, at least talk to someone else, too. Hans Mosberg would be the right man. He is smart and maybe you will listen to him." With these words, after embracing me, they left. That evening I telephoned Hans Mosberg.

Hans was a mysterious figure in the German community. He was a Jew, yet somehow was connected with the German Consulate. At a time when Jews were shunned by Germans, Hans was present at all German functions and his ponderous figure was always surrounded by some of the most influential German officials, who seemed to show deference to him. It might have been his conversation, spiced with the latest piquant gossip and news, that attracted them.

In any event, after Karl's death, Hans had invited me several times for dinner at various restaurants. Each time I found him a very pleasant, well-read, and highly educated companion. Now, he promptly responded to my call and paid me a visit.

When Hans was seated on my landlady's worn-out yellow sofa, I came to the point at once.

"Hans, I have been offered one of the Verdun Terrace town houses. Inna and Kurt Leuen say that I am crazy to consider it. What do you think?"

Hans raised his eyebrows. "You mean the Terrace on the other side of the wall of the French Club?"

"Yes."

Hans puckered his thick lips, sucked in some air, and rubbed his balding forehead with the palm of his right hand. "How much is the key money?" he asked.

"Only $300 U.S.," I answered.

He was thoughtful for a moment. Then a strange glint appeared in his small blue eyes as he peered at me through his glasses. "Well, that is not much, is it?" was all he said. But it was not just what he said that seemed important. It was the strange expression in his eyes and the half smile which seemed to convey something which he obviously did not want to express in words. I was certain that he knew something.

For some reason, I immediately felt assured of my decision and hastened to pay the present Russian town house tenant his key money. The lease was promptly changed to my name, and I moved in with my children the first of August 1945. On the 15th of August, the Japanese surrendered. The war was over in the Pacific.

Mosberg, who, as I found out later, was a high-ranking official of the German Secret Service, had known that Japan was about to surrender.

Naturally, with the end of the war, Verdun Terrace, next to the French Club, became a very desirable spot to live.

"You knew it all along. You knew it!" the former Russian tenant of my town house shouted angrily when I met him one day on the street. He looked furious, but I took satisfaction in knowing that his attempt to sell a town house to a naive young widow in what might have been a dangerous place had backfired.

48

Verdun Terrace

For me, Verdun Terrace was a timely miracle. Well-built, with windows facing the rising sun in the morning, the little town house became a cozy home for my children. It also was the beginning of a completely new life for me. To some extent, by now, time had healed the loss of my Karl, and the luxurious apartment with its plant-filled atrium on Great Western Road was slowly becoming only another cherished memory. I could not bring back what I had had before, but with a grain of effort, I could make our new home attractive.

Our main entrance, through a small fenced-in garden, had enough space for me to indulge my love for plants and flowers. The front door led into a medium-sized living-dining room. My old rose-colored velvet sofa, two comfortable matching chairs, and the glass-topped coffee table fitted in perfectly. An open staircase, with polished mahogany banisters, leading to two bedrooms and a bathroom upstairs embellished the setting.

In the dining area, at the far end of the room, I had the large glass window painted to simulate stained glass. The artist painted a tropical scene of a lagoon with a parrot on a branch in the foreground. He was so successful that from a distance, the window looked just like stained glass you see in cathedrals. At sunset, the sunlight filtering through it, creating a most striking effect.

Next to the dining area, the kitchen opened out into a small yard. Above it was a small servant's room where, very soon, an old Russian lady moved in. Her husband had deserted her and she had been forced out of her own small flat. I took her in with the agreement that, inasmuch as she was a masseuse, instead of rent, she would give me a massage on occasion. Eventually, we became good friends. She was the first addition to my household.

The second person to join my household was Sung, my cook-boy. How he found out that I needed someone always remained a mystery.

In any event, Sung appeared at my door, an unusually stocky, broad-shouldered Chinaman, with a big friendly smile, and eagerly accepted the meager wages of fifteen Chinese dollars a month which I offered him. But what a treasure he became! He proved himself to be an excellent cook and a meticulous cleaner, along with other unusual qualities which gradually manifested themselves. His wife did my laundry and at the same time his children played with Regina and Carola.

From the beginning, for some reason, Sung did not charge me for rice or bread. When I questioned him, he explained, his eyes twinkling with mirth, "Missy, no worry! No worry! We eat this together." Knowing the Chinese nature of frugality and practicality, I did not protest too much. I suspected that he was not incurring any loss and was balancing the ledger by adding to the cost of other items which he purchased at the market.

What I especially remember about Sung were his self-appointed duties as my protector, and his belief that he was an expert in women's fashions. Admittedly, I might have needed a protector, but his assumption that he was a fashion connoisseur tested my patience at times. For instance, when I had dressed and ready to go out, Sung would stop me and say, "Missy, this purse you carry no good with dress." Or, "Missy, that scarf no proper color." And he would promptly dive into my chest of drawers to choose something that he felt was more appropriate for my appearance.

Grandmother found him much too familiar for a servant, but I appreciated his attitude, understanding that in the old-fashioned Chinese households, servants were considered part of the family and their opinions were accepted.

On occasion, Sung would overstep his bounds when he would express disapproval of my friends—gentlemen friends, that is—and there were a few of them at that time.

It was often said: "Where there is honey there will be bees," and bees fluttered around me, understandably so, because I was young, attractive, and alone. Besides, what woman would not like attention? And this is when Sung asserted himself most definitely!

Not only was I "not at home" for some callers, but if the gentleman got as far as an invitation to the dining table and Sung judged him undesirable, the dinner would be served accordingly. Sung practically tossed the unpalatable food at the guest.

Understandably, the gentleman never returned. Strange as it may seem, I respected Sung's judgment because his acquaintance with the world was greater than mine.

Not always did Sung disapprove. One gentleman won Sung's approbation. "Missy, Mr. Armando belong for you," Sung told me one day. As usual, Sung had a point, for Armando de Zaldivar y Ruiz was special. How often did one meet someone with royal blood flowing through his veins? Armando de Zaldivar y Ruiz, on his mother's side, was a direct descendent of the Spanish Kings of Castile. I had met him in the house of my school chum Ludmilla. Ludmilla was now happily married to Osa Gonzales, a Basque, a champion Jai-alai player. Armando was introduced to Osa when he arrived in Shanghai.

Like most sons of Spanish nobility, Armando had been trained as a naval officer. But it was during Franco's regime, a most perilous time for the Spanish aristocracy, as Franco strove to weaken its power.

According to reports, including eyewitnesses on U.S. Navy vessels, Spanish ships, their decks crowded with young cadets and officers, had been seen sailing out of Cadiz in the direction of the Atlantic Ocean. These ships had returned empty. What had happened to those officers and cadets? None of them was ever seen again.

A few naval officers, like Armando, managed to survive. With the help of connections in high places, Armando's family was able to smuggle him out in time to escape this horror.

I will always remember Armando, a perfect image of a Spanish Grandee. Not tall, yet very handsome, with the typically Iberian features that you can see in the famous painting by El Greco, "The Burial of Count Argaz," now hanging in one of the chapels in the Toledo Cathedral.

Armando's proud bearing and his courtesy were both impressive and endearing. Sung had to have recognized them, as Armando never neglected to show his deference even to Sung.

I remember on several occasions while sitting at the Palace Hotel on the Bund, listening to music and sipping our four o'clock "spot of tea," Armando would suddenly arise from his chair. He would have espied one of his Spanish acquaintances entering the hall and prepared to greet him. As soon as the other gentleman noticed Armando, they ceremoniously bowed to each other in unison. Such cordiality may be considered outdated in our times, but how gracious and ennobling it was, and how it adorned our human intercourse.

When the Spanish Ambassador to China was recalled, Armando took his place as the "Chargé d'Affaires." He represented his country with distinction.

Armando's attitude toward me as a woman left nothing to be desired. He always arrived at my house with a bouquet of flowers or a box of chocolates or some other present. His English was far from perfect, yet we understood each other perfectly. As a lover, he lacked neither youthful vigor nor the proverbial Spanish passion. I enjoyed his lovemaking. Why not? "Youth passes so fast, bask and revel in it while it lasts" were my Father's words of wisdom. And mutual pleasure was all that Armando could offer at that time. He very frankly admitted that his financial position precluded all thoughts of marriage even though he would have liked a family and dreamt of having many children.

Our agreeable relations thrived until the advent into Shanghai of the Allied Army and Navy. This coming affected Armando's official position.

For Armando to find work in Shanghai with his limited English was like finding a needle in a haystack. He had to seek a livelihood elsewhere, and South America was one possibility. I encouraged this decision. Peru was what he chose. To help, I shared with him the little savings I had and he purchased a ticket on a freighter bound in that direction.

"You must be mad," my Father wrote me when he heard that I had given Armando $1,500 U.S. In the postscript of that letter, however, Father added, "But to the mad, life grants 'mad luck.'" Those were prophetic words, for the world would have frequently considered my actions mad. Yet, when I needed, life always provided timely assistance.

Two or three years later, upon establishing himself in Lima, Peru, Armando wrote that all went very well with him, and that he was representing a large American firm. He asked me to marry him, and with his proposal was a draft for $1,500 U.S., the sum I had loaned him.

Why I did not accept his offer I never understood. Perhaps I felt that he offered marriage more through a sense of "noblesse oblige" than sentiment. The proposal also coincided with my move to Tsingtao after my efforts to sustain myself as a secretary had failed, and after the Chinese Government, following Japan's surrender, had made Father the Councilor to the Governor of Shantung in charge of public relations with the American forces occupying Tsingtao, and given my parents a lovely house.

Many years later, when I was already in the United States awaiting the arrival of my future husband, Malcolm Norcross, and staying in Miami, Armando flew from Lima to see me. It was a short visit, and my future mother-in-law was highly suspicious of his motives, though she had been included at dinner in a fancy restaurant. The evening was hilarious.

49

Unexpected Assistance

With Germany's defeat, Karl's firm, the Farbwerke Hoechst, discontinued its operation. My pension stopped. Having no training to fall back on for employment, and having diminished my little reserves helping Armando, I found myself facing a most uncertain future. My household responsibilities and the cost of living, which rose steadily after the end of the war, made me more than anxious. I was lost for a solution and was contemplating letting go of my beloved little town house when most unexpected assistance came from the strangest of quarters.

Who should call me on the telephone but Vincent Dalton, the Irishman of Laoshan times. He had moved to Shanghai, had taken over the legal firm of a prominent French lawyer who had died, and was hiring a small staff: a secretary, a Chinese clerk, and a messenger boy. That was when he thought of me. He knew that I was a widow and living in Shanghai. He also correctly surmised that I had financial difficulties. Either prompted by kindness or frugality, or nudged by guilt for the past, whatever, he decided to offer me the job of secretary in his office.

I heard the phone ring. I picked up the receiver, "Hello."

A man's voice with an Oxford accent said, "This is Vincent Dalton."

"What is the number you are calling?" I asked, as the name did not register with me.

"Muse, don't you recognize me? This is Vincent. How are you?"

My God, I thought, recalling the past. What on Earth does he want after all these years? All I needed now was Vincent to add to my troubles, but I answered him cordially.

"Good to hear from you," I said.

He came to the point at once. "Muse, do you want a job?"

"A job? Well, what kind of job?" I wondered about his intentions, remembering him in Laoshan.

"I mean a real job, a clerical position as a secretary in my legal firm," Vincent hurried to explain.

I nearly lost my balance. What qualifications did I have to be s secretary in a legal firm? Not having received an answer, Vincent continued.

"Do you type? I need help typing documents."

"Type? Why, yes, I do, a little." I had taken typing classes in high school in Shanghai.

"Good, then come to see me in my office tomorrow morning. Fifth floor," and he gave me the address of a building on the Bund. "See you then," and he hung up.

Well, I said to myself, I cannot lose anything. At nine o'clock the next morning, I stood before the ornate bronze doors to the marble entrance hall of the building where Vincent's offices were located. The elevator slowly lifted me to the fifth floor. At the end of the corridor I saw a sign on the glass door in large letters: "Vincent Dalton et Cie."

It was not without trepidation that I placed my hand on the doorknob and entered the small waiting room furnished with a red and blue antique Chinese carpet and several comfortable chairs. Beyond was another door, which promptly opened as Vincent stepped out.

Despite the traumatic memories connected with him, I felt no resentment. Time had long ago erased the sharpness of the pain. My vision was more unbiased, more clear. Now what I saw was a short man with unkempt graying hair, dressed in a dark blue suit, a striped shirt, and a red bow tie slightly off center. His reddish face, lined with wrinkles, looked haggard.

"Ah, Muse! Good to see you," Vincent exclaimed. "How elegant you look!" Vincent's blue eyes twinkled with amusement as his gaze swept me from head to toe. "Come in, come in." He led me into his office. "Take a seat." He pointed to a chair next to his immense mahogany desk piled with books and papers.

"Your duty will be to type my opinions and various other legal documents. You understand?"

"But, Vincent, I have not typed for years." I had to be honest.

"You need the job. I need a good-looking secretary, an attractive addition to my firm. Nothing to it at all. I will pay you adequately and, should you have difficulties, Wong Lee, my Chinese clerk, will help you."

"But, Vincent..."

"Don't worry, my dear. With practice you will acquire proficiency," Vincent stated, and arose from his chair to indicate that we had reached an agreement. "Start tomorrow. Glad to have you aboard." With these words, he pointed to the door.

50

My First Job

The next morning I dressed myself in a navy blue skirt and jacket with a white blouse. For an accent, I took my red purse. Thus, with the colors of the Russian Imperial flag for moral support and Sung's approval of my outfit I was ready. "Missy look good," he told me, as I climbed into the pedicab that was waiting for me.

The distance from Verdun Terrace to the Bund was considerable and in this early-morning rush-hour traffic, it was difficult. But my pedicab driver, a strong young man, dressed as most pedicab drivers in indigo-blue trousers and jacket and a bell-shaped straw hat, made excellent progress.

Peddling like a demon, he darted through the pressing line of rickshaws, skirted with alacrity around cars, ignoring the maddened shouts and tooting of their drivers, dodged oncoming trams and buses, and finally delivered me to the entrance of Vincent's office building. I think I was more breathless than he was. In Shanghai, you took your life into your hands each time you ventured out into the streets. Amazingly, there were few accidents, or we did not hear about them, as the newspapers did not publicize them.

As I stepped into the marble entrance hall, glad to have arrived in one piece and on the dot of nine, I was full of anticipation of the new job ahead.

A pleasant-looking young Chinese gentleman, in a prim gray European suit, greeted me in perfect English. In a cordial manner he said, "Mrs. Spanier, I am Wong Lee, the clerk, at your service. Your office is here." He waved his hand in the direction of a glass door.

"Indeed, it will be a pleasure to be working with you," I replied according to the prescribed formula, as I entered the room Wong Lee indicated.

"This is your desk." Wong Lee pointed to a small black desk in the far corner of the room with a large typewriter on it. "Mr. Dalton requests that you type this 'Opinion' as soon as you can."

"Opinion?" I asked, fingering a pile of handwritten sheets next to the typewriter.

"Oh! It is a legal term; a document, advice about a case given by a barrister to his client," Wong Lee explained. "Two extra carbon copies, please, is the customary procedure." The way he tossed his words over his shoulder gave them a touch of derision. It annoyed me a little.

I sat down to try to accomplish my task. Needless to say, my performance was a total disaster. Not only did I have a terrible time reading Vincent's handwriting, but somehow my fingers just would not obey my commands, resulting in reams of discarded fine Bond paper. All the while, I had a feeling that Wong Lee was watching me with amusement. At last he got up, probably prompted more by fear of the cost of the valuable sheets that I had crumpled up than by sympathy for my plight.

"I shall do it." Wong Lee picked up the manuscript, his face a mask of composure. "Not to worry." He went to his desk.

That was easy for him to say, I thought. My job and salary were at stake. My only consolation was that I had warned Vincent, who in the meantime had remained diplomatically behind the closed door of his own office.

From then on, less important papers, requiring fewer carbon copies, found their way to my desk. By the end of a couple of weeks, my typing skills had improved considerably. At the end of the month, Vincent paid me appropriately for my performance. I was not paid too much during the six months I worked for him, I remember. But nevertheless, I welcomed every cent of it.

Meanwhile, as I was struggling to be a good legal secretary, things in Shanghai were changing at a drastic pace. Into our harbor, under the command of the distinguished-looking Admiral Cook, steamed battleships, heavy cruisers, light cruisers, destroyers, torpedo boats, submarine chasers, and tankers to serve them— the whole of the U.S. 7th Fleet.

With it, chocolate bars, cartons of American cigarettes, coffee, ladies' silk underwear, and many, many items of luxury that had been unavailable or too expensive for us during the war appeared in the PX's. For the young women of Shanghai, these items proved to be irresistible, just as they themselves became temptations to the men of the U.S. Navy, Marine, and Army Corps.

Officers of higher ranks, with these ladies at their sides, whizzed about in sedans and military jeeps. The rank and file, with their dates competed for military transportation as best they could. Nightclubs, bars, and restaurants resounded with the merriment of the uniformed clientele, who were spending their U.S. dollars as if they had been picked from trees.

After the many years of war privation, the sky suddenly opened to shower money, sex, love, and promises of a wonderful future in the U.S.A., a beguilement for the many very attractive—and even not so attractive—Russian women in Shanghai.

For me, too, Luck smiled, eventually leading me into the country where we all thought the streets were paved with gold. My channel to the "El Dorado" was through my friend, Deannie Fessler.

51

Deannie Fessler

My friend, Deannie Fessler, a tall, elegant, auburn-haired American, whom I had met through the Leuens, took upon herself the role of my comforter. When I was deeply involved in liquidating my Great Western Road apartment, she would breeze in with some kind of gift, a broach, a small bottle of eau de Cologne, or some other small present, to please me. Then, sitting down to a cup of tea, she would chatter about how lovely my legs were and how, in the United States, I could earn millions of dollars modeling nylon stockings and becoming a famous fashion model. Having distracted me from my worries, she would just as blithely breeze out, having left me in a much better state of mind. As everyone knows, there is nothing like a compliment to rejuvenate a dwindling sense of self-worth.

Deannie's own life was not happy, despite her brave front. Just before the outbreak of the war, her beloved husband had gone to Germany on a business trip and never returned. As a high official of the Farbwerke Hoechst, at that time the largest German dye manufacturer, which Karl also worked for, Fessler was put in charge of ammunition production, to which the factories had been diverted. These facts had been kept secret until after Fessler committed suicide in fear of the Nuremberg Trials at the end of the war.

When our pensions stopped, Deannie, like myself, found herself in financial difficulties, which were relieved by an interesting set of circumstances. Deannie's father was James Bryant Conant, the President of Harvard University. With his position as the president of an elite university, he naturally had connections with its alumni, some of the most influential citizens of the United States. As a result, he made sure that when the United States Seventh Fleet steamed up the Wang Pu River into the Port of Shanghai, its Admiral carried a letter to his daughter. What a stroke of fortune!

Admiral Cook needed to establish a command headquarters in the Port of Shanghai. Deannie needed money. The Admiral required a civilian clerical staff for his officers. Not knowing anyone else locally, he offered the job of "Civilian Personnel Director" to Deannie. Because she was acquainted with the local work force, Deannie accepted the offer even though she lacked experience.

In those days, who would make up the work force? It would be the Russians, a colony of twenty-two thousand. Deannie loved the Russians. She also had a big kind heart. So, whom did she start hiring as secretaries, typists, and clerks? Young Russian women, preferably pretty ones. But she also found places for those not as attractive. The news flew with the speed of a tornado that jobs were available in the Astor House, the former hotel overlooking the Yangtze Creek, now the Headquarters of the U.S. Port Command.

Meanwhile, desks, filing cabinets, and other necessary office equipment requisitioned from the local offices on the Bund, found their way to the second floor of the Astor House. In the Personnel Office, Deannie presided behind a large desk. Long lines of applicants had to wait their turn as the hiring proceeded full swing. The requirements, Deannie felt, were a pretty face and, most importantly, a well-proportioned figure.

"Dearie," she said to me, "the poor American boys have had such a bad time during the war. Now they need relaxation. You will like Lt. Drinkwater." With these words, she made me secretary to the officer in charge of the motor pool. I answered telephone calls and sometimes typed something or other.

One had to give Deannie credit. In no time, she filled all the positions, and before long the second floor resounded with vigorous action. Telephones rang incessantly, typewriters tapped without ceasing, filing cabinets opened and closed, and the Russian female staff of the U.S. Port Command applied all their great energy to the full benefit of everyone concerned. The Americans benefited by having the work done. Russian community benefited by the flow of U.S. dollars. My own salary, $150 U.S. a month, was a fabulous figure to me.

And all the while, the battle-fatigued men had plenty of opportunity for relaxation with their well-proportioned assistants.

52

U.S. Motor Pool Offices

My duties as Lt. Drinkwater's secretary at the Motor Pool were not difficult. By now, sufficiently proficient as a typist, I handled whatever crossed my desk satisfactorily. Where I ran into trouble was in answering the telephone and relaying the messages to my boss. In this situation I had a definite problem, yet not entirely of my own making.

In Shanghai we spoke what was called the "King's English." In the Shanghai Public School I had been taught to pronounce words clearly. But this was not so with the officers of the Port Command. Apparently, in addition to a predilection for chewing gum, the majority were from the Deep South of the New World. Their diction with gum and Southern drawl over the telephone left much to be desired and completely eluded my understanding.

The messages I wrote on little notes to be placed on Lt. Drinkwater's desk were unclear. My boss read my notes and would shake his handsome, short-clipped dark brown haired head and sigh. Being a gentleman, he said nothing.

I suspect that inasmuch as the Lieutenant was a Northerner from New York City, he secretly sympathized with me. Nonetheless, our operation with Lt. Drinkwater, a former banker, in charge, ran sufficiently well. There were no repercussions from those above, and all the higher-ranking officers had their jeeps and other vehicles delivered on time and in good condition.

Soon, I, too, became more accustomed to the manner of speech of the U.S. military personnel and, like many of us working for the Port Command, even learned to enjoy their foreign ways.

I, like so many of the other ladies, welcomed the chocolate bars, perfumes, and silk undies that our "dates" (a new word in our vocabulary) brought us.

I, too, listened to the stories about their vast, beautiful homeland and how prosperous it was. One strange thing about our dates, young or older, was that they all were unencumbered bachelors and all of them wanted to present us as brides to their mothers. Many women in Shanghai believed what their clean-cut, healthy, dashing dates said. Bitter disillusionment, however, would frequently follow. For suddenly these men, whom they had thought to be their serious suitors, would vanish.

"*Boje moy! Boje moy!* [My God! My God!]," the young woman, already pregnant several months, would cry out. "Go to Headquarters," her friends would advise. And off she would run to the Headquarters.

"Ver is my boyfriend?" she would ask.

"Miss, Lt. So-and-so's tour of duty ended, and so he was sent back home," a not-too-sympathetic military clerk would inform her.

"B-u-t, b-u-t, I am vit baby!"

"I am sorry. Lt. So-and-so has a wife in New Town on Lake Sawakakea."

"Vat am I to dooo?"

The clerk would wave his hands. "I am sorry," was all he could reply.

I, too, had a very similar experience, but not with such dire consequences. My romance with Lt. Samuel Osbarn ended, fortunately, with him at least telling me he was leaving. Sam proved himself an officer and a gentleman. At six feet two inches, blond, blue eyed, dapper in his well-pressed khaki fatigues, he could charm the devil himself with his suave manner. I was quite taken with him.

Sam would drive up to my gate in his jeep. ZOOM! ZOOM! I could hear him race his motor before switching it off. Being ready and waiting, I would run out and get in next to him, and off we'd go to one of the fanciest of restaurants in town. Sam would order only the best and most expensive dishes that money could buy.

At other times, we would drive to the Officers Club and enter hand in hand. There a party would be in full swing and the orchestra would be blasting away. Sam would swing me this-a-way and that-a-way, doing the Boogie-woogie. Accustomed as I was to the Old World dances—the waltz, foxtrot or tango—what my feet performed I was not quite certain.

Thus we "dated" for many months and, naturally, intimacy developed, which we both enjoyed. Then one evening Sam arrived as expected, but I did not hear him race his motor. He switched off his engine quietly and rang the doorbell. When I opened the door for him to enter, I noticed that he looked somewhat sheepish and his usually smoothly brushed hair was a little disheveled.

"Hi," he said, making a circle with his hand in the air, without giving me the usual peck on the cheek.

"Hello," I said. "Is anything wrong?"

"Oh, no, no." Sam did not look at me.

"Well, why not tell me. Perhaps you have had some bad news from home?" I prodded, sensing that something was definitely not right.

"W-e-l-l-l-l, no. Well, I guess I might as well tell you that I have my discharge papers. I will be leaving day after tomorrow."

"That's good news, isn't it?" I said, feeling an unpleasant sensation in my stomach. "You will be in touch, of course, won't you?"

Sam did not answer immediately. I asked him to sit down.

"Better not. You see, Muse, I came to say goodbye."

"You will write, won't you?" I repeated, yet something told me that this was the last time I would ever see or hear from him.

"No. You see, I am, uh, engaged to be married."

"Oh!" was all I had time to utter, because Sam was already out of the door and out the gate. I heard the jeep start and, with a raucous roar, it raced toward the street.

I must have stood there for some time, bewildered and saddened by the sudden departure of my "date," Lt. Samuel Osbarn. I really did like him a lot.

"Missy, dinner in dining room," I heard Sung say.

"Yes, please serve it," I replied automatically, making my way to the dining table.

"Have good fish." Sung placed before me a platter with a lovely trout, baked in a special brown sauce, mashed potatoes, and tiny sweet peas.

"Missy eat, good for you," he urged me, as he served my plate from the platter. "No worry, Missy," he consoled me. "Many other."

While we young Russian women were cavorting with the American "Tobacco Boys," as the "local yokels" called the American military personnel, in the German colony, traumatic events were taking place. Orders had been received confiscating their houses, apartments, and personal effects. Their possessions were to be distributed among the United States officers, and they were to be deported back to Germany.

As a widow of a German, I, too, fell into this category. But knowing that Father had connections with influential Chinese officials, I telegraphed him for assistance. It was just in time. Through his friend in the Shanghai Municipal Council, Father arranged for a young Chinese couple to move upstairs into my second bedroom. They claimed the house their domicile. In addition, my original Chinese citizenship, acquired through the Honorary Citizenship given by General Chiang Kai Shek to Father for his legal books and the other literary works on China, also helped.

But my dear friends, Kurt and Inna Leuen and Hans Mosberg, received just a few days to prepare to leave. Kurt had barely enough time to rush to his stables in the countryside where he kept a beautiful bay stallion. On weekends he used to enjoy riding in the field surrounding Shanghai. As a former German cavalry officer, the horse was very dear to him; therefore, rather than abandon it to an uncertain future at the hands of Chinese peasants, Kurt forced himself to do what every honorable officer in the same situation would have done. He placed his pistol to the horse's forehead and pulled the trigger. Other Germans also destroyed many of their animals.

The day of my friends' departure arrived. With great sadness, I stood on the wharf watching the line of weary-looking individuals weighed down with suitcases and bundles, the only belongings permitted, trudge across the gangplank to the deck of the immense former ocean liner.

I heard the ship's whistle shriek, announcing its departure. The mooring lines were released and slowly, slowly the vessel started to pull away. I heard no sounds of jubilation from the passengers. In silence, they waved with their handkerchiefs to those who came to see them off. I, too, tearfully waved my hand to my friends, and as they waved back to me, the ship made its way between Chinese junks on the Wang Pu River. Reaching a bend in the river, it disappeared behind the chimney stacks of the high gray factory buildings.

As I turned my steps back to the taxi stand, a sense of utter aloneness overwhelmed me. And I asked, where was justice in this world when good and honest people like my friends were treated in such a heartless manner? Why should millions who had nothing to do with the power ambitions of one crazed, evil man like Hitler, suffer? And a saying came to my mind: "When the forest is cut, splinters will fall."

"Oh, God," I prayed, "in thy infinite wisdom and power, keep my friends. Surround them by thy protection and thy guidance."

Years later I had an opportunity to be in Berlin where Kurt and Inna had settled. By then Kurt was retired and I had a pleasant visit in their comfortable, attractively furnished apartment.

Hans Mosberg's fate was not as good. He and his superior were tried at the Nuremberg Trials. The accusation was that they had supplied information about the location of a U.S. cruiser which Japanese torpedoes had sunk unlawfully, after the surrender. Hans was acquitted, but did not live long after that. One evening, returning home, he was murdered in the street. Why, how, and by whom, was never disclosed by the authorities. I heard rumors that it might have been revenge of some sort.

53

My Return to Tsingtao

My friends' departure in mid 1946, and the circumstances under which they had to leave filled me with insecurity. "What should I do?" was the disturbing question. Should I heed Father's letters advising me to move back to Laoshan where things were back to normal? The situation kept me in a state of quandary. I knew I had to decide, yet I kept postponing the decision until one day Fate itself, as it seemed to me, stepped in to guide me.

It happened one morning. Sung had just placed a tray before me with hot coffee, two soft-boiled eggs, toast, butter and jam, my usual breakfast. Then, instead of going back into the kitchen, he tarried, and cleared his throat several times. I understood that he had something on his mind.

"Yes, what is it?" I asked.

"Missy, maybe you sell house?" he asked with a sly expression on his face.

"Why you ask?"

"I think maybe Missy go to Tsingtao to Father, Mother. Good for children."

"Well, maybe. What will you do then?" I was surprised that he mentioned what I was thinking about myself.

Sung chuckled. "I? No worry."

"Then what about all this?" I waved my hand around my living room, while looking at the carved antique Chinese tables, chests, old rugs, and other curios which I had inherited from Karl.

"Maybe sell some. Some I keep for you my house."

Deep in my heart I knew that Sung was right. It was the sensible thing to return to my parents.

"Well, that sounds easy, but where I find buyer?"

Sung's face beamed.

"No worry. I know Chinese man, Mr. Lee. He give U.S. $3,000 for key money."

"Oh, Sung!" I exclaimed. Three thousand U.S. dollars was a tremendous sum at that time. How ridiculous, I thought.

"Missy, Mr. Lee no joke." Sung looked a little hurt that I should have doubted him. He lowered his head and puckered his lips.

"Well, all right, maybe you bring this Mr. Lee to see the house?"

Sung laughed. "*Ho! Ho!* [Good! Good!] He come five o'clock today."

The rascal, I thought. He knew all along what I would say and had prearranged everything.

Mr. Lee and his wife arrived promptly. They were a very demure, old-fashioned couple, dressed in traditional long black silk Chinese gowns. They bowed to me as they entered, and proceeded in silence to inspect every detail of the town house. Sung followed them respectfully at a distance. Finally, before departing, they consulted with Sung for a few brief moments, then bowed again in my direction and left.

"Well?" I asked Sung with some trepidation, as the possibility of selling at such a good price naturally appealed to me.

"Good, velly, velly good," Sung assured me. Like most Chinese, he had difficulty pronouncing the letter "R." "Mr. Lee say he take house. Pay U.S. $3,000 when have contract. Move after two months."

The result seemed like a miracle to me. With no difficulty, after a little greasing of the palm of the manager-in-charge of Verdun Town Houses, the lease was changed to Mr. Lee's name. Upon receipt of it, Mr. Lee, true to his word, counted out into a tidy pile thirty one-hundred-dollar U.S. bills. The two months permitted me time to arrange my affairs.

I found a good, kind, flaxen-haired Polish woman to be my little girls' nurse. Air transportation had recently been established between Shanghai and Tsingtao, so the girls left with their new nurse on a plane. My Father met them at the airport.

To take my furnishings to Sung's house, I hired a truck. We loaded it and I climbed up into the seat next to the driver. With Sung squatting among the furniture behind, we drove off.

Sung's house was at the end of Avenue Joffre. For a second, this surprised me, because Avenue Joffre was one of the most prestigious streets in the French Concession—a road with elegant shops, large apartment buildings, and houses of the rich. I did not dwell on this fact too long, however.

The driver abruptly turned the corner of Rue Albert, my road, and started down the four-lane Avenue. On both sides I could see big shops, important-looking restaurants, fine bakeries, and elegant furniture stores, with wide windows attractively displaying merchandise to tempt the eye of the pedestrian, as well as attract the attention of the occupants of passing vehicles. We drove on and on. Finally, we reached the residential section. Here, there were large apartment buildings and beautiful houses of European architecture.

I wondered if we had gone too far and was about to say as much to the driver, when I heard Sung tapping on the back window. Slowing down, the driver carefully guided his truck toward the sidewalk and stopped in front of a large iron gate, the kind one finds in China leading into old homestead compounds.

"You made a mistake. We must go back," I protested.

"No mistake, Missy. This belong the address," the driver assured me, pointing to the paper in his hand and the number on the gate. Imagine my astonishment. This place was indeed where Sung was living, and it was not a poor servant's house at all! Surrounded by a high masonry wall, Sung's family had lived here for countless generations. They had held onto this property despite offers of big sums of money for their land.

Climbing out of the back of the truck, Sung rapped the brass knocker several times. The gate slowly swung open and we drove into a spacious brick-paved courtyard, with a well in the middle, surrounded by several lovely old Chinese houses with slanting roof eaves and fretwork decorating their terraces.

"My home, Missy," Sung told me as he opened the car door to let me out. I heard a note of pride in his voice.

"Oh, Sung, why do you work for me as cook boy?" Looking around I saw the abode of a very well-to-do family. I also understood why he did not charge me for rice and flour and bread. He could afford it.

"Missy, if I no work, I play Mahjong, dice. Lose plenty money. Better work." He laughed as he hugged several children who came running and calling him "Pa, Pa, Pa." Behind them hurried several women of different ages. "My sisters, my Mother, my Number-One-Wife, my Number-Two-Wife," Sung introduced them to me.

I had encountered, with Mr. Wu's family, the Chinese weakness for gambling and the impoverishment that could result from it. My Sung had strength enough to realize it, and not having a profession, he did the next best thing. He took a job as a servant. The wages added to his pocket money. The work kept him busy and useful—a good, healthy, practical outlook on life. I was glad that he had found me!

Having shipped my children off to my parents and having safely deposited my valuable pieces of furniture in Sung's safekeeping until such time as it would be possible to have them sent up to Tsingtao, I gave my notice to the Motor Pool and requested that the young Chinese couple move out of my upstairs room.

Everything proceeded peacefully. The Chinese couple moved without protest. They were there just for appearances anyway. Nor did Lt. Drinkwater object to my leaving my secretarial position either. Perhaps he was even glad to get rid of me, as the choice of Russian women secretaries had no limit. He could hire another one with better qualifications—and not only in her clerical skills.

Meanwhile, Christmas was approaching. I hurried to buy everyone presents to take with me, before directing my steps to the airline office to purchase my ticket to Tsingtao.

From the door to the ticket counter, there was a long line of Chinese waiting their turn. In Shanghai, this was a time when we stood in lines everywhere. So, I, too, stood and waited. We moved very slowly, for the Chinese clerks were never in a hurry. For them, time was not equivalent to money as it was with the occidentals. China had lived for millennia within the concept of eternity. Besides, for a self-respecting person to hurry it was considered most undignified.

As a consequence, I crept along at the pace of a snail with the rest of the ticket purchasers. Eventually, even the snail reaches its destination, and I, too, was gratified to see just one man between me and the ticket window. I could even see my name on the list of reservations.

The man ahead of me bought his ticket and I was about to step up when suddenly someone came running into the office. It was a nun in the black habit of the Franciscan Order. In her hand she was frantically waving a telegram. Seeing a religious personage, everyone politely stepped aside. The man at the counter read the telegram and, without hesitation, crossing out my name on the waiting list, issued her a ticket.

I was furious. I demanded an explanation.

The explanation was that the Mother Superior of the Carmelite Sisters in Tsingtao had died. As the Order had a vow of silence, which allowed only the Mother Superior to communicate with the world, the convent was paralyzed. The nun in front of me was the newly nominated Superior of that convent. She had to get there in a hurry.

"Well, that is all fine and all right, but why cross my name from the list?" I demanded.

"So sorry, but that is the only ticket reserved for a European," the clerk explained, closing his desk with a slap.

As I was not easily intimidated, I demanded to see the manager.

"Please, through that door," said the clerk, pointing to a glass door at the end of the room.

The manager, a middle-aged Chinese gentleman in a dark blue European-style suit, listened to me patiently. He took off his glasses, cleaned them with his white linen handkerchief, and sighed deeply. "So sorry, but we have no more seats on that plane. Please come next week," he said politely in perfect English. At the same time he firmly grasped me by the elbow and led me out of his office.

There was not very much I could do but return home. I had previously informed my parents of the exact date on which I was to arrive. As we had no long-distance telephone service, I decided to notify them by telegram of the change of plans. There was really no hurry, as the original reservation was for a plane leaving in two days.

Strangely enough, though, the next morning I awoke with a start and a feeling of urgency. I felt that I should not wait, but should go immediately to send the telegram. Why? I could not say. I just had to.

Springing out of bed, I pulled on my clothes. I took the first pedicab to the telegraph office, and I sent, care of our friends, the Kushnareffs, the message that I would be arriving the following week instead.

The next evening on the radio, it was announced that a plane had crashed while approaching Tsingtao Airport. A treacherous fog had obstructed the mountain range over which the pilot had to fly. The plane struck the ridge. The announcer also mentioned that on this plane was the new Mother Superior of the Carmelite Convent.

When, a week later, I arrived in Tsingtao on another plane, my Father told me that he had been at the Kushnareffs in expectation of my arrival when they heard the horrifying news on the radio. Fortunately, my reassuring telegram had reached them almost simultaneously.

Then, as we made ourselves comfortable in the car to leave for Laoshan, Father looked pensively at me. "You know," he said, "I was thinking, you must not have been ready for the other world. That is why that poor nun took your place." As was his nature, he had interpreted and saw meaning in the remarkable way I had been saved from the plane crash. "There must still be much ahead of you," he added.

Indeed, how correct he was!

54

On the Road to Laoshan

But that day, as we were driving through Tsingtao on our way to Laoshan, my own thoughts dwelt more on the present than on the far-off future. My return to Laoshan was perplexing to me and the recollection of the isolation of former days was frightening to me. I kept these thoughts to myself, however, and was soon distracted by the sight of places which brought back pleasant memories. There on the right, I saw the wide show windows of the Peterhansel haberdashery, and I wondered what my handsome blond Peter Peterhansel, who had looked at me with such meaningful smiles while we sat in the gazebo overlooking the rivulet, in the days of my sojourn at Dr. Bergman's sanatorium, was doing now. Then, across the street from the store, was the German bakery and tea room, which had such delicious hot chocolate and pastries.

Now, as we were driving around a gray, circular, three-storied building, the town's market, I recalled how my mother and I used to browse along its maze of passages. Whatever you wanted for a sumptuous meal was there: live fish in buckets, live chickens and poults in cages, pigs, piglets, beef cut to your specifications, and, in addition, there were tons upon tons of fruit and fresh vegetables, all recently delivered from Formosa. Ah! What a delight for a discriminating cook!

Skirting the market building, we entered another street, a shortcut to the outskirts of Tsingtao. The street traversed the Japanese section of the city.

"My goodness! What has happened here?" I exclaimed, shocked by what I was seeing. The former area of tidy wooden Japanese houses with their miniature traditional gardens, and rows of shops well stocked with merchandise—an orderly community of Japanese residents and merchants—was now a scene of rubble. Doors and windows of every house hung loose on their hinges. Shattered glass littered the pavement. The shops, doors ajar, were empty and not soul was in sight. Only a couple of half-starved dogs and cats were scavenging among the piles of refuse. Fearing our approach, they hid themselves cautiously behind the debris.

"It is said, 'When a forest is cut down the splinters will fly!'" Father remarked sadly.

"What happened? And where are the Japanese?"

"They have been hurriedly repatriated to Japan," Father explained.

"How come?"

"When Japan surrendered and the American Navy steamed into the Tsingtao harbor, orders were received for all Japanese residents to be taken in trucks to the wharf to wait for their turns on the military transports. Meanwhile, their unprotected houses and stores were looted by the Chinese. Even on the wharf they were harassed. Gangs of Chinese snatched blankets, food, and their other meager necessities, until a few American officers formed a group to take turns patrolling."

"What a sad commentary on us humans." I could not help expressing my disgust.

"Alas, it is so." Father shook his head and, to change the subject, he continued, "We must be close to the country road. Yes, there it is." He pointed ahead where I could see the beginning of open fields.

The road had suddenly changed from asphalt to dirt, yet smooth enough for comfortable passage.

On both sides of us, as far as the eye could see, stretched miles upon miles of open fields covered with thick stubble left after the cutting of the crops.

Soon, I saw on the horizon the roofline of the town of Licun, the largest town between Tsingtao and Laoshan, and an important center of commerce and a stop for buses. Roads from various parts of the Shantung Province crossed here.

In the days of the Japanese occupation, Licun was as far as the car could go. From here donkeys or sedan chairs were the only means of transportation to Laoshan and Rock Mansions.

Now, as in those days, the bus depot had a crowd of recently arrived passengers and the town square was filled with travelers. Some were hurrying to the portable restaurants to sit under the white awnings and eat steaming hot noodles with tofu, rice with pork, or some other specialty of that particular restaurant. Others directed their steps to the open stalls, where I could hear vendors proclaiming, in loud singsong manner, the advantageous prices of their fabrics, spices, baskets, metal objects, and many other articles, anything a farmer or his wife might desire.

As we slowly progressed through the crowd, with our chauffeur tooting and shouting to clear the way, we finally reached the donkey square. Now as before these useful but stubborn creatures were giving trouble to their owners.

Loaded with baskets of eggs, cabbages, or sacks of grain, some with women and children on their backs, the beasts were resisting their masters' commands. No merciless beating with whips, prodding with rods, shouting, or pulling of bridles induced them to move forward until the notion came of their own free will. From that moment on the creature became the most patient, enduring, tireless, and reliable means of transportation and conveyance of goods. Besides the donkey, China had no other beast of burden except human backs. Horses were a precious commodity reserved for government officials and the rich. Both the Mongols and the Arabs had a bond with their steeds. The Bedouins depended on the camel. In China, the lowly donkey was all important.

Leaving Licun and the donkeys behind, we were again on the main road. Continuing in a north-easterly direction, we passed the family cemetery with its aged ginkgo trees behind the masonry wall, and in about an hour or so, we finally reached the first mountain range where the road zigzagged up to the pass overlooking the central Laoshan valley.

"Stop! Stop!" I cried out to the chauffeur, who was about to continue downward.

The car stopped. I got out. The air was filled with the scent of pines that covered the mountainside we had ascended and the panorama before me was just as beautiful as I had remembered. Step-like fields rose up from the very bottom of the valley where a rivulet meandered, to the very top, creating a picturesque effect. The moderate climate of Shantung Province, even during the winter month of December, permitted work to continue; and here and there I saw the peasants in their blue cotton-wadded coats and trousers tilling the land, in preparation for the next season's sowing.

Meanwhile, on open terraces, between great boulders, near mud-brick cottages, women, with tiny children strapped to their backs, busied themselves with their chores; some ground grain with mallets, others fed chickens or fanned their small outdoor charcoal stoves, preparing the evening meal, while above them, completing the picture, white puffy clouds drifted.

"How lovely and how timeless," I said, turning to Father, who was looking at the view through the open window of the car.

He nodded. "In China all is timeless. The Mongols, the Manchus, the greedy White Devils"—(the Chinese name for Europeans)—"or the Japanese can come and conquer. Without resisting and with great patience learned through the suffering of hundreds of years. Holding onto their ancient customs, the Chinese absorbed these intruders, whose monuments alone testify to their brief presence." For a few minutes Father was silent.

"China and the Chinese have stayed the same, an enduring culture resting on the principles of family loyalty and Confucius' precepts. Thus it was for hundreds of years and so it will continue. Maybe, on the surface, the outer trappings or manners will alter, in urban areas. But in the vast interior, the Chinese soul will remain as it has been from time immemorial." Lighting a cigarette, he inhaled from it deeply, and exhaled its smoke. "What a civilization!" Father shook his head with a smile.

In the tone of his voice I read the deep love he had for his adopted country that had so generously permitted the many poor Russian refugees to settle, live and prosper within its boundaries.

"Drive on, Wu," Father instructed the chauffeur. I climbed back into my seat.

With extreme caution, the chauffeur drove the car down the sloping road and into the parking lot in the center of Laoshan. We parked near several sedan chairs awaiting customers. One of the chairs was Father's. Bowing and smiling, his two bearers greeted him.

I looked around. It had been more than six years—and what seemed like a lifetime's worth of living—since I had been here, yet it was just as I had remembered: the rivulet gurgling as its waters washed over rocks and boulders, and there, on the opposite bank, was the clearing whence the path rose up the mountainside to the place where Karl and I had encountered Mao Tse-tung's sentinel, who had brought us to the Fifth Army's encampment. A nostalgia for those lovely, carefree days overwhelmed me.

I had to turn away, to distract myself. Forcing myself to look in the opposite direction, I was gratified to see that many of the summer houses strewn about the mountain slopes were being occupied. German flags, with black, red, and orange stripes, fluttered in the breeze. One flag, however, hanging from the balcony of the Swiss chalet which my family had occupied in the past, was different, with horizontal stripes of red, white, and blue.

"Father, what flag is that?" I asked, pointing to the chalet.

"That's the Netherlands'. And, by the way, a very pleasant lady from the Dutch East Indies is living in the chalet now. Make sure that you meet her." Father waved his hand to tell to the chair bearers to start.

"*Ho! Ho!*" called out the front carrier.

"*Ho! Ho!*" answered the one in the rear, signaling that he was ready. With another "*Ho,*" in unison, they lifted the chair and, before I could say another word to Father, they were carrying him away at a fast, steady clip. I followed, trying to keep up as best I could.

In less than fifteen minutes, walking a mile and a half on a winding trail, we had scaled a knoll, and were approaching the little "Miao," on the left. The small figurine of the protecting deity was inside, peering in the direction of Pei Chui Shui village and Rock Mansions in the distance. It was at this place that I had first met Karl.

I paused pensively near the "Miao." How unpredictable life could be. Who would have thought that some six years later I would be standing in the same place looking over Pei Chui Shui's straw-thatched roofs at Rock Mansions, as his widow. Just as at that first meeting, the setting sun was coloring Rock Mansions' silvery granite walls golden, while on the upper terrace, from a tall flagpole, our white flag with my initials and crown in blue was waving in the wind.

Father had not neglected to hoist our flag and it greeted us as we approached. It was our banner and a symbol of courage and challenge to life's adversity.

"*Ni Hao ma Xsiao Jie?* [Are you well?] *Ni Hao ma?*" several peasant women, clad in their gray wadded cotton winter jackets and trousers, called out from their doorways. They had recognized me as I walked through the narrow street of the village and were greeting me according to propriety.

"*Hen hao xie-xie ni* [Well, thank you]," I answered, waving back to them as I hurried through the dust-filled passage onto the trail which led to the waterfall and passed the entrance to Rock Mansions. In a few minutes I reached the first of our one hundred and twenty-nine steps.

As I started to climb, I was pleased to see the tall lilac bushes which I had planted near the stairs when the house was built. They had grown from tiny one-foot plants to more than six feet. The climbing roses on either side of the entrance to our widest terrace above, had also spread. "What a mass of pink blooms it must be in May," I said to myself, pleased with the results of my careful planting and recalling how I used to collect the donkeys' and goats' droppings on the road into a basket to use as fertilizer.

And what a surprise awaited me on the terrace just below the house! The two arborvitae I had placed in the round beds in the middle of the lawns had grown from three feet to over twelve feet.

"Mama, Mama!" I heard my girls shouting excitedly. Stesha, their Polish nurse, was helping them down the last flight of stairs.

"My darlings! My darlings!" I grasped them close to me, hugging and kissing them.

"They watched for you the whole day," Stesha laughed. "Now, girls, let's take Mama to Grandmother. She is waiting upstairs."

Regina and little four-year-old Carola obediently took me by my hands and we slowly walked up to where my mother was standing. I noticed how much thinner she was and how her face was lined with wrinkles, making her look older and haggard.

Poor, poor woman, I thought, putting my arms around her tenderly. In the past, we had never been close. Her difficult temper and unpredictable moods had always created a barrier between us; but at this moment, after my own sufferings, I had more compassion and understanding for this sick woman, who had endured with my crippled Father the pressures of the times since leaving Russia, and had stood firmly by him as his nurse and constant companion. In her own way, she had displayed fortitude every day of her life.

"Where are you all?" I heard my Father's voice coming from the great room, bringing me back from my dreaming to my surroundings.

I entered the cathedral-ceilinged living-dining room and was immediately enveloped in the pleasant warmth coming from the burning birch logs in the fireplace. The flickering and sputtering of cinders also added a joyful note to the austere, dark-wood paneling of the large room.

At the far end of the room, Father had already taken his usual observation post, in his favorite chair, to the right of the wall-to-wall picture window. With cigarette in hand, he was watching the eastern valley where the last sun rays illuminated the mountain's peak. For a few minutes, the peak flashed bright yellow. Then, as the sun hid itself behind the opposite range, the light faded away. The view of the rivulet, the winding trail, and the valley's oblique slopes gradually began disappearing into the evening shadows, leaving a feeling of sadness—the end of another day.

Then, suddenly, I was aware of how much we depended on the sun, how all life depended on it, and how it influenced our moods. When the sun was in the sky, our spirits soared. With the sun hidden behind the clouds on rainy days, we might feel depressed...

"Call Hsiao Lee. He must light the candles," my Father's voice interrupted my thoughts.

Father's request came just as Hsiao Lee, our Number-One-Boy, brought in a ladder, and in a few seconds was climbing it and lighting one by one the twenty candles in the wrought-iron chandelier hanging from the ceiling. What a glow they produced in the room!

There is no illumination as soft as the light coming from burning candles. It seems to soften hard edges and makes people, especially women, look younger and lovelier.

That evening, after dinner and after my two little girls had been snugly tucked into their beds, Father, Mother, Stesha, and I sat chatting for quite some time in the comfortable overstuffed chairs by the fireplace. The candles and the glow from the burning logs lent a cozy and secure atmosphere around us.

On the other side of our picture window, it was pitch dark, awaiting the sunrise of a new day.

Because of the absence of guests that holiday season, our family celebrated Christmas and New Year's Eve quietly.

As tradition called for, we had decorated a medium-sized spruce with ornaments kept since my own childhood days. Strings of tinsel, glittering crystal stars, multicolored balls of various sizes, and little Santas hung on the branches. At the very top of the tree we placed a lovely toy angel with a trumpet.

Regina and Carola were delighted when they awoke on Christmas morning and everyone was pleased with the presents: scarves, gloves, and blouses for the adults, and toys for the children.

According to an old Russian custom, on New Year's Eve at midnight, we wrote down our wishes for the following year and, as the clock was still striking twelve, we burnt the paper over a candle. A superstition? Who knows? But it had never failed me.

Regina, Carola and Marianna's daughter, Helen - 1947

55

Lili Van Ditmars

The month of January went by with no change in our quiet daily routine. Lunch followed breakfast, a brisk walk in the afternoon, some reading in front of the fireplace in the great room, dinner, and off to bed by eight-thirty.

Father must have noticed my ennui because, one afternoon while I was reading, he interrupted me.

"Have you been to see Lili van Ditmars?"

"No, I have not," I answered.

"Why not? You might find her a pleasant friend. It may be worth your while to make the effort."

I did not answer. I did not want to tell him that the memory of the unhappy events during our residence in the chalet made me reluctant to go there.

But Father persisted. "I have a feeling it may be worth your effort," he repeated.

Hmmm…There he goes again with his feelings, I thought. So, to please him I said, "All right, I will go to see her tomorrow."

The next day I did go up to the Swiss chalet. With somewhat mixed feelings, I knocked on the entrance door. After a few minutes I heard brisk steps and the door opened. Before me stood a striking-looking lady in her early fifties, I guessed. She was about my own height, five feet seven inches, with shoulder-length snow-white hair. Her features were not particularly beautiful, but she had the darkest, most piercing black eyes. Dressed as a man, in trousers, turtleneck jersey, and tweed jacket, she was very different in appearance and composure from anyone I had encountered so far.

"I hope I am not disturbing you. I am Muse Spanier," I introduced myself. "My parents own Rock Mansions."

"Lili van Ditmars," she said with a heavy Nordic accent, extending her hand. She grasped my hand firmly. "Pleased to meet you. Come in."

I entered the living room. It all looked the same as when we had lived there—the natural pine paneling, the small round three-legged tables, the slant-front pine desk in the corner, and the cuckoo clock ticking over the mantel.

"A cup of coffee or tea?" Lili offered. "I have just baked some good old-fashioned Dutch cookies."

"A cup of tea would be splendid and I will certainly enjoy your Dutch cookies," I replied.

"Then I will hurry," Lili laughed, as she abruptly made a roundabout turn, disappearing into the next room. In no time, she returned carrying a large black-lacquer tray. On it, under a yellow and green floral tea cozy, I saw the teapot, cups, and a plate with dollar-sized round cookies sprinkled with powdered sugar mixed with cinnamon. I found them to have a delicious flavor as they melted in my mouth.

Listening to Lili and how she escaped to China from Sumatra and eventually came to Laoshan was fascinating. The afternoon flew by. As the days were short, I had to depart.

"Be sure to come back soon!" Lili called out as I hurried down the path from the Swiss chalet.

"I will, I will!" I shouted back. I hurried to the left, around a group of rocks, and entered the clearing which led to the parking lot from where the wider trail took me to Rock Mansions.

Thus began my friendship with this very interesting and unique lady.

"Well, how did it go?" Father looked eager to know the results of my visit to Lili. I recounted to him the details of our meeting.

"There must be an interesting story about why she is here from the Dutch East Indies," Father concluded, as he braced himself to rise from his armchair to go to the dining table, where Hsiao Lee had arranged our dinner around the silver candelabra with eight burning candles.

My friendship with Lili van Ditmars grew. Once or twice each week I would visit her. Lili always greeted me in a most warm and friendly manner, making my visits comfortable and enjoyable by preparing and serving exotic East Indian dishes.

Whenever I ventured to inquire how she had found her way into our distant mountains, she tried to evade direct answers. I could see that speaking of her home was painful for her, so I did not press her. With time, however, as we became better friends, Lili told me her sad story.

She was from Holland originally, where she had married a Dutch rubber planter from Sumatra, who had come in search of a wife. It was a custom in the colonies to bring wives from the homeland, thereby retaining the purity of blood.

"I had adapted easily to the isolation of a vast rubber plantation near Medan on the Island of Sumatra. I helped my husband to manage the natives who worked on the plantation. I also became proficient in delivering babies. With my knowledge, I introduced hygiene into the nearby villages, and helped many of the native women who otherwise might have died in childbirth, a common occurrence in that tropical environment. I was much respected and many a time was called to assist even on the other plantations. Sometimes I had to ride a horse for several hours to get there," Lili told me with great satisfaction in her voice. She turned her head to look out of the window and her dark eyes filled with tears. Slowly, absent-mindedly she refilled her cup.

I sensed that she wanted to share with me some painful memories. Respectfully, I kept my silence, waiting for her to begin. After a while, she cleared her throat.

"You cannot imagine those horrible days of fear and uncertainty when the Japanese forces took Sumatra. Like locusts, their soldiers scattered over our island, knocking on doors, rounding up any Dutch men they could find, including my husband and my son Philip, incarcerating everyone, into extremely primitive camps in the jungles. The bare rations and harsh treatment took their toll. Many prisoners succumbed to disease and died. Those remaining met an even more tragic fate when news reached the Japanese garrison that Japan had surrendered.

"The Medan Camp's commander, a crazed, sadistic, man, ordered all the prisoners to be decapitated. My husband, too, was slated for decapitation. Philip managed to survive, however. He hid during the ensuing turmoil. That night, with help from a native boy, he escaped into the jungle."

Lili got up slowly from her chair, went to the slant-front desk, and took a photograph out of a drawer. "Here is my Philip." She handed me the picture. "This was taken four years ago as I was leaving. Isn't he handsome?"

I looked at the photo and had to agree wholeheartedly that indeed Philip was handsome. Smiling pleasantly, he stood against the backdrop of foliage in a white sports shirt, with his strong muscular arms showing.

"Philip is six feet tall. He has dark hair and my eyes." Lili gave a funny little laugh. "'You are thirty-three years old,' I keep writing to him. 'You must find yourself a good wife.'" She looked at me and paused to be sure I caught her meaning. "Now he is managing a large rubber plantation."

"You certainly can be proud of him. But tell me, how did you get away?" I changed the subject. But Lili did not answer immediately. She arose to arrange the burning logs in the fireplace. Then she turned to me.

"Well…you see…we all knew what to expect. In 1939, my husband insisted that I leave. At that time, we could transfer our savings out of Sumatra through the Dutch Bank to Holland or Hong Kong. I went first to the Philippines. Then I flew to Hong Kong, Shanghai, and finally a friend suggested Tsingtao as a good, quiet, inexpensive place to live. I met Mrs. Bernhard. She offered me her Swiss chalet. So here I am."

"Well, I am glad you are here! However, it is getting late and I must be on my way," I said, hearing the cuckoo in the clock announcing five. As I got up to leave, Lili stopped me.

"Wait a minute. Before you go, I would like to ask you if would mind if Philip writes to you."

The question somewhat startled me. Yet, at the same time, the thought was appealing. "Why not?" I replied.

Several weeks later, during one of my visits, Lili, with a grin like a Cheshire cat, placed into my hand a small white envelope. "From Philip. He had inserted it with his letter to me. If you want to answer, I can send yours with mine. It's simpler that way." Then, after clearing her throat, she added, "Let me assure you my son is an honorable man."

I could see that she was apprehensive that I might misinterpret Philip's good intentions.

"I have no doubt that he is," I hurried to reassure her mother's fearful heart, "and I certainly will answer his letter."

Thus a correspondence between Philip van Ditmars and myself was initiated.

Philip wrote in a small, bead-like handwriting, which, to me, showed his precise, careful nature. He described in great detail how he managed the large rubber plantation and took responsibility for the well-being of the natives who worked for him. All alone, his only satisfaction was in doing his duty to keep up his family's holdings. It was not an easy life, surrounded for miles by jungle and cut off from civilization on the exotic island of Sumatra.

I read Philip's letters with fascination. They introduced me to a world so unlike my own. Little by little, I developed a warm, loving feeling for this obviously very fine man. His interest in me also lessened by pain of aloneness, giving me hope. The letters were like a shaft of light cutting through the clouds of my and my girls' uncertain futurity. I waited eagerly for them.

56

Some Unusual Guests at Rock Mansions

Meanwhile, due to the improved roads, business at Rock Mansions that Spring improved considerably. A steady trickle of weekend guests kept us busy.

Father assigned to me the duty of greeting and seeing to the comfort of our visitors, a sort of maître d'hôtel.

"This will be a great opportunity for you to learn more about human nature. You know, managers of hotels acquire such an insight that, at a glance, they can tell precisely the balance in a patron's checking account."

Why I should develop the skill of knowing people's finances was not clear to me. On the other hand, understanding people and developing insight might be of great help in my future. Therefore, I took Father seriously and, as guests arrived, I carefully noted their peculiarities and found many opportunities to observe human behavior.

As an example, consider Mrs. Bluitz. The day before she arrived, a runner brought us a telegram: "WIFE, CHILD, NURSE ARRIVING MARCH 10. REQUEST ROOMS. WILL REMIT PAYMENT WHEN NOTIFIED. SIGNED SAM BLUITZ."

"Strange. No mention of the duration of stay," Father remarked, rubbing his chin thoughtfully. "Well, give her the two adjoining East rooms and the bathroom," he instructed me.

As time was short, Hsiao Lee and I rushed to arrange the accommodations. We polished the floor, shook the rug, dusted, washed the windows, fluffed up the pillows, and spread our best linens on the bed. As a final touch, a vase with lilacs from one of our bushes was placed on the dresser. Looking around, I thought the room was more than adequate. The second room for the child and the nurse was just as carefully prepared.

The following day, Mrs. Bluitz, a petite, peroxide blond in her late thirties, arrived in a sedan chair, holding her three-year-old daughter. Behind her walked the Chinese nurse and two coolies bent over under the weight of two huge suitcases.

"Looks like she is here to stay," Father observed, placing his monocle to his eye as he sat on our top terrace.

I greeted Mrs. Bluitz cordially. She returned my greetings with a nod of her head.

I said, "May I escort you to your rooms, Mrs. Bluitz?" She nodded as she got out of the sedan chair.

"Hope the beds are soft. I have difficulty sleeping, you know," she began as we were walking down the corridor.

"Our mattresses are horsehair, not spring. But the guests have not complained," I answered.

"Oh, well," she shrugged her shoulders. "I presume your closets are sufficient for all my dresses?"

"We have garderobes."

"What's that?" Mrs. Bluitz, asked, raising her eyebrows as she entered the room and pointing with her finger to the large piece of furniture with a mirror on the door in the far corner.

"The French call them garderobes. In English it is a wardrobe." As I was speaking, my heart sank at the sight of Hsiao Lee dragging in Mrs. Bluitz's large suitcases. "There is another wardrobe in your daughter's room," I quickly added. "The two will be enough."

"I certainly hope so," Mrs. Bluitz sighed.

"Mrs. Bluitz, these are rustic surroundings, but we will do our best to make you comfortable." I bowed, making my exit. When I told Father about my first experience with Mrs. Bluitz, he shook his head ominously.

"I wonder why her husband sent her here? We may have trouble."

However, the first week of Mrs. Bluitz's stay went by tolerably well. She took several long walks into the mountains, which gave her a good appetite. She appeared at dinner beautifully attired and ate whatever was served with relish, retiring to bed early.

Another week passed. Mrs. Bluitz took her walks as usual. Her appetite was quite good, but she began inquiring if there were any letters for her. There were none. Meanwhile, Mr. Bluitz had sent money as Father requested.

The third week began. Mrs. Bluitz was changing. Usually immaculately dressed at dinner, she now came carelessly clothed and she barely touched her food.

"Aren't there letters for me? I want to go home," she kept telling me. I became worried.

"Father, shouldn't you write to Mr. Bluitz? His silence is strange."

"Well, it is really not our business to get involved in family affairs," Father answered.

But as the days went by, Mrs. Bluitz started to take her frustrations out on Father's most sensitive spot, his pride and joy in his menus and our cook's culinary achievements. As soon as Hsiao Lee would place her plate in front of her, she would sniff loudly.

"Feeh! This smells!" she would comment, wrinkling her nose as she poked her fork into the meat or vegetables. Nothing can be so contagious at a communal table than a finicky neighbor's remark. Before I knew it, the other guests, too, would examine their plates and this one would find his meat underdone, another, just the opposite.

One evening Father's menu called for filet mignon with a special truffle sauce, which he considered a pièce de résistance.

"These mushrooms are spoiled. Look! They are black!" Mrs. Bluitz said, raising her voice, and scraped the precious fungus off the meat. "Hsiao Lee, take it back to the kitchen!"

Later, when I described the situation to my Father, he took it as a personal affront.

"What ignorance!" he said. "Truffles are always black. Our Tah Po is the best of cooks and your Mother, who supervises the kitchen, is very careful about the freshness of every product that is served. This cannot continue. Mrs. Bluitz will have to leave."

"But, Father, how can we get rid of her? She has no money to buy her tickets on the ship."

"I will see to it." Father's voice sounded determined. He sent Mr. Bluitz a short letter saying that he was sorry, but Mrs. Bluitz would have to go home. He wrote that if he, Mr. Bluitz, did not wire the money for her passage, Father would pay for it himself—and how would that look when people heard about it? This little bit of blackmail worked. Mr. Bluitz telegraphed the money. Several days later, Mrs. Bluitz was able to go back to Shanghai on one of the Japanese marus.

It was with mixed feelings that I waved goodbye to Mrs. Bluitz as she stepped into the sedan chair with her child. As her sedan chair, followed by the nurse and the two coolies with her heavy luggage, disappeared down our one hundred and twenty-nine steps. Though I breathed a sigh of relief, and was glad that she had left us, I wondered with sorrow what the future might hold for this unhappy woman.

Of course, not all of our guests gave us serious problems. Some difficulties had a touch of humor. Mr. James Brown's visit comes to mind. Mr. Brown, a prosperous Shanghai jeweler and a most cordial gentleman, breezed in unannounced.

"I need a few days of rest. I do hope you can accommodate me." He bowed politely as he entered our great room. He was a tall, decorous gentleman with black shiny hair, slicked down with pomade.

"You are most welcome," Father said, arising from his green chair to shake Mr. Brown's hand.

As Mr. Brown walked across the room, I noticed a unique fragrance.

All went very well. Mr. Brown liked his room, bed, and our service. At the first meal he consumed more than his share.

"Now *that* is a guest! And what a connoisseur of cuisine," observed Father, quite pleased.

Everything was progressing satisfactorily. The next evening, however, Mr. Brown entered our hall waving his arms, swatting the left and right sides of his neck and face.

"Is anything wrong, Mr. Brown?" I asked, somewhat taken aback by his behavior.

"Forgive me, but the bugs, you have so many bugs!" And smack went his right hand on his forehead.

I looked around. Everyone else sat quietly. Bugs? I thought. What bugs? We were at a high, dry, mountain elevation with window screens.

"No one has ever complained of bugs before," Father reacted angrily when I told him of Mr. Brown's discomfort.

But high mountains and screens or not, there sat Mr. Brown in obvious agony, pursued by insects, waving his arms to chase the nasty varmints away.

I decided to look into this puzzlement, suspecting that it might be his imagination. But as I approached him, I found, to my surprise, that there were, indeed, several flies and mosquitoes, even a ladybug, flying around him. But why were the insects bothering him and not the others? Then it dawned on me...

"Mr. Brown, what is that lovely smelling eau de cologne you are using?"

"That's Olympia, an exceptional oil for my hair. I brought it from Greece."

"You don't think it might be attracting the bugs like a love call?"

"You know, strange that you should mention it. I thought of it yesterday," Mr. Brown admitted. "I will try not using it for a few days."

Being a reasonable man, he stopped using the Olympia and, miraculously, the bugs stopped gathering around him. Mr. Brown did have some difficulties keeping his thick hair in place, but in our bucolic surroundings it mattered not.

When Mr. Brown came to bid goodbye, his hair was again slick and shining, and as he walked away down our steps, the alluring of Olympia drifted toward me, spread by the gentle mountain breeze.

I also found some of our guests' national traits worth observing.

I remember particularly our German visitors who had frequented our Laoshan mountains during the war years of 1939–1940, when I had met Karl Spanier. Many were distinguished-looking diplomats. We received their reservations for rooms and private baths way in advance, always written in the most precise and polite terms. On the date specified, undaunted by the bad roads, our German guests would arrive in sedan chairs or on foot, usually in parties of four or six.

After taking their showers, and unpacking in an orderly manner according to lists which remained visible on the chests of drawers, at five-thirty in the evening it was time for "schnapps" in our great room. After that, we were requested to serve dinner precisely at six-thirty, which ended, in the winter months, with a demitasse of coffee and a small glass of a liqueur in front of the fireplace. By nine o'clock, everyone retired to be ready and in full strength for the next day's enjoyment—mountain climbing.

The next day started again with showers, breakfast on the dot of eight, followed by a day-long excursion with a box lunch, which Mother would be careful to fill with every kind of delicacy, including various sandwiches, potato salad, deviled eggs, and fruit—grapes, peaches, pears or apples, according to the season. Water and a thermos of hot coffee completed the provisions for the knapsack.

Our German guests returned from their walks in good time for another shower before schnapps, and after dinner, they would again retire early to bed. As long as we were punctual, the high quality of food maintained, and plenty of hot and cold water for showers supplied, we heard no complaints from our methodical guests. Nor were there any problems to interfere with their obvious love and enjoyment of nature.

To our surprise, however, during their stay we suddenly experienced difficulties from the most unexpected quarter, our water carriers. We had four strong men who carried water from the river all day. Due to the fastidious use of water by our German guests, plus the normal consumption in the kitchen, our five large water tanks, converted from former diesel oil barrels, would empty too fast, to the total frustration of our carriers.

Each of the four men carried two five-gallon buckets filled with water on wooden poles slung over their shoulders. They would struggle up the one hundred and twenty-nine steps, and then forty more steps up the wooden stairs to the top of the house where the water tanks were located. From there the water ran through the pipes into the kitchen and the three bathrooms. Hour after hour the men carried and poured, carried and poured—a non-stop, back-breaking labor. Then, just when the tanks were full, the water level suddenly dropped, which always took place during the morning and evening hours. Something had to be wrong...

The water carriers ran to Tah Po, our cook. "A pipe is leaking! A pipe is leaking!" they shouted. "We stop! We stop!"

In a panic, Tah Po rushed to Father. "The water carriers don't want to work!!" he said, wringing his hands nervously.

"Calm, calm, Tah Po. It's only our German visitors are very clean," Father tried to explain, understanding what was happening. "Our guests like to wash in hot baths and showers."

"Cannot, cannot! How can people wash so often?" Tah Po could not understand, nor could the water carriers. How could they be expected to? They, like all peasants and common folk in China, undertook a trip to the public "hot baths" only rarely, maybe once or twice a year, before the Chinese New Year or some other exceptional occasion. The rest of the time, an occasional rubdown of the body and the most important parts with steaming hot wet towels was considered more than sufficient. With difficulty, after a great deal of bargaining and a raise of several coppers per hour,

Father succeeded in persuading the carriers that no leakage existed, and they reluctantly resumed their duties.

When the time came for our German guests to leave us, having packed their belongings according to their lists, and leaving adequate tips for our help, the water level in the tanks returned to its normal levels at the different times of the day. The water carriers had fewer trips to the rivulet, and calm and serenity were restored to Rock Mansions.

When the war ended in 1945, and most Germans in Shanghai and Tsingtao were deported to their homeland, the American ships dropped their anchors in the Tsingtao harbor. In the meantime, our country roads were repaired by the new Chinese government of Shantung Province. So, in late 1946, when I returned to Rock Mansions with my children, we had a different type of visitor. American naval personnel and their families drove in their jeeps to Laoshan.

These people were young, healthy, energetic, and full of life. A fixed schedule meant nothing to them. They filled every hour with excitement. Instead of hot showers, they went swimming in the mountain rivulet, and enjoyed picnics on the bank. They hiked for hours to different temples, and returned invigorated and ready for cocktails, which they drank to all hours of the evening.

When we finally served dinner, they ate with gusto. They tipped Hsiao Lee generously, as though money grew on trees for them, nor did they forget our kitchen staff and the water carriers.

Hsiao Lee, Tah Po, and the four water carriers would line up on the top terrace to see the *Yung-wen*, the Americans, leave. They would bow and bow, and wave and wave their hands, shouting, "*Ten hao xie xie!* [Good, very good, thank you!]"

One of the memorable American families who visited us after my return, were the Ramosas. They left an impression on me.

A naval officer, Captain Ramosa was eventually promoted to admiral. In appearance and bearing, he reminded me of a proud American Indian Chief, and later I learned that he, indeed, had Indian blood. His Spanish wife had an alabaster complexion, dark brown hair, and large black eyes that sparkled when she laughed. I especially liked their daughter, Agnes. She was a beautiful tall girl with thick wavy black hair falling down to her shoulders.

During the several weekends that they stayed with us, Agnes and I became great friends and took many walks together. Soon after, when my Father received an offer to be the Councilor to the Governor and we all moved to Tsingtao, the Ramosas invited me several times to their parties, where I met the "brass" of the

United States 7th Fleet. This relationship enabled me to get a much needed job in the Fleet Headquarters.

Though delightful and generous people, the visits of the United States naval officers and their families were infrequent. Yet our considerable staff had to be fed and paid, and our family sustained. This required substantial, steady income.

Father continued to advertise in the Tsingtao and Shanghai papers, meeting with no response. The foreign residents of these cities were too preoccupied with rebuilding their businesses and had neither the time nor the money for pleasure trips.

To help, I dipped into my own savings, the "key money" for my house, but could not continue to do so indefinitely, as it was the only small security that my girls and I had. Our future looked bleak. To add to our fears, we also kept hearing persistent rumors that the political situation in China was explosive and that a confrontation between the Nationalist forces of Generalissimo Chiang Kai Shek and the Communist Fifth Army of Mao Tse-tung was inevitable.

Mother and I felt that we should make a decision as to whether we would continue to stay in Laoshan or not. She had an idea that might meet with Father's approval. I agreed with her totally, urging her to speak to him without delay.

Mother seldom offered advice, but when she did, I noted that it always had considerable practical merit. No doubt she had inherited this practical side from her shrewd peasant Father, who had become a very rich manufacturer before the Russian Revolution.

One morning, when Father, awaiting the letter carrier, was sitting on the top terrace in his usual place, Mother decided that the time was right to speak to him. I was watching from our entrance doorway, as Mother pulled up one of the deck chairs.

"Tolichka," as she always called Father endearingly, "I was thinking," she began in a timid sort of way.

"Yes, Dear, what about?" Father answered absent-mindedly, without taking his eyes from the trail beyond the roofs of the Pei Chui Shui village.

"Well, I really believe that we should move to Tsingtao. It would be wise, you know. All these disturbing rumors of what may happen in China are frightening."

Father glanced at Mother, obviously surprised. "Now, now, Lubochka, it may all blow over. The Chinese are sensible people." He patted her gently on the arm. "Remember, we have weathered tougher times."

"Tolichka, listen to me. Now is the time. You have connections in Tsingtao. All of our guerrillas are now officials in the Shantung Government. You may get a job there or you can start again your legal profession and…"

Father regarded Mother with sadness. "Lubochka, even if we should move, where would we find a house big enough for our family and cheap enough that we could afford it?"

I felt that this was the time for me to step into their discussion.

"Father, I totally agree with Mother. It makes sense."

Father puckered his lips as he stroked his short-clipped moustache. "Well, maybe, but…," and his voice faded away. He looked sad and dejected, and his lower lip kept twitching.

I knew what that meant. It was so difficult for him even to think about leaving his beloved Rock Mansions. "My last creative endeavor," he called it, in a "life of a man full of great designs and insignificant achievements." Father even desired this to be his epitaph on his tombstone.

To show that I understood him, I put my arms around his shoulders and kissed him lovingly on the forehead.

"Thank you, Dear," Father said, smiling at me sadly. "Any suggestions?" He looked at me searchingly.

"By the way," I said, "Lili van Ditmars told me yesterday that she was moving and that she found a house large enough for a bed-and-breakfast business." I thought this news might encourage him toward Tsingtao and lift his spirits.

"And how is it going with Philip?" Father chuckled. "Is Lili still pursuing her matchmaking?" Father adjusted his monocle to his eye to observe me better. He was highly suspicious of the whole idea of Sumatra.

"Why, don't you remember that I told you that Lili has had several letters from Philip for me?" I answered casually, not to show my own deep interest in Philip.

"Does he know that you have children?"

"Why, yes, Lili told him. In his last letter to me, he mentioned that there are two excellent boarding schools for girls in Singapore."

"So…" Father knitted his brows. "What did you answer?"

"I really have not decided anything. Yet, as things look at present, if he should propose marriage, don't you think it is worth considering? Philip seems honest and sincere, and he is well established with his rubber plantation."

"Well…, well…" Father scratched his moustache as he looked away from me. His gaze wandered over our terraces and on toward the distant western range of mountains. Thus he sat for several minutes, miles away in his thoughts.

"Well what?" I finally asked, trying to bring him back to the subject of our conversation.

"Yes, Tolia," Mother nudged him, "what were you going to say?"

Father slowly lifted his right leg with both his hands to cross it over his left leg. Then he shifted himself to a more comfortable position in his chair.

"Well...I think the place for Muse and her children will be in America. Yes, I can see it clearly...That is the logical place. You will marry an American, a naval officer. That is what I see."

"Oh, please, Father, stop!" I interrupted him. Suddenly, I had a strange sinking feeling in my stomach as I recalled that day when he had so accurately predicted my meeting Karl. In my mind flashed every detail of that meeting near the "Miao," Elena and I and the donkey, and Karl walking toward us.

Without taking notice of my reaction, Father continued: "America is a great country, where you will do well. Remember our trip in 1935? Holland or Sumatra is not for you. There, a woman must be a 'homebody,' and you are not disciplined enough for that." Father made an effort to get up from his chair, indicating that our conversation was over. Mother and I helped him up and into the house.

57

Stormy Weather

The conversation with Father left Mother and me in a very uncertain, anxious frame of mind, and the change of weather added to our melancholy. Our blue skies had suddenly turned steel gray and the soothing sunshine hid behind billowing dark clouds. Torrential rains blew in from the Yellow Sea. This condition was most unfavorable, as we desperately needed good weather for our weekend guests.

Father sat in his chair next to the picture window in our great room, smoking one cigarette after another and morosely staring out toward the distant mountain range, now hardly visible because of the sheet of rain.

Mother, whose moods had never been too stable even in good weather, roamed idly from room to room like a ghost in her black kimono dressing gown. The children, rambunctious from being confined indoors, ran about like wild Indians, giving Stesha a hard time. Even Hsiao Lee, normally a cheerful man, sensing that something was not right, went about his household duties with a glum expression on his face. Tah Po, our cook, must have been anxious, too, because now and again the sound of a falling metal pan reached me. I surmised the reason to be his anxious thoughts as he handled of the utensils while preparing our meals.

To distract myself, I tried to read. We had many books, on all subjects, stored in the low cabinet with glass doors in the entrance hall. But hard as I tried to concentrate, my disturbing thoughts and the drumming of the rain on the window panes interrupted my reading. I looked at my watch. It showed two-thirty. Ah, I thought, just the right time to start out for Lili van Ditmars and be back before dark at five. Perhaps a hot cup of tea with a Dutch cookie would lift my spirits, and maybe I would be able to persuade her to tell my fortune with cards.

I remembered the times she had entertained me by laying a deck of cards out on the table and instructing me in the intricacies of predicting the future by the way the cards fell in various combinations. She was a wizard with the cards, a talent she had acquired from gypsies long ago in Holland.

"Let it rain," I said to myself, "but I have to do something to distract myself, and what can be better than to take a long walk alone, have tea with a friend, and have a peep into the future, perhaps, at least in the cards, a better one than expected."

So I grabbed my raincoat out of the wardrobe, slipped into it, fastened the rain bonnet under my chin, and, so as not to disturb anyone, tiptoed through the great room to the entrance. Father, however, had noticed my departure.

"Be careful, watch your step," he called out.

"I will, I will," I answered, a little annoyed that he should admonish me like a child. "I'll be back before dark." I shut the door behind me.

Keeping my head down so as not to be blinded by the rain, I started down our main steps to the larger of our terraces—and then I discovered that Father's advice was well given. The waters from the torrential rains had seeped under the granite slabs of our walk and stairs, and had raised and shifted them here and there, disturbing the even surface. I had to be careful, and especially alert on the staircase.

Eventually, I made it to the trail below, which was a narrow path of beaten down clay. But here, too, I found obstacles. The hard clay had turned into mud, making my passage, even here, hazardous due to the steep drop to the rivulet to the left of me.

Nevertheless, undaunted, I continued toward Pei Chui Shui village and soon stepped onto its cobblestone passageway meandering between the houses. Not a soul was in sight, not even a wet chicken or a pig. The yards adjacent to the dwellings were deep puddles and the animals had been brought into the houses where they were together with their masters. Not only in bad weather, but even at night, livestock (fowl, pigs, goats) were precious enough to have them share the protection of a roof and bolted door of the one- or two-room cottages.

The only animals I encountered on my way were donkeys, tethered to posts, while the rain drenched them. Perhaps it was not a totally ungratifying experience. Judging by the animals' half-opened mouths and eyes, and their long ears pulled back, which gave them an almost pleasurable expression, they seemed to be enjoying the cool waters running down their muzzles and through their matted coats down to their skins. At long last they were receiving a washing, a rare happening in the lives of these exploited and neglected creatures.

Leaving the village, I hurried past the little "Miao," around the mountain slope, on and on until finally I was in the central valley where the cars parked. Here I had to cross a fifty-foot-long granite bridge to reach the other side, where the path to the Swiss chalet started. But when I looked where the bridge should have been, I was taken aback. The bridge was totally submerged under the fast-flowing sheet of water. The rivulet had overflowed its banks.

My first thought was to turn back, as any sensible person probably would have done. But, being foolhardy at times, I said to myself, "I can do it." Taking off my shoes, I picked up the hem of my skirt and my raincoat, and resolutely stepped into the water. The current was swift; however, the rough surface of the granite paving under my feet gave me a foothold. Besides, I found the water level to be not as deep as I had thought. It was just several inches below my knees. It permitted me to move forward at a shuffling pace. Thus shuffle, shuffle, stop…shuffle, shuffle, stop, I crossed the bridge.

I will never forget the look of amazement and fright on Lili's face when she opened the door. I must have looked quite a sight standing there shivering, dripping water, my wet hood hanging low over my eyes, my raincoat clinging to me.

"Good heavens, girl!" she exclaimed when she recognized me. "Are you all right?"

"Lili, I had to get away from the house. It is so depressing!"

Lili did not let me finish. Without a word she pulled me in, took off my wet raincoat, hood and shoes, and draped them on the back of a chair in front of the hearth where a fire was burning. "Now you just sit in here and get warm, and I will prepare us some hot tea." With these words she pulled up an armchair.

"Don't forget the Dutch cookies," I called after her as she disappeared through a doorway leading into the kitchen.

"But, of course, of course!" she laughed. She was soon back with a tray with cups, teapot under a tea cozy, and, on a crystal plate, the cookies. "Here. Drink. It will make you feel better."

I don't remember when again I enjoyed as much the hot liquid going down my throat and having my body warmed in front of the fire. Lili let me relax. She sat quietly sipping from her cup, waiting for me to start the conversation. After a while I turned to her.

"You are leaving Laoshan. But Father cannot decide what to do. This worries me. Nothing worse than indecision, you know."

"Yes, I know. Sometimes it's difficult…The unknown can be very threatening," she sighed. And then suddenly her eyes had a spark in them. "How about a peep into the future?"

"What do you mean?"

"Let's look into what the cards will tell."

"That is just what I was hoping you would offer." I immediately felt better, hoping that the cards might predict a future better than what was at present.

Lili reached out to the small drawer of the lamp table next to her. Out of it she took a deck of green playing cards, closed her eyes, and began shuffling the deck in her hands. Having done this for several minutes, she placed the cards face down on the round coffee table standing between us.

"Cut them into three equal piles and think," she instructed. By the serious, concentrated look on her face, I could see that she really believed in the cards.

Fortune telling with cards had been practiced, especially by gypsies, from time immemorial. I guess that when uncertainly or trouble enters our lives, we all would like to have some assurance and solace. China had its **I Ching**, the "Book of Changes," compiled by Confucius. Even the highly civilized Greeks had the Oracle of Delphi, where priestesses, the sibyls, inspired by the god Apollo, told their obscure, ambiguous predictions as they sat in a trance induced by vapors seeping from the ground. Many of these prophecies did come true.

We Russians are particularly superstitious, and I am no exception. So there I was cutting the deck, waiting for wonderful revelations. Lili gathered the cards together and started to lay them out on the coffee table, each card face up from left to right, into four rows of eight, thirty-two cards from the aces to the sevens. Having done this, she touched the cards with her index finger to count to the ninth card. Now and then she would nod her head or sigh.

"Well! What do you see?" I asked impatiently.

"I see a long trip." Lili pointed to the ten of clubs. "This will lead you to better times." She indicated the ten of hearts. "One of the best cards in the deck."

"Good. We are going to move to Tsingtao then," I added.

"No, much farther. There will be a change of residence. You see here the ace of hearts that stands for your home. It is upside down and it has a seven of diamonds next to it. But then there is also the king of clubs next to your own card, the queen of hearts."

"Ah! What does that mean?" I was starting to get excited.

"It signifies a gentleman in your life," Lili explained.

"A good man? How old?"

"Hard to say, but not very young. The clubs are cards of business, social position..." Lili knit her brows and became suddenly silent while she gathered the cards together.

"Something wrong? You have not finished."

"It's enough for today. Besides, I forgot, I have a letter for you." She rose, went to the desk, and came back with an envelope which she handed to me. By the precise handwriting on it, I recognized it to be from Philip.

"Give a serious thought to his offer."

I was about to open the letter when there was a knock on the front door. Lili hurried to open it. It was Hsiao Lee with a sedan chair and the carriers. Father had sent them to be sure I got back safely. I was glad that he had.

After tucking the letter under my now dry raincoat and thanking Lili for her hospitality, I climbed into the sedan chair. The rain had subsided somewhat. The sedan-chair carriers crossed the river over the bridge with no trouble and I was delivered home safely and in grand style.

After dinner, alone in my room, I opened Philip's letter. Though Lili's remark, "Consider it seriously," made me guess its content, I was, nevertheless, full of excitement when I read that Philip wanted me to consider coming to Sumatra with my girls and marrying him. How wonderful! A grand vista for the future opened before me. At last my humdrum existence in Laoshan would end, and...

And suddenly, with a dull thud, I was brought back to reality. I asked myself, "Could you leave your parents here in Laoshan under the present circumstances? Of course, you cannot..."

With sadness, I reread Philip's letter, and something that I had overlooked drew my attention. On the last page there was a postscript: "Should you accept my offer, I need your passport from the Chinese government to petition the Dutch authorities in Sumatra for permission for your entrance. This may take a while." It gave me hope.

I breathed a sigh of relief, realizing that it also gave me time—and with time, things could happen and my parents' predicament could be altered. This thought silenced my fears. Nevertheless, I felt it advisable not to make any commitments to

Philip and, for a while, not to mention his offer to my parents. I knew that it would only disturb them and add to their worries.

However, I had to answer Philip, so I wrote to him, describing our difficulties, and said that I would have loved to come to Sumatra, but at present, I could not make such a move. Should the conditions change, I would let him know. I hoped that he would understand.

Philip understood and suggested we continue our correspondence.

58

Father Accepts a Government Position

Then, something unexpected occurred. A messenger arrived to announce to Father the arrival from Tsingtao of two government officials. The messenger intimated that they were important. Therefore, according to prescribed customs, Father prepared himself to greet them on the threshold of the entrance to Rock Mansions.

Imagine Father's amazement when, on the day and hour specified, who would walk up to our top terrace but two of the former guerrillas, not as Father remembered them in the tattered clothing of poor peasants, but in trim gray officers' uniforms with gold on their caps' visors. Approaching Father with great dignity, they bowed before extending their hands to shake Father's in a most formal manner. When they saw Father's surprised look, however, their formality changed to friendly merriment.

The older of the officers addressed Father in Chinese, "It is such an honor to be here again and to see Honorable Sir looking so well." An interpreter, with a briefcase slung across his shoulder, stepped forward from behind him to translate what he had said into excellent English.

"I thank you. You pay me honor with your visit. Much water has poured down the river since the time you were here," Father answered. The interpreter translated this response into Chinese.

"Indeed, indeed," the two officers sighed, inclining their heads. Father invited the gentlemen into the house.

"And how is the honorable Taitai [lady of the house]?" one of the officers inquired, as he made himself comfortable in one of the chairs in front of the picture window.

"My wife is very well, thank you," Father replied, lowering himself into his own green armchair.

"And the young lady, your daughter?" the other officer asked. "We hear she has now two children."

"She, too, is well, thank you. Her children give me much joy," Father answered in the proper Chinese manner, understanding that these questions were only customary politeness before speaking about what had brought them here.

While the exchange of courtesies proceeded, Hsiao Lee had poured hot tea into cups and now was serving them on a tray. Each officer and the interpreter took a teacup into both hands and silently began to sip from his cup. Father did the same.

After a few minutes, having done as etiquette prescribed, the older of the officers cleared his throat, nodded to the interpreter, and indicated that he was ready to proceed with business. The interpreter reached into his briefcase and extracted a large, pale yellow envelope bearing a large vermilion seal. The older officer arose and ceremoniously handed it to Father. Father accepted it with his head bowed, showing his respect, but he was puzzled by what it might contain.

"This is a formal offer from the Very Honorable Governor of Shantung, your friend, General Wang Yao-wu, the former officer in command of us guerrillas. He is inviting the Honorable Sir Ko-te-ne-fu [Kotenev] to accept a position. The Very Honorable Governor needs help in conducting some of the duties that now rest heavily on his shoulders," spoke the officer through the interpreter.

Father was stunned. "Me? But!—how can I be of service, handicapped as I am?"

The older officer listened to the translation and then drew in his breath to emphasize the importance of what he was about to say. "You see, the American Fleet is in Tsingtao Harbor. Many problems." He shook his head meaningfully. "So, it is only proper to create good relations with our visitors, entertain them, attend to misunderstandings and difficulties, yet preserve friendly connections. Your Honorable Sir has much experience and can assist us so that the dignity of China is preserved."

Father understood that what the Governor needed was a public-relations man.

"I am greatly honored by the confidence bestowed upon me by the Very Honorable Governor of Shantung, but I have a big family," Father tactfully approached the subject of remuneration for such a job.

"No problem," the officer nodded, and added, "An appropriate house has been prepared. We have not forgotten your help during the war and we know your difficulties. Now it is our turn."

"I accept the Very Honorable Governor's offer and will do my best to serve him," Father responded, clasping his palms together, showing his gratefulness.

The officers arose, bowed in unison, and slowly withdrew out of our great room.

Mother could not suppress her tears of happiness when she heard what had happened and that we were moving to Tsingtao. The prospect of Father being a counselor to the Governor made her even more ecstatic. "God has heard my prayers!" she exclaimed in exaltation, raising her arms heavenward.

Now full of energy and expectations, she discarded her black Japanese kimono, dressed herself in a pink and orange house dress, and began hustling and bustling about. Here she was wrapping and packing figurines, bric-a-brac, crystal decanters and bowls into boxes. There she was supervising the selection of paintings to be taken down from the walls. There was not a corner in the house that she did not look into to be sure that we did not leave anything useful behind.

In the meantime, the children ran about gleefully, singing a ditty that Stesha had taught them. "We will be building castles in the sands. We will be swimming in the sea. Oh! how happy we all shall be," they rejoiced.

Father, who should have been the happiest and proudest of the Governor's confidence in him, was the only one who did not take part in all the activities. He sat pensively in his overstuffed green chair, thoughtfully smoking one cigarette after another.

"Why are you so pensive? Isn't it marvelous how everything came about and the possibilities opening for you? Just think how timely it is." I hugged him tenderly to cheer him.

Father inhaled deeply from his cigarette, exhaling a cloud of smoke before he answered me. "Yes, marvelous, and timely it certainly is. No doubt of that. But who knows what lies ahead…?" He turned his head toward our picture window to look out at the distant valley and the meandering rivulet far below.

"Why think of what might be? Think of the present." I kissed him on the forehead.

"Present? What is the present?—only a fleeting moment between the past and the future. And at this moment I am bidding farewell to all that I love." Slowly, he waved his hand in the direction of the valley and then to the great room around him. "I have a presentiment that I will not see Rock Mansions again," he concluded in a low voice, his eyes filled with tears.

"Oh, Father, stop that Russian pessimism," I exclaimed angrily, and then, like a flash, I, too, sensed a foreboding that I, too, was in Rock Mansions for the last time. It came to me clearly, almost audibly.

"What is it?" Father's voice brought me back. He was looking at me oddly.

"Oh! Nothing. I was just thinking what I must do next." I hoped my voice had not betrayed my own fears, as I hurried off to help Mother.

Several days later, three trucks loaded with our belongings left the central Laoshan valley. Mother was next to one of the chauffeurs with two of our dogs. Father and I sat in the other truck. In the third truck were Stesha and the girls.

Hsiao Lee sadly waved to us as the chauffeurs accelerated their engines to climb up the steep grade to the overpass in the mountains. Hsiao Lee had been retained as the caretaker of Rock Mansions. Tah Po, our cook, was to follow us to Tsingtao on his own. The water carriers were dismissed. We gave them two months' salary as severance pay, which left them not completely unhappy. Much later, Hsiao Lee, visiting us in Tsingtao, told us that the water carriers had found new jobs. We were all very glad to hear this.

59

Tsingtao in 1947

We found our new home on Honan Road, the better residential area of Tsingtao. It was a well-constructed, two-storied white shingled house with a black-tiled roof, standing above the street on a knoll. A stairway of wide concrete steps led up to the garden, with forsythia bushes close to the house and an old maple tree in the background.

From this height we had a good view of the surroundings. Across the street, to the east, stretched an extensive yard with a four-storied red building, which was the former German military hospital, and now barracks for the U.S. Marines. Beyond this we could see part of the esplanade with consulate buildings facing the open sea.

The interior of our house was comfortable, provided one could adapt, which we did with time, to some of its strange features. Moving into 15 Honan Road, we moved into a world completely different from our own. The house had been designed and built to accommodate a Japanese life style. Its former owners had been a prominent Japanese family who adhered to their national traditions.

There were wooden floors only in the two corridors and up the stairs. The seven rooms, four on the ground floor and three above, had "tatami" flooring, replaceable woven-reed matting, padded and stretched on frames which lay on an invisible supporting grill. Beautiful and soft to walk on, it was meant for shoeless inhabitants who sat on cushions and ate from low tables.

We soon discovered that hard-soled shoes with ladies' sharp heels damaged the tatami fibers, not to speak of what Father's heavy desk and our chairs and chests of drawers did to the lovely flooring.

One of the most attractive areas in two of the rooms, in the front parlor and on the second floor, were the slightly raised, cage-like partitions with decoratively grained platforms four by three feet in size, with delicate carved wooden columns up to the ceiling, the "takanomas."

Here was where the Japanese lady of the house displayed her proficiency in flower arrangements, and where, with a painting appropriate to the time of year, a silk scroll was hung on the wall. In front of it an appropriate vase with just the right flowers, or cunningly twisted twigs, would be placed. It was an art all its own, requiring exquisite taste and knowledge, which is part of the education of every upper-class Japanese girl.

We enjoyed all these architectural details. Our difficulty, however, arose where we least expected. The problems were the two bathrooms, and they were baffling. These were two small square rooms, one on each floor, with a small washbasin on the wall, no bathtub or shower, and for a toilet, an oblong hole was cut out in the corner of the tile floor with a water faucet.

The lack of bathtubs presented little difficulty. We had found a round wooden tub in our basement, which would be brought into the bathroom. Into this tub, we would scramble to squat on a small stool while an accommodating servant poured hot water over us from a pitcher, drenching us from head to toe. That situation was not too bad, and we quickly adapted to this procedure. On the other hand, we all had serious problems when nature called. To relieve ourselves there was no other way but to hover eagle-like over the oblong hole in the floor.

This performance required not only strong leg muscles, but also a precise aim, qualities that every Japanese acquires from childhood by sitting cross-legged on pillows and cultivating dexterity by arising without help or leaning, just unfurling upward cobra-like.

One sees it done in the movies during a tea ceremony when the Japanese hostess, with a cup in both hands, arises from kneeling on the floor.

Alas, I never could master the technique, and was always glad that there was no one present to watch my performance.

For my Father's convenience, a special large metal basin was made to take the place of a tub, and a portable commode was provided, which, when required had to be brought rapidly into his room. Remembering King Louis XIV of France, the "Sun King," receiving ambassadors while enthroned on a latrine, the whole thing added importance to this necessary function.

We adapted ourselves to our new abode and some of its inconveniences. Father hung his collection of oil paintings and placed his desk and a sofa in the second room facing the parlor to the right of the entrance, making it into his office. Mother distributed our furnishings throughout the house. The three rooms on the second floor were assigned to me and my girls.

In my rooms I covered the tatami flooring with my oriental rugs and in the "takanoma" hung a cherry-blossom scroll with a Christmas cactus in a pot before it. Not quite according to the Japanese discipline of traditional flower arrangement, it nonetheless lent an attractive touch. Stesha and my girls had the large room across the hall from me, where they had ample room for games.

Tah Po, our cook, made himself comfortable in the servants' quarters at the back of the house, and, with time, after burning a few meals, got used to cooking over a gas burner, a concentrated heat that necessitated a more watchful handling of victuals.

Having assigned proper space for everyone in the family, there were two rooms left unoccupied. One was on the ground floor to the left of the entrance and the other was an odd room built under the cement stairway leading up to the house, originally a cave-like enclosure, which had been converted by the original owner into spacious living quarters with a kitchenette and a shower/toilet. A large window and the entrance door of this apartment faced the street. This unusual living space my Father rented to two sisters, who opened a small Russian tea room. A young, attractive brunette whose name was Margot, moved into the other room.

Father was exceedingly pleased that we not only had a pleasant home but also a source, however modest, of greatly needed additional income. The reason being that Father soon learned from the Shantung Government that his remuneration ended with the use of the house. It was also imperative for him to establish his legal practice and for me to find a job.

To practice law in the Chinese Tsingtao Court, Father had to hire a Chinese interpreter and secretary who knew not only the legal procedures, but also the Russian and English languages. What a requirement!! It was like looking for the proverbial needle in a stack of hay. To our amazement, Father found such a treasure, a shabbily dressed elderly Chinese gentleman with a few hairs for a beard and a long moustache. He spoke Russian and wanted to be addressed as Stepan Stepanovitch in the proper Russian manner, because he originally came from Harbin, a Russian-controlled city in Manchuria.

Not only was he proficient in the languages, but, as Father soon found out, he was a wizard in the "know-how" required to circumvent Chinese red tape by greasing the right palm of the right official, thereby speeding the required receipt of the necessary papers, permissions, or whatever the petition, filed by my Father for his clients.

Fortune smiled on me, too. A minor secretarial job at the U.S. Port Command opened. I was hired through Captain Ramosa's introduction. My salary was $60 U.S. a week, a handsome amount in those days. Much later, I discovered that I got that job because of my Father's Chinese connections. It had been reported by U.S. Intelligence that I was a Chinese spy, and they wanted to keep me under close surveillance. I thought it was rather illogical, taking into consideration that, if, indeed, I had been a spy, I would have had access to all the files and confidential correspondence in the Port Command.

The humorous part about the whole circumstance was something that the U.S. Intelligence agents did not know, but we did, which was that the private secretary to the Chief-in-Command was a young Chinese lady who was also in the employ of the Chinese Government. Whatever directions had been received or whatever happened that morning in the United States Navy or in the Marine Corps were reported to the Governor's Office before evening. Eventually, it trickled down, even to Father. In addition, many of these directives, orders, and instructions came from Washington and were crucial to the future of China and the safety of Tsingtao.

60

Life under the Protection of the U.S.A.

In 1948, Tsingtao was basking in the glow of prosperity. After the days of austere living during the Japanese occupation, the heavens had suddenly opened to shower "manna," in the form of United States dollars, on the impoverished residents. Not only did jobs for every profession become available, paid in U.S. currency, but more importantly, dollars were spent by the American soldiers and sailors who had saved their pay while on active duty in the war zones. Starved for drinks, sex, and "good times," they were now spending these dollars without reservation. The restaurants overflowed with military personnel. The bars could not stock enough liquor, and when it came to sex, it seemed that Tsingtao had become one big red-light district.

Formerly, everyone was used to the highly disciplined Japanese forces which had needed no local services in this respect, since they had been wisely provided with "camp followers" and prostitutes, who were under constant medical supervision. What we were witnessing now, the "free-for-all," horrified us. Drunken misbehavior, rape, and even the murder of women were not isolated cases. The Chinese authorities were helpless and the U.S. military patrols were too few to preserve order.

The Governor asked Father to make an official complaint to the commanding Marine officer, Colonel Griffith, so Father paid the Colonel a call. Father politely drew his attention to the lack of discipline and to the excesses of the marines and sailors on furlough.

Colonel Samuel Griffith, a scholar of military tactics and later the author of a book dealing with Chinese martial arts, listened to Father attentively, but shrugged his shoulders.

"But you cannot ignore such behavior," Father protested. "It undermines the respect that Orientals have had for us Europeans—and the United States in particular. There may be serious implications in the future, even in diplomacy."

Colonel Griffith waved his hand disdainfully. "You must understand. All these poor men are battle fatigued. They need an outlet," and again he shrugged his shoulders.

Father left greatly disturbed and puzzled by such short-sighted policy. Remembering the care that the British gave in handling themselves to maintain the respect and fear of the populations in the colonies, thereby sustaining peace and order, Father felt that the Colonel's lack of action was tantamount to madness or pure naivete. He returned home depressed.

While all this was going on, my friend Lili van Ditmars had moved to Tsingtao, and my correspondence with Philip continued. As Lili had told me in Laoshan, she was now managing a bed-and-breakfast place, an attractive yellow house with a red entrance door on the road to the Strand (beach). Her business prospects were not too promising and I suspected that, in keeping with the times, and in order to adequately subsist, she had to resort to renting more of the beds, than making breakfasts. Ah, well, sometimes floating with the current might be the wisest.

My family, too, ironically found itself in an interesting situation. We began noticing that our tenant Margot, the attractive brunette, who had the large room to the left of the entrance to the house, was having an unusual number of visitors. The two older, and not so attractive, ladies in the apartment on the street level were also having a steady stream of visitors.

With Margot, the visitors stood, two or three at a time, in our corridor waiting for the one inside to come out. When he did, he was smiling and looking contented. Margot's capacity to satisfy was certainly impressive and, like the two sisters below, she was obviously prospering. Our location across the road from the Marine barracks, the former German military hospital, was a definite advantage to the trade.

"Tolichka, under our roof is a house of prostitution!" Mother screamed, livid with indignation.

"We need the rent. What can we do?" Father sighed, shrugging his shoulders.

"Do something, do something!" Mother pleaded. So Father did. He raised the rent. All the ladies brought their money, pleased to stay. Business was too good to argue with the landlord.

"If you can't beat them, join them," Father told his friend, a Russian Orthodox priest, Father Inokenty. "God will forgive you and I absolve you," said the priest, making the sign of the cross in the air.

Father Inokenty, the Russian Orthodox priest of the local Russian church, was a frequent visitor to our house. He was a colorful individual, fat and untidy looking in his gray cassock, which smelled of perspiration. With a bushy black beard, he exuded with each word a strong spiritual presence from his every breath. He was a well-read and fast-thinking man, however.

Our dog, Mebzig, a Llasa, also developed a great attraction to him, or maybe to his gray cassock. Whenever the two men were deeply engrossed in a philosophical discussion of some highly ethereal matter, Mebzig would stealthily approach, lift up one of his hind legs, and spray the hem of the fragrant gray priestly garment.

I always wondered if either of the men noticed this transgression or, perhaps, sign of respect. Neither of them moved an eyebrow, Father, maybe not to embarrass Father Inokenty, while the priest, perhaps, deemed it an inspiration enacted by God through a lowly canine creature.

Our own need, plus sympathy and understanding for our tenants' dire circumstances due to their total lack of education and training, forced my Father to tolerate the unsavory practice in our home. We continued to coexist amicably under the same roof, with everyone in his own area doing his own thing. My parents were in their two rooms to the right of the entrance, where Father had his legal practice. Margot, relieving battle fatigue, was across the hall. Stesha, my girls, and I were upstairs, where I occasionally had parties for my U.S. Port Command friends. The two sisters, on the street level, ran their small Russian tea room, restaurant, and whatever...

I must admit that our tenants, appreciative of being able to remain, did make every effort to be discrete. Thus, all went smoothly for several months until one day when, had it not been for a most fortunate coincidence, a tragedy would have occurred.

It happened one Saturday evening. I was returning home after supper with friends. It was getting late. Normally, I never ventured from home after dark unless I was escorted, but this day my friends had persuaded me to stay later than I intended. Enjoying their company, I did not notice how time had flown. My friends found a pedicab for me, which was considered a reliable means of transportation. I gave the driver my address and we started off along the esplanade.

I still recall the street lanterns on the corners lighting their perimeters, and the flickering lights hung close to the wheels of the passing rickshaws and bicycles.

We were nearing the corner leading to Honan Road. My driver was just turning to the right when I became aware of something going on at a little distance behind us. It was another pedicab. Its passenger was a man in a military cap with a visor, intensely waving his arms as he urged his man to hurry in our direction.

This behavior seemed strange to me, but I quickly forgot about it. My thoughts were still dwelling on the pleasant time that I had just had with my friends.

A few minutes later, my pedicab drove up to the front of our stairway. I paid the driver and started up the stairs. Having reached about the tenth step, I heard angry voices coming from below. I looked down into the light of the street lamp. Near our entrance was the pedicab. Its driver was off his bicycle, holding out his hand to a man in uniform.

"One dollar! One dollar!" he kept shouting. His passenger said something angrily, and reached into his trouser pocket. The passenger was in uniform and his cap had a visor.

"The marine barracks are across the street! Why stop here?!!" flashed in my mind. I sensed danger. Instinctively, I started to run up the rest of the steps. I heard footfalls. They were close behind me.

"Quick, quick, to the door, to the door!" kept pounding in my head. Now I was on the path. I could see the door of the house. I rushed toward it. I reached out for the doorbell, but I could not press it. Someone gripped me around my waist. I tried to struggle.

"Keep quiet, or I will kill you," the man snarled close to my ear. I could smell liquor on his breath as he clasped his hand over my mouth. He was pulling me toward the bushes. Cold terror seized me and with all the strength I had I tried again to resist being pulled into the bushes.

"Keep still!" I heard the man hiss like a viper. His fingers tightened on my mouth and nose, making it difficult for me to breathe. I felt my strength waning.

Then, suddenly, a light flashed. Our entrance door opened.

"Who's there?" I heard Margot's voice. "What are you doing, Lieutenant Andersen?" Margot had recognized my assailant.

"I'm...I'm..." stammered the man, caught by surprise, and, having been recognized, he let go of me.

Before we knew it, he turned and disappeared down the steps. I stood, shaking, unable to move or speak.

"Come, dear," Margot told me as she put her arm about my shoulders. "You were lucky that I was near the door and heard the strange shuffling noise outside. That officer is known for his strangeness."

Margot assisted me into the house and up to my room. Not wanting to disturb anyone, I quietly crept into my bed, thankful to Margot for having been in the right place at the right time.

That night in bed, I tossed about, exhausted yet unable to sleep. It must have been daybreak, for I heard the crowing of a distant rooster, when, completely spent, I finally dozed off, only to be awakened by Stesha's voice.

"Musa Anatolievna! Musa Anatolievna!" She always addressed me in the patronymic Russian manner. "Are you all right?" And she gently shook my arm.

I opened my eyes. My rooms were flooded with sunshine. Stesha was bending over me, her blue eyes full of fear. "It's eleven. You have missed the Sunday church service! Can I bring you some coffee?"

"Yes, please, a cup of coffee is what I need."

As Stesha hurried out of the room, I closed my eyes again, feeling listless. It had been a fretful night. I was also aware that I should tell Father about my experience, and was worrying about the consequences. Nonetheless, I had to tell him.

Meanwhile, Stesha was back with coffee, toast, and two soft-boiled eggs on a tray, my usual breakfast. She poured me a cup of coffee, urging me to eat. To please her, I ate one egg and a piece of toast.

"That's better," Stesha said, looking satisfied. "Now, I must go to see what our girls are doing," and she left me.

The food had somewhat restored my energy. I decided to dress and go downstairs.

I found Father at his desk, writing. Mother sat nearby, embroidering a tablecloth. This was her hobby and her work was very fine.

One look at me and Father must have seen by my appearance that something was wrong. "Why such big rings under the eyes?" he asked.

Mother, too, was examining me carefully. "*Dooshenka chto s-toboy?* [Dearie, what's the matter?]"

"I had a very bad night," I answered and related my evening experience.

"*Boje moy! Boje moy!* [Dear God!]" Mother jumped up. "You see! You see! What did I tell you?" She turned on Father, waving her hands and raising her voice.

"Quiet, quiet, Luba," Father tried to calm her.

"This is no place for our daughter and her children, no place," Mother shouted as she paced the floor. "You must move, move from these sordid surroundings!" She stopped in front of me, with tears in her eyes.

"But where can I go?" I murmured, taken aback at the thought. I looked at Father. He was sitting, with his head down and a frown on his face, rubbing his moustache. At last he looked up and, with a faltering voice, said, "Mother is right. I shall speak with Stepan Stepanovitch. He will find you something suitable. I will also speak to Colonel Griffith." To indicate that the discussion was over, Father resumed his writing.

Father's interview with the Colonel was unsatisfactory. The Colonel just waved his hands in silence. Lieutenant Andersen was not even reprimanded. No action materialized—until the local newspaper printed the story of a young woman's body being found on the beach. The paper reported that the woman had been seen leaving a bar that evening in the company of a Marine lieutenant. Who had committed the crime? It remained a mystery to the public.

Through the grapevine at the Port Command, I eventually heard that Lieutenant Andersen had been discharged from duty, and returned to the United States.

61

I Meet Captain Norcross

Stepan Stepanovitch was given the difficult task of seeking a suitable dwelling for me. As he was well acquainted with Tsingtao, Father thought that he might be just the man to find a centrally located flat in one of the houses owned by Chinese. There were several of these large residences that belonged to formerly affluent families who, due to the war, had lost their wealth and were now forced to rent part of their houses.

Meanwhile, Stesha, the girls, and I stayed in our second-floor rooms. As before, our lives continued in the same pattern. Stesha took care of the girls. I worked at the Port Command from eight in the morning until four in the afternoon. Sundays we attended Russian church services. Once in a while I participated in various social functions frequently held at the Edgewater Hotel.

As a single, young, attractive woman, I, as were a few other Russian ladies in Tsingtao, was invited there, not so much to embellish the evening with our charm and beauty but, as I believed, to be a dancing partner for the single officers. Whatever the reason may have been, I thoroughly enjoyed these elegant evenings.

At one of these dinner dances, my life took an unexpected turn. I have always found it remarkable how some incident, of not too great importance, could, in the process of time, predetermine events in the life of an individual, and this is exactly what happened. Though I could not have divined it at the time, one evening at the Edgewater Hotel determined not only my children's and my future, but also changed of the fate of my parents.

The Ramosas had invited me to a Saturday night dinner dance at the Edgewater Hotel. I was told that a Captain Eddy Pierce, the Chief of Intelligence on the Admiral's Staff from the flagship *Estes*, was to escort me.

On the date specified, at six-thirty in the evening, Captain Pierce arrived in a chauffeured official car. What a distinguished-looking man he was—tall, blond, and handsome, with a proud military bearing and many decorations for valor blazing with gold on his dark blue naval jacket. I was impressed and delighted to have such an outstanding escort to match my own finery, which was a chic lavender chiffon evening gown from the Shanghai days with Karl, and which I had resurrected out of my chest. Looking in the mirror, I was pleased to see what was reflected back to me.

In due time we arrived at the hotel, where the ball was in full swing. The orchestra was playing. The ladies, in colorful evening gowns, were swirling on the dance floor in the arms of gentlemen in tuxedos, naval and marine officers in full dress uniforms, and adjutants with gold braids over their shoulders. I could see that every one of any consequence was present. It was a grand affair.

Captain Pierce led me to a large round table where he introduced me to several naval officers, their ladies, and two single naval captains.

Soon cocktails were served, followed by hors d'oeuvres. The Edgewater was renowned for its cuisine and the dinner was excellent. Just as outstanding was its famous orchestra, which was playing the latest dance pieces.

I loved to dance, but to my chagrin, after Captain Pierce had invited me two or three times, he started to show more interest in his whiskey.

On the dance floor he became awkward and less in tempo with the music. By eight o'clock, he stopped asking me to dance. He just sat there, leaning with his elbows on the table.

Contrary to our Russian custom, where a lady could be invited to dance by men other than her own escort, that evening I had to have been considered Captain Pierce's "date" and therefore his partner only. Besides, everyone was also tactfully ignoring the Captain's obvious inebriation.

So, there I sat, watching the dancers on the floor, chatting with the lady next to me and trying not to show not only my own embarrassment, but also my anxiety as to how I would be getting home. As my gaze wandered around, my eyes met the eyes of an officer across the table from me. He was a pleasant-looking man with a small, well-trimmed moustache. He smiled. I smiled. Suddenly, there was a commotion near me.

Captain Pierce had lost his balance, and two young lieutenants from a neighboring table had jumped up to help him. Captain Ramosa said something in a low voice to the officers.

"Aye, aye, sir," they replied as they grasped Captain Pierce under his armpits, and proceeded to carry him out of the hall.

"What a predicament!" I said to myself. "What am I going to do?" Then I heard a voice behind me.

"Captain Malcolm Norcross. At your service."

I turned. It was the man with the neatly trimmed moustache. "May I have this dance?" He bowed gallantly.

"With pleasure," I answered.

Captain Norcross was about my height. He was a splendid dancer. I complimented him on it. He explained that as a midshipman he had been trained to dance at the Naval Academy in Annapolis. It was one of the prerequisites for his future career. I noticed that he also had several decorations for valor on his chest. Captain Norcross was not as handsome as Captain Pierce, but he compensated for this lack with his jovial manner. He drank sparingly and was eager to please.

"Would you please see that I get home?" I asked him.

"I would be glad to," he replied, with a note of pleasure in his voice.

Not only did Captain Malcolm Norcross see to it that I got home safely that evening, but several days later, he paid me a formal visit. I introduced him to Father. They chatted amiably for some time, and when Captain Norcross left us, Father had the strangest expression on his face.

"What are you grinning like that for?" I asked, a little irritated at the way Father went overboard by inviting the Captain to come back soon.

"Well, I certainly think that you should not overlook the possibilities here," Father replied.

"What do you mean?"

"Didn't you hear him say that he was divorced?" Father cleared his throat. "And such a gentleman. Not only an Annapolis graduate, but also fourth generation Harvard University. A very desirable possible husband."

"Oh! Father!" I said, thinking of my correspondence with Philip van Ditmars. "He probably has a lady in America and this may be the last time we see him."

"I don't think so," Father smiled.

"How do you know?"

"By the way he was looking at you."

"There he goes again," I said to myself.

Father was right, however. I saw Captain Norcross soon after, and again and again. As a matter of fact, he became not only a frequent visitor to our house when my parents were sure to have him stay for lunch or dinner, but he also invited me to attend with him many of the military receptions and private parties.

I became accustomed to him and developed a liking for this well-mannered gentleman who never appeared without a bouquet of flowers, chocolates, or some other token of attention.

Captain Norcross's rank and position on the Admiral's Staff as Chief of Supply and Logistics for the Seventh Fleet, gave him stature in the eyes of Tsingtao society. He had been a supply officer with Admiral Byrd during "Operation Deep Freeze" at the South Pole, and he was the supply officer who had established the Guantanamo Bay Naval Base in Cuba.

These positions certainly showed that Captain Malcolm Ambrose Norcross, forty-two years of age, was a very capable man, in addition to being a distinguished officer. Everywhere we went together his peers treated him accordingly. I had to admit that being escorted by him no doubt appealed to my vanity, aside from the fact that he was a pleasant and accommodating man to be with. Amazingly, all his achievements did not make him boisterous or overbearing. He conducted himself simply, even seemed to be at times self-abasing.

His courtship continued. Father encouraged it. As I was still corresponding with Philip, my close friendship with Malcolm Norcross and his attentions presented a problem, especially because Philip lately had been advising me to acquire a passport to be able to travel.

Philip had read the reports in the newspapers of the confrontation between the communists and the Nationalist Government of China. Mao Tse-tung's Fifth Communist Army was surrounding Nanking, while some of his forces were in Shantung Province, close to Tsingtao.

Philip worried about this dangerous situation. He wrote, urging me not to tarry any longer because it would take some time to get the necessary permission from the Dutch authorities for my entrance into Sumatra.

62

Political Situation in China

In the meantime, the American envoys were endeavoring to persuade the Nationalists and the Communists to form one ideal democratic government.

Invited by the Nationalists to one cocktail party after another, and one banquet after another, where they gave inspired speeches proclaiming the utopia that could be created by such a coalition, the Chinese officials listened attentively with broad smiles and elated expressions on their faces as they refilled the envoys' glasses, and, because they needed America's financial aid, outwardly showed every respect. But the Chinese could predict, as could all clear-thinking individuals, that the well-meaning American efforts were doomed to failure. Two such disparate ideologies as communism and capitalism could never live amicably together.

As each side played for time, vessels of various sizes kept mooring at the Shanghai wharves. Their cargoes of flour, cement, and clothing, sent by the American people, were for the devastated Chinese villages in the interior.

An organization called UNNRA also arrived in Shanghai. UNNRA established its headquarters in the four-story building next to the Shanghai General Post Office overlooking one of the canals. After settling its extensive staff in luxurious apartments, UNNRA began its operation, the distribution of the commodities. While their intentions were laudable, what transpired was quite disappointing.

Cargo of flour and cement often arrived in the same ships' holds. Unloading the ships, the inexperienced Chinese coolies handled these cargoes carelessly, which resulted in a considerable loss of freight.

When the boxes of clothing sent to the villages were opened, among the useful items, the peasants found, to their utter amazement, women's wigs, long nylon stockings, and nylon underwear, leaving them completely baffled as to what to do with these strange contraptions of the "white devils."

But what was indelibly etched on my mind was even worse. On the outskirts of Tsingtao, standing in long rows, were idle trucks, jeeps, weapon carriers, and tanks— all rusting away. The reason was that these vehicles had been shipped to the Chinese government, minus the necessary engines and parts, with no provision to correct this lack.

The scenario we were witnessing, and the knowledge of the state of Chiang Kai Shek's forces and government, filled us with considerable apprehension for our own future, particularly since we knew the Communists were receiving abundant help from Soviet Russia.

What made us all even more fearful was what Malcolm Norcross confidentially disclosed to my Father. The Captain explained that the reports sent by Admiral Cook to Washington had indicated the lack of an immediate threat to Tsingtao from the very limited Communist forces. In response came directives showing clearly that no one had even read the Admiral's information, or that it had been intentionally ignored. In addition, orders had recently been received to prepare to leave Tsingtao on short notice. For the Fleet to abandon Tsingtao and its excellent harbor was tantamount to handing over the city, an important strategic location, to the Communists on a silver platter.

63

Captain Norcross's Proposal of Marriage

Meanwhile, my friendship with Malcolm Norcross deepened. He visited me often and we spent many pleasant hours riding in the jeep, picnicking on the beach, and having dinner and dancing at the Edgewater Mansion.

One afternoon, Malcolm arrived unexpectedly.

"The afternoon is lovely," he exclaimed. "Let's go for a ride."

"Sure. Why not!" I answered, as I snatched my overcoat off the hook and tied a pink kerchief around my head.

As we drove off, I began suspecting that Malcolm had something on his mind. It was the way he kept clearing his throat as he maneuvered the jeep around ruts in the dirt road running past the old German fortifications to the observation point at the end of the road, our favorite spot for picnics. Here the view was spectacular. Below the embankment, where we parked, waves were splashing against the huge rocks. Before us the sparkling Yellow Sea, with several dark silhouettes of tiny islands in the distance, unfolded as far as the eye could see.

"Muse," Mal turned to me, as he suddenly took my hand. "Muse, you must know by now that I love you. Muse, will you marry me?" He was looking searchingly into my eyes.

His sudden proposal surprised me. For several minutes I could not find words to answer him. I did like him a lot...

"Do you think you have enough time to get the necessary permission from the High Command to marry me?" I asked him. "I am a Chinese citizen, you know. It will take time to get my papers ready. What about the political situation?"

"If you say yes, then you must get your passport.

You and the children must leave for the United States as soon as possible. We have no time to lose."

I wanted to say yes, yet I felt confused. "Mal, can I give you my answer tomorrow?"

"Certainly, dear. But remember, we have little time," and he started the jeep's engine.

Malcolm's proposal of marriage threw me into a quandary. I was torn between him and Philip van Ditmars. Though I had never met Philip in person, from his letters and photograph I felt I could judge him to be a good young man. Malcolm Norcross was perhaps not as attractive physically, and was somewhat older, but he was a fine gentleman in whose presence I felt comfortable. He was willing to adopt my girls to facilitate my entrance into the United States. However, one difficulty with marrying Malcolm arose quite unexpectedly.

To marry me, Malcolm had to obtain official permission, and there was a six-month waiting period. Everyone suspected that the rule had been enacted to prevent military personnel from bringing home their Russian and Asian girlfriends. The only way to circumvent this new rule was for me and my girls to enter the United States on a tourist visa. After marriage on United States soil, I would then be allowed to remain as a permanent resident. It all seemed so complicated! I also felt that I was betraying Philip.

"What shall I do?" I turned to Father for advice.

"Daughter," Father answered, "you must go to Nanking immediately. I will get you an introduction from the Governor to the Minister of Foreign Affairs, Wang Shih-chiah. This will speed up the processing of your passport."

"But, Father, what about Philip van Ditmars?"

"My dear, you are a widow of twenty-nine years of age. Your husband, may his soul rest in peace, left you with no financial security. America is the place for you. It is your duty to save your children from the doubtful times ahead under the

Communists here." Father's voice was deep with uncompromising emotion as he spoke. "Yes, in the United States you will be safe. Make every effort to get there. There is no other way!" he insisted. "Be courageous! Live honorably as your Mother and I have always done. Life will lead you as it has us. Trust it."

I accepted my Father's advice and acquiesced to his wishes.

Meanwhile, Malcolm had arranged for me to stay in Nanking at the American BOQ (Bachelor Officers Quarters), so as soon as Father obtained the letter of introduction for me from the Governor and our passport photos were ready, I took a plane to Nanking.

We landed late in the afternoon on a dismal, dusty runway on the outskirts of Nanking. The airport had several corrugated metal Quonset hut hangers, and a long, low, black-tar-roofed receiving center. Alighting from the plane, I noticed several military aircraft near the hangar. A crew of mechanics was feverishly working on the engines and propellers.

Having only a small suitcase, the customs officer waved me through, and soon I was in a taxi on my way to my lodging, an attractive sand-colored, two-storied building surrounded by a carefully tended evergreen hedge. The manager, a gray-haired gentleman in civilian clothes, greeted me cordially, but coolly, and led me to my room.

"I trust you will find this adequate?" he said with a wry expression on his face. I surmised my feminine presence was probably contrary to the intentions of the establishment.

"Yes, thank you," I replied. "Kind of you to let me stay here."

"Glad to be of assistance. We serve meals at regular hours. Breakfast starts at seven. The room will be available for a couple of days." As he spoke, he was edging towards the door.

"Only two days?" I asked, surprised, and a little worried.

"Yes, I'm afraid we're booked." Without further ado he closed the door behind him.

"I hope that will give me enough time," I said to myself, feeling rather disconcerted by the manager's curtness.

Looking around, I found the room to be without frills, but well furnished. A chest of drawers with a mirror stood between the two windows. Two chairs and a small round table were in the far corner. Near the bed, there was a night stand with a decorative, colored cut-glass lamp. The bed was delightfully soft and comfortable, so I slept well that night.

The next morning, after breakfast, I took a taxi to the Ministry of Foreign Affairs. Despite the early hour, the streets were surprisingly congested. It looked like a general exodus. Trucks, cars, wheelbarrows, and donkey-drawn carts were piled high with boxes, bales, mattresses, and other household items, with children perched on top, their parents on foot.

My driver, in desperation, was frantically tooting his horn as he slowly made his way through the crowd.

"What is happening?" I asked, startled by what I was seeing.

"No good. No good." The driver shook his head. "People hully out, velly, velly scared. Mao Tse-tung soon come. Velly close," he said angrily, as he pressed long and hard on his horn to scare away two rickshaws that were in our way.

Eventually, we arrived at the Ministry, a dignified granite edifice with a high arched entrance, guarded by soldiers. One of the guards led me down a long corridor to the designated Department of Passports and Visas.

Upon entering the large, well-lit room, I found myself amid another scene of frantic activity. Clerks were clearing desks, sorting and shredding documents, and packing office equipment into crates.

I tapped on the long mahogany counter to draw attention to myself. After several minutes, an elderly clerk in a gray European suit came up.

"Yes, Madame?" he inquired, knitting his brow.

"I have a letter to the Minister of Foreign Affairs, Wang Shih-chiah, from the Governor of Shantung," I said, showing him the letter with the Governor's seal. "I need a passport. Is this the department?"

The man stared at me as if I had dropped from the planet Mars. I handed him the letter. After fingering it for a second, he turned to his colleagues and said something in Chinese. They all laughed.

"Sorry, no time," the man told me, and then turned his back on me.

I was near to tears. My God, what am I going to do now? I thought.

"Please, please show me the way to the Minister's office," I pleaded. "I have two little children."

Not one man looked up...Finally, I decided to find the office myself and was just about to step into the corridor, when I heard a low voice behind me.

"Look, there, there down the staircase. The man in the middle is the Minister," a young clerk informed me. He must have followed me. He was pointing to the right. I turned to thank him, but before I knew it, he passed me and was gone.

At the end of the corridor to the right, I saw a white marble staircase down which three men in black suits were running. As they came closer, I stepped forward, barring the way. With surprise on their faces, the men stopped.

"Please forgive me. I have a letter from General Wang Yao-wu to the Honorable Minister," I said as I handed my letter to the gentleman in the middle.

"Ah! From my friend!" the gentleman exclaimed as he broke the seal and searched the contents. "Good to know that my friend is well," he said in perfect English. "You will have your passport." He smiled and nodded. Then he said a few words in Chinese to the man standing to his left, at the same time giving him the letter. "He will attend to this," he told me. "And now, Madame, please excuse me. I have important matters to attend to." He bowed politely and proceeded down the corridor.

"Kindly come this way," the man holding the letter instructed me, and led me back to the room I had just left. But what a change of attitude we met!

Everyone stood up as we entered. Everyone listened attentively to my escort's instructions.

The elderly clerk asked for my photographs and I handed them to him.

"You may pick up your passport in seven days," he said without looking at me.

"But, sir," I said, "I do not have seven days. I can only be here for two."

"Then perhaps a friend can pick it up for you," my escort interjected. "I am afraid it's regulations," and he waved with his hand, showing that he could not change this.

"But what about all this?" I gestured at the packing in the room.

"It will be all right," my escort nodded assuringly.

Fortunately, I did have a friend in Nanking whom I had planned to visit. She was Ludmilla Saloff, who, with Marian Schwaikowsky, had been a witness at my marriage ceremony. At this time she was employed as a governess to the daughter of an American diplomat stationed in Nanking.

What a stroke of luck that she is here, I thought. I was able to call her on the telephone.

Ludmilla invited me to visit her. When I told her of my problem, she immediately volunteered to help, assuring me that she would do her best.

"However, we also are packing," Ludmilla said. "The Diplomatic Corps has received orders to be prepared to leave in ten days; so I will have no difficulty picking up your passport."

Thus reassured, I breathed a sigh of relief.

I left the BOQ the next morning and made my way in a taxi to the airport. As we drove through the streets, just as congested as they were the day before, I heard strange sounds. They came from a distance at regular intervals. Could they be explosions? I thought, and tapped the shoulder of my driver.

"What is that noise I hear?" I asked him.

"That belong guns, big guns," he replied.

"Guns?! Whose guns?"

"Belong Mao Tse-tung."

"My goodness! Please hurry," I urged him, realizing that, apparently, Nanking was under siege.

My driver speeded up and, using his horn, delivered me to the airport, another scene of bedlam. Small, twin- and single-engine airplanes kept landing and taking off. Crowds of people with luggage kept rushing toward them and scrambling in behind them, pushing their children and their older parents in through the open doors.

I stood bewildered as the ticket clerk told me, "Not here, not here. You pay inside plane when you get in."

"What planes are these?" I asked the man. "They look like military craft."

"They are General Chenault's airplanes. The pilots are called Flying Tigers. Flying to Shanghai. Helping people get away."

So, like the others, I ran to the runway and, as soon as one of the planes landed and the doors opened, I dashed forward, shoved someone out of my way, and scrambled up the flimsy ladder. The copilot pulled me up and pointed to one of the seats against the uninsulated metal wall inside the aircraft.

As more and more people crowded in, I began to worry that we might not get off the ground because of the weight of bodies and baggage. This situation, however, was quickly corrected.

The chief pilot, a tall, lanky man, emerged from the cockpit, went up to the wide open door of the plane, and pointed to one box. "Out," he ordered with a Southern drawl, and the copilot pushed the box out.

"Out! Out! Out! " He pointed, and out of the door went suitcases, boxes, and duffle bags, in spite of the desperate pleas and entreaties of their owners.

Unperturbed, having lightened the craft of excessive weight, the pilot commanded, "Okay! Close!" The copilot pulled the door, closing it with a bang. A hush fell over the passengers as both pilot and copilot took their seats in the cockpit.

With a deafening roar, the two engines started to turn over. Shaking and trembling, the plane first slowly, then faster and faster, began rolling down the runway.

"It will never make it," an old Chinese gentleman in a long black silk gown, sitting next to me, exclaimed, as he clung to his seat. "Man is not made to fly. He must crawl on the earth. Crawl."

This must have been his first experience in an airplane, and terrifying for him. Just as terrifying as it was for me. The plane lifted and we were in the air, a seeming miracle to me, when one considered the number of passengers and the amount of baggage still on the plane.

Needless to say, the Flying Tigers' planes that had fought the Japanese throughout the war were sturdy pieces of engineering, and their pilots, battle-scarred veterans, were expert at handling these planes.

Shaken by the vibration of the plane, deafened by the roar of the engines, my back chilled sitting for two hours against the uninsulated metal sheeting, nevertheless, when our plane touched the ground with a bang in Shanghai and I stepped onto the solid earth with wobbly legs, my heart overflowed with gratitude for having successfully completed my mission in Nanking.

I drove straight to the apartment of Elizabeta Mihailovna Tokmakoff, my Father's ancient friend, where I thought I could stay. As I rang the doorbell unannounced, I was not certain how she would greet me. I should not have worried, however, because, when she opened the door, I found myself clasped in a warm, loving embrace to her ample bosom.

"Muzachka! What brings you here?! Come in, come in," she greeted me, taking my small suitcase in her hand.

I told her of my visit to Nanking, my adventures there, and the reason why I had to wait ten days in Shanghai until Ludmilla Saloff arrived with my passport.

"But, of course, you must stay here!" Elizabeta Mihailovna exclaimed. "My little room upstairs is vacant. Follow me," she said as she went up the staircase. I followed her, observing how frail and old she looked and how unsteady her legs were as she climbed the steps.

"I hope I am not inconveniencing you."

"How can you?! What are friends for if not to share and help when needed? Now have a rest. You look peaked." She closed the door, leaving me in the same little room that I had occupied many years before when Father had sent me the long list of plumbing equipment to buy for Rock Mansions.

The room was exactly as I remembered it, with the same white frilly chintz curtains on the single window overlooking the backyard. There were the same white cotton bed cover on the brass bed and the same little Delft lamp with the blue and white picture of a Dutch windmill on the base, standing in the middle of the marble-top bedside table. All at once, I felt at ease and at home. Yes, indeed, I thought, what would humanity do if there were no true lasting friendships?

At that moment, suddenly, in my mind's eye arose a scene of Father sitting at one end of a large dining table covered with a linen table cloth, and Mother at the other end. Eight guests, with me, a little girl of seven, next to Father.

Everyone was a friend, everyone sharing our meals, not just once, but many times, sometimes daily. Why? Because they had fallen on difficult times, and Father, who by then, had a good job and could afford it, felt it his sacred duty to have an open house for those in need. He was not the only one known for hospitality in the Shanghai Russian emigrant community during the twenties and thirties.

Friendship was what had sustained and made it possible for many Russians to survive during their difficult days after the revolution in Russia. Now I, too, had no doubt that my friend, Ludmilla, would not fail me and would bring me the all-important passport. I had given her Elizabeta Mihailovna's telephone number, and I confidently awaited her call.

Meanwhile, Elizabeta Mihailovna and I sat near the radio, listening to the latest news. In Shanghai, an international city of five million, including the Chinese residents, the foreign community showed little concern for China's changing political situation. Business progressed as usual. Shops sold their merchandise and manufacturers produced their goods. Import and export firms continued to place orders and distribute their wares. The majority of people were closing their eyes and ears to what was transpiring in the rest of the country. Besides, the news over the radio and in the newspapers minimized the threat from Mao Tse-tung. It might have been censored, but after what I had experienced in Nanking, I feared the worst.

On the third day of my stay with Elizabeta Mihailovna, my fears proved correct. A most frightening communiqué was announced over the radio.

NANKING HAD FALLEN TO THE COMMUNISTS! Chiang Kai Shek's government had fled to Taiwan on the island of Formosa. I felt dizzy, hopeless! "My children and I are trapped!" I exclaimed.

I must have looked terrible, because Elizabeta Mihailovna jumped up from her seat. Hastening to the buffet, she took out a bottle of brandy and two glasses.

"Drink this, the color will return to your face," she told me as she filled a glass with the brandy.

I drank, but it did not alter my frame of mind, as I realized that there was no chance now of getting my passport.

"What now? What now? What now?" I kept repeating, as my hostess poured glass after glass of brandy for me, while also helping herself to several.

I do not remember how I stumbled to my bed, but I distinctly recall the splitting headache with which I awoke the next day. I dressed, washed, and shuffled down to the living room where Elizabeta Mihailovna sat at the table. A pot of coffee, cups, and a dish with Danish stood on the table next to her.

Age had not changed her love for fastidious appearances; just as I remembered her in the past, so now, too, she sat, a picture of cultivated taste, with her snow-white hair in a French twist, a demure, purple silk dress buttoned high at the neck, and a long, shimmering string of pearls tied in a knot.

"Here, sit here," Elizabeta Mihailovna gracefully waved her bejeweled hand in the direction of the chair opposite her. "Have some coffee," she said as she poured a cup for me out of an ornate porcelain coffee pot. "I also have something to tell you," she continued, as she puckered her lips in a peculiar manner, seeming to suppress a smile.

More bad news, I thought. "Please, Elizabeta Mihailovna, don't jest."

"I'm not jesting," she interrupted me. "You will not believe who telephoned this morning."

"Don't have the slightest idea," I answered, aware only of my throbbing head.

"LUDMILLA SALOFF." She pronounced every syllable slowly, stopping to see what effect it had on me.

"So, I am glad that she got out of Nanking so fast," I said without much emotion.

"My dear Muza! Don't you understand what I am trying to convey to you?" Elizabeta Mihailovna sighed impatiently, seeing me calmly pick up my cup of coffee. "Ludmilla has your passport."

I nearly dropped the cup. "What, what are you saying?!"

"You heard me."

Everything around me suddenly started to spin. Tears of joy were choking me.

"I'd better bring you some valerian drops to calm your nerves," Elizabeta Mihailovna said as she hurried to the cupboard. From a shelf she took a small vial of golden-colored liquid. After measuring six drops into a glass of water, she gave me the milky-looking substance. "Drink it. You will feel better."

I drank it without quibbling. My Grandmother used to give this age-old remedy to me whenever my Mother had one of her fits. It did the trick then and, after a while, it calmed me now.

"How did she manage to get it on such short notice?" I wondered aloud.

"Ludmilla will tell you herself. Now have a Danish." Elizabeta Mihailovna placed a vatrushka, a cheese Danish, on my plate.

Ludmilla Saloff arrived late that afternoon and, with a wonderfully glowing smile, handed me a large brown envelope containing a small blue booklet with the star in a circle of China's nationalist government on the cover. It contained my children's and my passport, No. 16732.

How Ludmilla obtained it was remarkable and due entirely to the help of her kindhearted American employer. The morning of the day the American diplomats were to be hurriedly evacuated, Ludmilla asked if someone would drive her to the Ministry. She felt that, though chances were slim, my passport might be ready. As a friend, she had to try. In spite of the pressing, fear-laden atmosphere, her employer consented to drive her, and they were pleasantly surprised to find that the passport was ready.

"Your friend is a most fortunate young lady," the elderly clerk told Ludmilla as he gave her the envelope. "If you had come tomorrow, it would have been too late. We are closing today. Inscrutable is the way of Tao," he added as he nodded his head thoughtfully.

Yes, indeed, inscrutable it is, I thought then, and still think now.

Having this document in hand unfortunately did not end my troubles. At the American Consulate I was advised that I would have to obtain another visa to some South American country. This precaution was necessary because, after the expiration of my six-month tourist visa, when I was supposed to leave the United States, the additional visa would serve as a guaranty that I would be able to go to another country if I was unable to return to China.

This advice sounded simple to undertake, but, as I found out, it was not.

After making inquiries, I found out that the Venezuelan Consulate would be the easiest place to obtain this visa. The Consulate had been recently established on the sixth floor of a multi-storied pink building on Bubbling Well Road near Wei Hai Wei Road, and was open for business five days a week from ten in the morning until four in the afternoon.

I arrived there promptly at ten on a Monday. The elevator took me to the sixth floor. When I entered the Consulate's reception room, I was struck by the luxurious surroundings. Particularly striking on the white Carrara marble floor was the set of sofas and armchairs of soft black Moroccan leather and the carved teak desk of the receptionist by the frosted glass door.

The clerk arose to greet me and inquired politely as to the nature of my business. I explained what I needed.

"Someone will be with you very shortly," he said as he picked up the telephone to announce me.

Immediately, the frosted glass door swung open and a gentleman in a pinstriped suit, who looked remarkably like Adolphe Menjou of film fame, came out. I could not suppress a smile at how strikingly similar were his dark hair and small, fastidiously groomed moustache to those of the movie star.

"Ricardo de la Riva," the gentleman introduced himself with a slight accent as he clicked his heels. "How can I be of service?"

I told him that I needed a visitor's visa for my children and myself.

"So you vont to travel in our beautiful contrée?" he asked as he looked me over from head to toe.

"Well, not exactly," I said honestly.

"Not exactly?!" The gentleman raised his eyebrows. "May I ask what passport do you possess?"

"Chinese," I answered.

"Hmm...I sée...May I know vy you vont the visá?"

I told him the truth.

"So your fiancé ées Americaine Capitan?"

"Yes, but what has that to do with my getting the visa?" I asked, a little perturbed by his questions.

He did not answer me.

"Is there a problem?" I asked apprehensively, seeing that he was rubbing his meticulous Adolphe Menjou moustache thoughtfully.

"No, no, that ées, not exactly. You are, of course, prepared to pay a fee?" he lowered his voice as he glanced in the direction of the clerk, who was busy typing.

"But naturally." I was surprised that he should ask me. I did not think that I looked so poor.

"Ah! Madame, then there ées no problém. The fée is two thousand dollárs."

"Only two thousand?" I was amazed. At this time, in China, the Chinese dollar (called "Yuan") was so completely devalued that everyone was used to paying in hundred-dollar Chinese bills. For this reason, everyone carried large bags to fit in the bundles of this worthless currency. So, without further questioning, I opened my own ample bag and counted out four five-hundred Yuan.

"Oh, Madame, you do not understand! No, no, not these—Americaine!"

"American two thousand?" I was stunned. "But this is extortion!" I raised my voice indignantly, realizing what he was doing.

"Madame! Not so loud!" Adolphe Menjou straightened himself. "That ées the price if you vont thée visá." His voice sounded uncompromising.

"But I do not have such money!"

He shrugged his shoulders, bowed, turned on his heels, and disappeared through the swinging frosted glass door.

What now? I thought as I walked back to the elevator. Suddenly, I heard someone behind me. I turned. It was the clerk.

"Madame, this is the address of the Brazilian Consulate. You may be luckier there," he half whispered as he pushed a folded piece of paper into my hand. Meanwhile, the elevator door had swung open.

"Good luck." The clerk smiled pleasantly as I stepped into the elevator.

Outside the building I looked at the address. The Brazilian Consulate was beyond the International Concession on the outskirts of Shanghai. Nevertheless, I knew that time was of the essence. I hailed a taxicab and, after a long ride, we arrived at our destination, a lovely English villa surrounded with a barbed-wire fence. The iron-gate grill was open.

At the entrance to the house, I had to ring the doorbell several times before I heard steps and the door was finally opened by a small, pudgy, bald-haired man in a white shirt and black trousers.

"Yes, yes, what is it?" he asked me impatiently. I explained who had given me his address.

"Oh! Señora. We are not open," the man sighed. "And my baby is sick. Very, very sick. I have to go. She is crying."

From the interior of the house came the shrill cry of a baby in pain.

"Come tomorrow. Tomorrow," he told me as he was about to close the door.

"Oh, Señor, I do not have tomorrow. I, too, have two small children and need your help. I am a widow."

"You widow with two children?"

I nodded.

"Dios mio!" he exclaimed, shaking his head in sympathy. "Can you type?"

"Yes."

"Then come with me. My secretary not here today." He took me by the hand. We entered the next room. It was filled with unpacked crates, several file cabinets, and several desks standing helter-skelter. On one of the desks stood a typewriter. "Copy this into your passport," and he handed me a sample page. It was not difficult to follow his instructions.

"Now I will place the Consulado de Brazil Seal and sign it. I am the Consul. Here you are." With a big grin, the Consul gave me back my passport. "Visa No. 7."

"How much do I owe you?" I asked.

"Four dollars."

"American money?"

"Of course not, Chinese," he replied indignantly.

"But it is like nothing."

"You have worked for it," he laughed, patting me paternally on the shoulder. Just then the air was again rent by the cry of the baby. "Oh, my poor, poor baby," he exclaimed as he hurriedly led me to the entrance and closed the door behind me.

I stood on the doorstep for several minutes, giddy from what had just transpired. How fortunate I had been to be led to this little Brazilian with such a compassionate nature.

64

Visas to the U.S. Denied

Now, full of confidence that all was in order, I hastened to the United States Consulate. A blond, curly haired receptionist ushered me into the office of the Vice Consul. An elegantly clad, attractive, middle-aged, Semitic-looking lady in a tailored blue dress, wearing heavy-rimmed glasses, arose from her seat behind her desk.

"Please be seated." She directed me, pointing to the chair across the desk from her. She peered through her glasses as I sat down in the chair she indicated. "What can I do for you?"

I told her that I needed a visitor's visa into the United States. "Here is my passport," I said as I gave it to her. "You will find everything in order."

"You are a Chinese citizen?" she asked as she glanced into the little blue booklet.

"Yes, and I also have an additional visa to Brazil. I understand it is required."

"Well, yes, but?" She tapped impatiently on the desk with her pencil.

"But what?" I asked apprehensively.

"Well, you see, you are not Jewish."

"No."

"Then I am afraid I cannot issue you the visa."

"But what has my not being Jewish to do with this? My Grandfather in Russia was one of the few lawyers who specialized in laws applicable to Jews and defended them. My Father was a member of the Jewish Club in Shanghai. His best friend was a rabbi."

I thought all these facts would show how sympathetic and friendly our family had been to her people and would turn her in my favor.

"You see, the synagogues in the United States provide a guaranty for their people," she explained. "If you were a Jew I could issue you the visa right away, but you are a Chinese citizen with no one standing behind you. Sorry. I advise you to go back to Tsingtao where you have connections."

The Vice Consul stood up. She rang a bell summoning the receptionist, who showed me out.

Needless to say, I was completely disheartened. It was now the end of December. I had a feeling that time was running out on me.

I dragged myself back to Elizabeta Mihailovna, who was ready with her encouragement.

"Now don't you worry, dearie. All will work out. But now you had better hurry to the airplane ticket office," she advised me.

"Elizabeta Mihailovna, do you know that in Tsingtao the Vice Consul in charge of visas hates Russian women? Rumor has it that a Russian woman with whom he was in love left him for another man. What chance do I have?" I despaired.

"So now is the time to rely on miracles." Elizabeta Mihailovna's voice took on a religious fervor. "I will go to the cathedral and place a candle before the icon of Saint Nicolas, the Miracle Worker of Russia."

"Do you think one candle will be sufficient to obtain his intercedence?" I asked, a little incredulous that placing candles might influence events.

"Well, perhaps I had better place two."

"And please, one before our family's patron saint, Saint Serafim. My parents believe in him," I added, remembering my Mother on her knees before the icon of the saint.

"Good idea. Now hurry to the ticket office! After all, we have to do our part. In Tsingtao you and your family are known. Besides, Malcolm Norcross will be able to help you." Elizabeta Mihailovna, both the daughter and former wife of practical merchants, had her feet firmly on the ground. Yet, as a true Russian, her nature was also deeply rooted in religious beliefs.

At the airport I had no difficulty purchasing the next available seat on a plane, but due to the few planes flying to Tsingtao, the Chinese agent told me that I would have to wait several days. I would be notified the day before in the event of a cancellation.

"What does this mean in time? Please, I must get to Tsingtao as soon as possible. It is an emergency," I pleaded with tears streaming down my cheeks.

"Madame. Look!" He showed me a two-page waiting list. "Everyone claims it is an emergency," he chuckled.

"I suppose that you are aware of the critical times in China?" I could not help showing my annoyance at his chuckle.

"Madame, everyone is. There is nothing I can do at this moment." He scowled at me.

I realized that I had to control myself. So, I thanked him politely, and emphasized how grateful I and my two little children would be should he find a way to help us.

"I will see what I can do." He nodded and smiled in a more friendly manner, as he turned to the man next in line.

The next several days were nerve-wracking. What particularly increased my fears was a telegram from Father telling me that Malcolm Norcross had informed him of a freighter with a cargo of wheat from the United States that was expected to arrive in Tsingtao. He urged me to move heaven and earth to get there before its scheduled departure on the 15th of January.

My goodness, I thought. It is already the 10th of the month. How will I be able to do this?

But lo and behold, without moving heaven and earth—or maybe Elizabeta Mihailovna's candles did influence the saints to assist me. Whatever it was, I received the confirmation of my seat on the plane to Tsingtao on the morning of the 11th. I had a place on a plane the next day. I immediately sent a telegram to Father informing him of my arrival.

The morning of my departure, Elizabeta Mihailovna embraced me tearfully. "May the saints and angels take care of you, dearie," she whispered as I climbed into the taxi. "And you yourself do your best," she added just as the taxi started.

Before we turned the corner, I glanced back. Elizabeta Mihailovna stood at the black iron gate of her sand-colored town house. Her aging, frail figure was wrapped in a blue velvet house robe, and her long string of pearls hung around her neck. I waved to her. She responded with a slow, graceful wave of her bejeweled hand.

That is how I will always remember her. What happened to her after Shanghai was taken by the Communists, I do not know.

65

Last Days in Tsingtao

My flight from Shanghai to Tsingtao that Saturday the 12th of January was pleasantly uneventful. The small, two-engine plane had all the conveniences of a passenger craft. The walls were insulated, the seats were comfortable, and the steward even served us tidbits and a cool drink. In two hours we reached the mountain ridges surrounding Tsingtao Airport and swooped over them with no difficulty, touching down on the runway on schedule.

To my pleasant surprise, there, awaiting me, stood Malcolm Norcross, Stesha, and my girls.

"Mama! Mama! Mama!" Regina and Carola shouted. They broke away from Stesha and came running towards me as I stepped off the stepladder of the plane. I hugged and kissed them. How good it felt to feel them close to me.

"Now, now, let your Mother go," I heard Stesha say, as she tried to pull the girls away from me. "Captain Norcross is waiting to say hello to Mother." And there was Malcolm Norcross, distinguished looking, with gold braid on his visor and medals on his uniform.

"I thought you would never get here," he laughed as he embraced me. "Is this all your luggage?" He picked up my small valise. "Let's go. Your grandparents are waiting," he said to the girls as he gently pushed them toward the entrance of the air terminal, leading us to the official car he was driving. He helped us get in. With me sitting next to him, he started the engine.

"I am glad you are here. You're just in time," Malcolm said as he turned to me. "The freighter, *Empire State*, on which you will be sailing has just arrived. I made reservations for you."

"Mal, I do not have the United States visa. In Shanghai I was instructed to seek it here."

"But you must purchase the tickets on Monday, or it will be too late. There is a panic in Tsingtao. Your tickets are the last available." I could see drops of perspiration on his forehead.

"All will work out, Dear. Don't worry," I assured him. I, too, however, felt just as anxious, particularly after he hurriedly related to me that Admiral Cook had received orders to have the ships' engines ready. The fleet would leave as soon as all the belongings of the American citizens' were taken aboard...

"We are packing the Consul's household now," Malcolm concluded, as he drove up to the entrance of our house.

My parents were naturally glad to have me back. Mother tearfully hugged and kissed me. Father's cheeks were also moist with emotion. The next day, Sunday, I went with Stesha and the children to the Russian church. Besides us and the priest, there were very few parishioners, and these were old and decrepit. Everyone who could had fled from Tsingtao. The sight of these poor forsaken souls brought tears to my eyes.

At home, everyone was also full of sadness, yet trying to put on a brave front by keeping the conversation revolving around trivia.

As for myself, I was dreading the next morning and my trip to the American Consulate. That Sunday night was the longest and most painful night I can remember. I tossed about in my bed awaiting the break of day, and, at last, the sun's rays did finally creep in and light my second-floor bedroom. Sometime later, I heard footsteps on the stairs. It was my Mother. She knocked on my door to tell me that breakfast was ready.

After forcing myself to eat and gulping down a cup of coffee, I was ready at nine o'clock to sit down at Father's desk to pick up the telephone. I dialed the American Consulate. As I had previously met Carl Hawthorne, the Consul, and he was acquainted with Malcolm, I asked to speak to him. In a few seconds the Consul was on the line.

"Hawthorne here."

"Good morning. This is Muse Spanier," I greeted him, making my voice sound as cheerful as I could.

"Ah, Muse. What can I do for you? " I thought I heard a tense note in his question.

"I need a tourist visa for myself and the girls. What time can I come to the Consulate?"

"Well, you see, Muse, the Vice Consul, our man in charge of the visas, is in Tientsin, and is unexpectedly delayed. However, I expect him back soon. I will let you know."

My heart gave a skip of joy. I knew then, with the Vice Consul away, that I had a chance of getting the visa.

"Carl, I cannot wait. I need it today." I emphasized the "today." "You can issue it yourself."

"We-l-l-l, not really," he answered. "It will be better to have him do it."

"Carl, you know yourself that the freighter is my only chance and will be gone by the time he returns."

"We-l-l-l, yes, but, but...," he started to stammer.

I remembered a motto of the Jesuit religious order: "The goal absolves the means." This was when I decided to play all my trumps, as we said in Russian. So I charged ahead, come what might.

"Carl, I hate to mention it, but you know I am engaged to Captain Malcolm Norcross, and if I do not get this visa, who knows what a man in love might do. He is the Chief of Supply, and the shipping of household goods comes under his jurisdiction. Do you know what this means?" My God, I thought, I am stooping to blackmail.

He was silent.

"Are you there, Carl?" I asked, fearful that he had hung up.

"Yes," he replied, with obvious annoyance.

"Carl, I must insist. Please, please help me and my children today."

There was no answer. My heart sank. Then, suddenly, I heard the sound of his throat being cleared and after a few seconds, Carl's voice came over the line.

"Oh! All right! Then come right away. Best during lunchtime," he told me And the receiver clicked off.

At ten o'clock I stood in Carl Hawthorne's office before his desk.

"Where is your passport?" he asked me without lifting his head.

"I also have another visa, which I understand is required," I tried to reassure him. Carl waved his hand impatiently as he reached out for the American Consulate seal in a box. Pressing it on the ink pad, he stamped one of the pages of my passport. He wrote in by hand, "14th January 1948," and signed it.

"Thank you so much. Words cannot express what this means to me," I told him.

"I wish you all the best. You will be on the same ship as my wife." He stood up and cordially shook my hand.

That afternoon Malcolm and I hurried to the shipping agent.

The agent carefully counted the U.S. bills that Malcolm paid. "You are just in time," he said. "These are the last. I had several people who would have given double for them." He handed me a folder with the long yellow slips of paper. "You and your children have a cabin all to yourselves," he told me. "The **Empire State** leaves at noon tomorrow. Bon voyage."

After all the difficulties that I had encountered, to finally hold these three precious pieces of paper was overwhelming. I cannot describe how elated I felt. Now, however, as I suddenly realized that I really would be leaving—leaving my parents and China—I had a presentiment that it was forever. My throat tightened and I found myself overwhelmed with grief.

Malcolm must have guessed my feelings. He drove me home in silence.

"See you later. I know you have important things to attend to," he said, as I got out of his jeep.

He was correct. There were three things. First, I had to make arrangements for Stesha, second was packing, and then I had to write to Philip van Ditmars. This last, I knew, would be the hardest. I hoped that he would understand why I had made the decision to leave for the United States, and forgive what, to him, must seem a betrayal.

Stesha's wish had always been to return to Poland, her native country. In anticipation of my departure, she had already applied to the Polish Consulate in Shanghai for reentry papers and had received them. Now all that was left was for me to give her her severance pay.

Now that I was leaving, I gave Stesha several months' wages from what was left from the sale of my town house. Though not a large sum in United States currency, it was, nevertheless, enough to make sure that she had the means to realize her desire.

Next was my packing. This was simple. The girls' and my own clothing fitted into a trunk, two smaller suitcases, and a hat box. The rest of my possessions—several antique oriental rugs, oil paintings, valuable curios, and a few carved Chinese chairs and other pieces of furniture—Malcolm had had crated some time ago, and now they stood waiting to be picked up.

All that remained was the letter to Philip. After several unsatisfactory attempts, I finally wrote honestly and to the point why I had accepted Malcolm's offer of marriage and why I was going to the United States.

By the time I had finished what had to be done, it was evening, and time for supper.

For our last meal together, Mother took special care in setting the table. On her favorite embroidered tablecloth, she encircled the silver candelabra with branches of green leaves. At each place she placed our best silver and crystal goblets. Mother also prepared the traditional Russian dish for special occasions, the *pirog*, a pie with beef, eggs and rice filling, her specialty.

Father said a short prayer and we began eating our dinner quietly, silently.

I remember the circle of light from the candles on the white linen tablecloth and the sparkles along the edges of our crystal glasses, while, in the far dark corner of the room, before the effigy of our patron Saint Serafim, the little oil lamp flickered.

I was also aware of how momentous this supper was for each one of us in the room. Not only were we gathered together as a family for the last time, but each of us was standing on the threshold of the unknown future.

Father noticed that I glanced in the direction of our icon. Breaking the silence, he said, "Muza, in times of need, turn to him. He will help you. He has never failed me."

I nodded, but kept my silence, not wanting to break the reverence of the moment.

That night I had an unforgettable dream.

I dreamt that I was in a large cavern with an arch-shaped ceiling of granite. Holding the arch together was a triangular keystone. Suddenly, I heard a thunderous noise, as the walls and ceiling of the cavern started shaking. To my dismay, the keystone was slipping out of its place. Then I saw it hanging halfway out.

"If it falls, I will be lost—buried alive," I said to myself, as horror seized me.

As the earth continued shaking, I kept watching the keystone. "Now. Now," I kept saying to myself. There was another thunderous convulsion and suddenly I heard a voice: "You will be all right. You are in a special place." Everything around me calmed down. I looked up. The keystone was halfway out, but it was still holding up the arch that supported the ceiling of the cave.

I remember awakening greatly relieved. The dream seemed so real and so appropriate to what I had experienced in my life so far.

The next morning I related my dream to Father. He smiled before replying, "Whatever it might mean, it is encouraging. You can face life confidently."

It is curious how we perceive the passing of time. Anticipating something pleasurable, the clock's hand moves much too slowly. Awaiting an unpleasant or dreaded happening, the same hands on the clock's face are racing; and that is how that morning I awaited the time of my departure.

The hands on the wall clock above my Father's desk were moving much too fast. Before I knew it, the clock was striking ten times, and it was time for me to leave.

Malcolm had telephoned the night before to tell me that he regretted that an important staff meeting was to be held the next morning because of the critical situation. He had to be present and therefore could not see me to the ship. He had, however, arranged for a cab to pick me up. Several sharp toots of the horn had just announced the cab's arrival.

Parting is always sorrowful, but parting with your dear ones, and feeling that it might be forever, is excruciating.

I will never forget the anguish on my Father's face as I kissed him goodbye, and my Mother's sob as I embraced her as she knelt before the icon of our saint.

Stesha awaited me outside. I hugged her tenderly and wished her happiness in Poland. What a kind-hearted young woman and what a good nurse she had been to my little girls. I left her, sure that all would go well with her.

The taxi brought my girls and me to the wharf and we went aboard the *U.S. Empire State*.

After arranging our belongings in our cabin, the girls and I went on deck. In spite of the cold wind, we stood there watching for a very, very long time. First, there were the other passengers coming on board. Among them I saw Mrs. Hawthorne, the Consul's wife. Then we watched as a sailor cast the line off the capstan.

Unmoored from the wharf, the ***Empire State*** began moving away, and with its moving, I, too, felt that my own ties with China were being severed. As I stood bracing myself against the gusts of wind, I looked up at the steel-gray sky as gusts of the northern wind shook our ship. Wrapping my blue fox jacket more tightly around my shoulders, I turned to check on my two little girls.

Now hugging the shore, the ship was passing the hill slopes of Tsingtao, speckled with multicolored roofs, and farther away, on the portside, was the Strand Beach and the red roof of the hotel. Then I could see what used to be the Kushnareffs' farm, and still farther, on a promontory, stood the tall pink building, the Edgewater Hotel, with the First World War German fortifications clearly visible behind it.

As the ship progressed toward the open sea, the steep embankment of the Laoshan Mountains arose, with several Taoist monasteries clinging like gulls' nests to the upright slopes. I remembered that this was where Karl and I had had our picnics on the terraces of some of these temples in these lovely mountains...

As our ship slowly took its course northward around a precipitous cliff, the wind increased.

"Mama, Mama, I'm cold!" Regina cried out, shivering as she clung tighter to me.

"I'm cold," Carola also whimpered.

Just then the sound of cymbals announced lunch. The girls' cries and the cymbals brought me back from the past.

"Yes, let's hurry. Lunch will warm us," I told them. I took them by the hand and led them toward the door and down the corridor to the dining room.

Our Passage to the United States lacked nothing to be desired. The Pacific Ocean was as smooth as a tabletop and our ***U.S. Empire State*** cruised steadily at its normal speed of eleven knots, trailing a V-shaped wake behind it. At times, a school of dolphins swam alongside the ship. They were seemingly enjoying the competition of a race with the slow-moving dark object in their domain.

My sixteen fellow passengers were pleasant. Whenever we assembled, and it was mostly at meals, everyone tried their best to be congenial. To everyone's contentment, the food far surpassed everyone's expectations.

As in 1935, when I traveled to the United States with my parents, our **U.S. *Empire State*** also stopped for cargo and provisions in Japan before it directed its course eastward across the Pacific.

After fourteen days at sea, we saw, at last, in the distance the shoreline of California and the Golden Gate Bridge spanning the entrance to San Francisco Bay. Sailing under it, we soon passed the little island of Alcatraz, with its concrete fortress structure, the famous prison. Before we knew it, our ship was preparing to moor at a San Francisco wharf.

It was with mixed feelings of joy, to have arrived at our final destination, and fear of the unknown before me, that I stood with my girls on deck, watching as our ship's line was cast to the dock, where if was secured. Next I heard the scraping of the gangplank as it was placed into position.

I watched as a young man in a blue business suit, with a briefcase under his arm came aboard. I soon found out that he was from the FBI. He had come on board to check the passengers' passports.

Over the loudspeakers the Purser instructed all passengers to assemble in the dining room for passport and visa verification.

With perfect assurance that my credentials were in order, I stepped into the dining room and took my place with the other passengers. When my turn came to approach the official, he invited me to sit down.

"Your passport, please," the young man requested, smiling.

I gave him my little blue booklet. After quickly flipping over several pages, he came to the U.S. seal, my United States visa.

"Hmmmm…," he mused, and began searching through a small pile of papers next to him on the table. Apparently, he found was he was looking for. I could see from where I was sitting that it was a sheet with several single-spaced, typed paragraphs.

"Hmmmm…" came from him again as he skimmed over them. "Ma'am, what is the purpose of your visit to America?" he asked, looking at me in a strange way.

"Why, isn't it clear? Don't I have a visitor's visa?" I answered, with a sensation that something was amiss.

"So-o-o, you are a Chinese citizen…and you have a visa to Brazil?"

"Yes."

"Well, Ma'am, I am obliged to detain you," he told me, emphasizing the last two words. "Kindly take a seat at the other table while I process the others and then I will take care of you."

"But why? What is the reason??!" I asked, feeling as though the ceiling was collapsing on me.

"Please, Ma'am, no scenes," the man spoke sharply. "There are reasons. Please do as I say."

"Mama, what's wrong?" Regina asked, tugging at my sleeve.

"All will be all right," I said in Russian, trying to calm her, as I noticed the strange glances from the other passengers.

After the official finished his work, he turned to me. "Get ready to come ashore. I will be taking you to lunch," he smiled politely but coolly.

"But what about my luggage? Shouldn't I go first to a hotel?" I asked, completely puzzled by his behavior.

"The Purser will take care of it," he replied curtly.

I turned to the Purser, who was standing nearby at the door. He looked just as perplexed as I was.

"Ma'am," the Purser nodded, "I will take care of it."

I found myself being driven in an official car through the congested traffic of the streets of San Francisco. Baffled by what was going on and full of anxiety, I sat quietly next to my girls. After weaving in and out of the long line of cars, busses and trams, and in and around corners of streets, we arrived under the portico of a white building, surrounded by large trees, with a large sign which heralded the building as the St. Francis Drake Hotel.

To my great surprise, as soon as we took our seats at the table in the dining room, my escort's attitude changed. He suddenly took on the manner of a most charming conversationalist, very concerned with my welfare and my activities in China. He wanted to know all about how we lived there, what I did there, my Father's position in the government, etc., etc. There was no end to his questions.

I told him about our life. I even honestly shared with him the reason why I had come to the United States. He joked. I laughed and he laughed.

"Isn't it funny? You know, someone had reported to us that you were a spy in the employ of the Chinese Government," he explained. He looked straight into my eyes, to see my reaction. I forced myself to smile. Realizing how important it was for him to believe me, I explained in detail how these accusations might have originally started.

I told him that it was rumored that a young Russian woman, in desperate financial straits, was supplying elaborate stories about other Russians to a U.S. Secret Service man, who paid for this information to be included in his reports. Because of her need, she became a stool pigeon. This was the truth and, fortunately for me, the man believed me.

"Well," he said thoughtfully, after listening attentively, "do you have U.S. $600 for a bond?"

"I do not have much, but $600 I do."

"You see, I realize that all the allegations against you are nothing but vicious calumny. But in order to approve your entrance, however, I will have to go according to one of our ordinances, which requires that you post a bond as a guarantee that you will leave after the six months."

I must have looked alarmed, because he immediately assured me that once I was married to Captain Norcross, I would be able to remain in the United States.

After lunch, the man drove us to his office. I counted out six one-hundred-dollar United States bills. I was left with just enough money to stay overnight in a hotel and then buy tickets on a train to Miami, Florida, where I was to be met by Malcolm's Mother, with whom we would be staying. I handed the $600 to him.

The man took my passport, turned it to the last page, and, with a large seal, stamped: "Entrance to United States. Date: 29 January 1949."

Epilogue

While my life in the United States took its course, what happened with my dear ones in China was tragic.

Mao Tse-tung's victory changed everything. The house which Governor Wang Yao-wu had given to my Father was confiscated. Father and Mother had to move into a room of a kind Russian friend. Because of Father's previous connections with the Nationalist Government, he was imprisoned, and shortly thereafter died.

Left destitute and alone, Mother became a public nuisance. She wandered in the streets of Tsingtao begging for food. The police picked her up and, not having any other place to put her, took her to a labor camp for female Chinese convicts. Fortunately for her, the Russian priest, who was one of the few Russians who remained in Tsingtao, heard about her situation and succeeded in having her shipped to a Shanghai hospital for the insane. Here she lingered until the Organization of World Churches found a home for her in Denmark.

Because my own circumstances did not permit me to take her in, and because United States immigration laws did not permit the entrance of emotionally disturbed people, Mother spent the rest of her days near Copenhagen on the shores of the Baltic Sea in a well-provided Danish home for the aged. Toward the end, she closed off the world around her. She became totally blind and deaf.

My Grandmother's fate was just as sad.

Considering her too old (she was ninety-two) to move with them to the United States, my Uncle Vsevolod arranged a place for her in Hong Kong. She had lived all this time with my Uncle in Shanghai. It must have been a heart-rending experience for the proud old lady to sail alone into the unknown. I want to believe that she bore this rejection stoically, as the true descendent of her courageous Teutonic ancestors.

As for myself and my children in the United States, however difficult were the times and situations, whatever challenges life presented, I managed to overcome and surmount them. Just like in my dream, the keystone never fell out of its position supporting the archway that held up the granite ceiling—the ceiling of my endurance.

LaVergne, TN USA
18 February 2010
173572LV00004B/25/A